C000254445

Tuesday's Child—
The Life and Death of Imogen Hassall

Tuesday's Child—
The Life and Death
of Imogen Hassall

by Dan Leissner

Midnight Marquee Press, Inc.
Baltimore, Maryland

Copyright © 2002 Dan Leissner

Without limiting the rights under copyright reserved above, no part of this publication may be reproduced, stored in or introduced into a retrieval system, or transmitted, in any form, or by any means (electronic, mechanical, photocopying, recording, or otherwise), without the prior written permission of the copyright owners or the publishers of the book.

ISBN 1-887664-47-5
Library of Congress Catalog Card Number 2002113487
Manufactured in the United States of America
First Printing by Luminary Press, September 2002
Revised Printing by MMP, December 2008

Fear—fear of loneliness, of old age, of death, of love and of hostility—And from this Fear springs the only positive passion which can be permanent in such a nature, the pitiable longing, more childlike than womanly, for protection.—Christopher Hassall's description of his heroine in Walton's *Troilus and Cressida*

For my Mother and Father
my friends
and
for all members of the acting profession:
without you the world would be a much duller place

Table of Contents

INTRODUCTION

There is a certain, secret satisfaction in being all alone on New Year's Eve. A smugness even. Turning it around—the epitome of loneliness becomes a declaration of independence. Let the common herd gather at its watering holes, seeking reassurance in numbers. I am self-sufficient. I shall relish this precious opportunity of complete solitude, suspended in a womb of unique emptiness, that perfect quiet at the top of a large and empty house.

Other New Year's Eves had come and gone, insignificant. But this New Year's Eve of 1996/97 was inescapable. It crept up the stairs and under my door; and in my solitude, made for contemplation, it shone a spotlight on me. New Year's Eve is a time for taking a long, hard look at one's life and finding it wanting.

But what did I want? Spiritually and materially, this society offered me little or nothing to aspire to, other than my basic creature comforts and the odd toy to distract me. Not since 1976, when I was a student, was I in any way pressured by my peer group—I had no peer group. I fell in and out of love, or lust, every now and then, and put some hapless female up on a pedestal. Someone once warned me that all that such elevation achieved was to place the lady's feet level with my teeth. I usually deserved it. However, the one time that I didn't left me determined never to trust my judgment or my instincts again.

So, at age 42, my sole achievement in life—and a considerable one, I think—was to have sustained the close friendship of a few rare individuals.

After much contemplation, between tinkering with my toys, I surprised myself by making an actual New Year's resolution. And it was one that I intended to keep.

I arrived at my decision just before the distant hooting and hollering of the first drunks of the New Year, staggering down the street below my window, broke the spell of silence.

I was going to find a project, a challenge, something to exercise my mind.

My work, as a freelance copy editor and proofreader in law publishing, was just that, work, a necessary evil; although I could take some satisfaction from my gamble in going freelance—if I had to work for a living at least I could try and do it on my terms. I had no interest whatsoever in climbing the career ladder. The grinding ordinariness of office culture had become a nightmare.

> I can't live with ordinary people. I always end up hating them.
> —The late Kurt Cobain

The sheer stress and desperation of it reduced me to a state where I could barely function in the job and shuffled home zombie-like to sit and stare all evening at a point somewhere behind the television set. This mental and physical exhaustion, plus a fatal combination of laziness and arrogance on my part, inevitably drove my employers to invite me to jump before I was pushed.

Freelancing, therefore, was a matter of survival. I had, in retrospect, narrowly avoided a nervous breakdown—no way could I go back to an office. But, while I marveled at the energy and tenacity with which I endeavored to make a go of my new lifestyle and recognized a newfound space and time and self-respect, freelancing didn't solve the essential problem—I had no purpose in my life.

So, I intended to stimulate my dulled brain with something extraordinary.

But what?

My creative juices had run dry. In my 42 years human society had tossed up only two occupations that I felt genuinely suited me: photography and writing.

The only benefit of working in an office was that a regular salary allowed me to afford photography. I applied myself to it diligently and even sold a few pictures. I experimented with so-called glamour photography and found it to be enormous fun and extremely therapeutic. The wit and wisdom of the models was a refreshing antidote to the humorless political correctness that I had to endure daily in the office. However, when I went freelance, photography was relegated to a mere occasional hobby.

I have been writing, semi-seriously, since I was in my early 20s with the usual heap of unpublished novels to my credit, moldering in the attic. I did receive the odd enthusiastic response from a publisher's in-house reader, but not, it would appear, from its marketing types and accountants.

But, by January 1997, I hadn't written anything of substance for quite some time; a few fragments, no more.

I was, however, determined to find my project. And, this time, I wasn't going to let it fade away, or talk myself out of it, like I usually did. I wasn't going to be lazy, or give up, or be sidetracked.

"Eighty percent of those who want to be photographers never make it," I had read somewhere. "Because 80 percent of that 80 percent never actually get round to taking any photographs."

It was a revelation. I stopped talking about it and talking myself in and out of it, and thinking about it and reading about it, and went out and did it. And, lo and behold, I sold some pictures!

Action not thought! I was determined to find my project.

Very good. But what?

"To know and to love another human being is the root of all wisdom," wrote Evelyn Waugh, or words to that effect. And so it has been with my friend Caroline.

Caroline is a happily married woman with three beautiful children and has been my friend for 15 years. I have no religion and no politics and I adhere to no prescribed morality. Friendship is my only faith and I have faith in Caroline. Uniquely, I have absolute confidence in my feelings for her. She is the only woman with whom I have succeeded, more often than not, in behaving as an intelligent adult, which says a great deal about her.

This book began with Caroline.

For some considerable time, Caroline had been researching her family tree. It is a tale of romance, intrigue and mystery, but I am sworn to secrecy. Out of the blue, Caroline asked me to pop into the Public Record Office and look something up for her. I enjoyed it, searching through those mighty, evocative registers.

Caroline's researches appeared to be doing her a world of good, stimulating and entertaining her at a time when she was in dire need of light relief. And the story that was unfolding for her was extraordinary and full of surprises.

That's it! A research project. So far so good. But what was I going to research?

No sooner said than done. Enter Imogen.

One January morning in 1997, I returned from the corner newsagent with a glossy video magazine, an idle impulse, one of those cheap productions whose mainstream content is rapidly being supplanted by horror and pornography.

In the letters column, there was a small photograph of an attractive young woman with a mane of combed-back black hair, a big grin and an astonishing cleavage. The photo was attached to a reader's letter, inquiring as to the availability on video of the film and TV

credits of an actress called Imogen Hassall.

Imogen Hassall. I remembered her. I was 15 in 1970, when Imogen, bikini-clad, lit up the pilot episode of my favorite TV series, *The Persuaders.*

Although I was, superficially, a teenage, suburban hippie, it was the Playboy Club, jet-set glamour of *The Persuaders* that formed my secret fantasy world. Its leading characters, played by Roger Moore and Tony Curtis, were an English aristocrat, Lord Brett Sinclair and Danny Wilde, a rough-diamond from the Bronx. International playboys from opposite ends of the social spectrum, they were forged into a team of crime-busting knight-errants, devoted to righting wrongs and rescuing beautiful women.

Lord Brett Sinclair, as personified by Roger Moore, was my wish-fulfillment figure, my fantasy self. Externally a scruffy hippie, flapping about in my surplus RAF greatcoat and two-tone crushed velvet loons, internally I yearned to be cruising down the leafy lanes to the front gates of my stately home in my gleaming Aston Martin DBS with a lovely Chelsea Girl by my side.

I envied Brett's lifestyle, but above all I longed for his benign outlook on life, the way that he could look down on humanity and smile, because he could afford to be benevolent.

I rediscovered *The Persuaders* when they released the series on video, as the great nostalgia boom erupted in the 1990s and immersed us all in the 1960s and '70s. I still envied Lord Brett Sinclair. At the conclusion of each absurd episode, I still had that great bittersweet ache inside, like that awful moment when one wakes from a wonderful dream, still warm all over, only to realize with cold abruptness that it was only a dream.

And there was bikini-clad Imogen. After re-reading that letter in the magazine, I went back and watched her again—in *The Champions* and *Carry On Loving.* She was unusually beautiful.

She had hovered somewhere far at the back of my mind, on and off, since 1970, my adolescent dream girl, suffused by the same golden glow of nostalgia as the 1966 World Cup winners. I had a vague notion that she had come to a sad end, but I knew absolutely nothing about her.

I had found my subject—no sooner said than done.

Or she had found me.

Delving into the *Writer's Handbook* and the *Writers' and Artists' Yearbook* for 1997, I searched for likely sources of archive material.

The British Film Institute Library was my first port of call. On microfiche, they held a file of old newspaper clippings, going back only as far as 1969. I was surprised and delighted that there was anything at all and disappointed that there was no more.

It was, however, enough to tantalize me, to hook me. Immediately, there were surprises. She was the daughter of the celebrated librettist Christopher Hassall, who had written the lyrics for Ivor Novello; her grandfather was the important graphic artist John Hassall ("Skegness Is So Bracing"). And what was all this, about the Royal Ballet School, the London Academy of Music and Dramatic Art and the Royal Shakespeare Company?

I read on...

It was a tale told by *The Sun*, *The Mirror* and *The News of the World*. But what I read there, reading between the lines, made a considerable impact on me. It was the obvious force of a compelling personality; and the hint of a far deeper tragedy than I expected.

I rushed home with my treasure and, over the next few days, wrote a long essay, based on my initial response to what I had read. I surprised myself.

As I wrote, Imogen emerged—an Imogen, my first Imogen, the first of many. An emotional bond was forged. Her presence was immediate and overwhelming.

The clippings told me that Imogen had lost a baby shortly after its birth. My friend Caroline had also endured that most terrible loss. From a distance, I had fumbled, inadequately to do and say the right thing. I thought of Caroline as I wrote about Imogen—how I'd wished that I could simply ride in on my white horse, like the hero in a Western, and put all to rights; and how I despaired impotently, because life just isn't like that.

I thought about another friend, as I wrote about Imogen. The emotional resonances, the coincidences, were powerful.

As I wrote my essay, and as Imogen emerged, I sensed the frustration and guilt of her friends, unable to help her. How can you help someone who won't help herself?

Jeff has been my best mate since the day we met, as schoolboys in 1969. We were Butch Cassidy and the Sundance Kid. Jeff was Sundance because he was faster on the draw. I was Butch because I did all the talking—"I got vision and the rest of the world wears bifocals." We were amazed when we saw the movie. It was about us!

We will always be Butch and the Kid, but at 43 reality had a way of closing the old range down.

And reality came crashing down on Jeff. It was a case of everything happening at once. Professionally and privately, everything that could go wrong did go wrong, one on top of another.

I gradually became aware that I hadn't seen or heard from Jeff for weeks, then months, straddling Christmas 1996 and on into the New Year. I knew that things were going wrong, and that a crisis was brewing. But, as weeks became months, I did nothing. I don't know why.

I was certainly preoccupied. And I suppose I assumed that he would inevitably resurface and we could resume, carry on where we left off, playing our guitars and riding the range.

I had my project. I had something to do. You have to sacrifice your time and energy, if you want to achieve anything, even the time and energy you might have to spare for your friends. And the longer this break in communications lasted, the more I just let it go on, especially as it seemed obvious that it would be up to me to end it.

Perhaps I was afraid of bad news and just hoped that it would all go away and he would show up again, guitar in hand. I didn't want any bad news, not at this crucial, formative stage of my project, when it was essential that I focus and accentuate the positive.

Quite simply, I was bewildered. I didn't know what to do. Imogen's friends must have gone round and round in similar circles.

Then, all of a sudden, impelled by thoughts of Imogen, I found myself on the bus to Jeff's workplace. There I found him, and it all came out. He was undergoing a slow, prolonged breakdown, which would soon accelerate and have him off work for many months, and which still recurs and hangs on to this day.

At least we overcame our mutual embarrassment, but I still don't know what to do or say; and we both know that no one can help him if he can't help himself.

I think of Imogen, and her friends, their helplessness and frustration.

By the time I brought myself to find out what was happening with Jeff, I had finished my preliminary essay. I had no idea what this project might amount to. Obviously, it deserved to be more than a mere mental exercise for its own sake.

A magazine feature, perhaps? The *Reader's Digest*?

I returned to the Public Records Office and ordered copies of Imogen's birth and death certificates. She was born in Woking and died in Wimbledon. Conveniently, I lived in nearby Surbiton — she was a local girl, which was going to make life a lot easier than I had feared. In between her birth and her death, Imogen's life revolved around the Swinging London scene; I was walking in her footsteps.

"Killed herself" said the death certificate, starkly. Her last home, where she died in 1980, was next door to the Crooked Billet pub in Wimbledon Village. I used to drink there occasionally during the time that she was a regular. Who knows, we may even have rubbed shoulders at the bar. I wouldn't have recognized her, she was so far back in the dusty vaults of my memory.

I went to the Gap Road cemetery in Wimbledon to look for her grave. I walked right past it twice before I found it, a simple white marble slab, now dark and discolored, inconspicuous.

Short of wishful thinking about the bar at the Crooked Billet, it is the only physical proximity I will ever have to her. Sometimes, when I stand there, I feel nothing. At other times, it is as if she is standing beside me. It is unpredictable, just as she was.

When I first located the grave, the marble was solid black, coated by an unpleasant dark slime. From that day, and with each successive visit, the stain retreated inwards from the edges of the slab, which has become distinctly brighter.

Tentatively, I placed adverts in *The Stage* and in Imogen's local newspapers. The response was instant, and trickled on over the following weeks. It was an intriguing cross-section: a fellow pupil at the Royal Ballet School; a cult TV buff; the lady who owned Imogen's corner pet shop; a purveyor of theatrical memorabilia; an ordinary theatregoer; an actor who worked with Imogen in 1973.

Some over-eager sub-editor decided that I couldn't spell, and amended Imogen's surname to Hassell. I was incensed. I will always wonder whether someone of crucial importance, unknown to me, decided not to bother getting in touch, because I was plainly an idiot, who couldn't even spell her name right.

Nevertheless, the response pleased me. But such a haphazard selection was never going to amount to anything of real substance. I needed a method, a strategy.

My first major breakthrough came quickly in the form of John Foster, of Durham, theatre archivist extraordinaire. John provided me with a detailed list of Imogen's theatre credits, complete with cast lists — names to chase — a potential mine of information.

Equity very kindly agreed to forward my mail for me. Now I was up and running.

Hot on the heels of John Foster, came David Daly, Imogen's last agent. He suggested that I speak to a friend of Imogen's, Jackie Ingham.

The first friend—I had found one of Imogen's friends!

Speaking to Imogen's friends is a magical experience. As actors when they speak of her, they become her—imitating her voice and body language. They bring her to life. They often used various nicknames for her such as Imo and Jenny.

Jackie, who up to this point had been quite serious and intense, suddenly brightened and said:

"She would be delighted to know that we're all talking about her."

I swear I saw Imo sitting there with us at Jackie's kitchen table, grinning like a monkey.

From that moment, Imogen was alive. She walked beside me all the way back to Putney Station; and she has walked beside me ever since.

Jackie gave me names, who gave me more names, and so on, on and on. It's been that way with almost everyone I've spoken to. The effect is like tossing a handful of pebbles into a pond, watching the ripples from each pebble spread and interconnect.

Sometimes, the coincidences and connections were startling. An actress who knew Imogen briefly in 1958 was able by sheer chance to give me the address of a friend from 1978. Another, who had worked with Imo in 1980, put me in touch with Jenny's lover at LAMDA in the early '60s.

And so it went, the ripples fanning outwards, connecting. I began my research proper in January 1997 and by April I was ready to start writing. The results impressed me. I had barely begun, but already I had a first draft of some 120 typed pages.

It was going to be a book. I was going to write Imogen's biography.

I was writing a lot of letters and traveling on buses, subways and trains. My phone kept ringing and my correspondence file expanded. I was acquiring an impressive autograph collection and Imogen was putting on weight daily.

I'm not normally starstruck, but when Charlotte Rampling called I turned into a tongue-tied idiot. She was very nice about it. I was well and truly Rampled over the telephone.

One important breakthrough was eluding me, and I knew that without it the book could never be.

"Have you spoken to the brother?" I was asked again and again.

To date, it seemed as if the world was beating a path to my door. I'd had it easy. My contacts were making contacts for me; Equity was forwarding my mail to the names on the cast lists painstakingly handwritten by John Foster. I was depending heavily upon the kindness of strangers.

It was about time that I did some of the real spadework myself. I took myself off to Wimbledon Reference Library and barricaded myself behind a tower of telephone directories. Eventually, I emerged with a long list of Hassalls nationwide.

I typed a single letter, and gave thanks for the invention of the photocopier. All kinds of Hassalls responded, but none of them was one of *the* Hassalls. Then, my persistence paid off. Mark Hassall was Imogen's cousin. He was also an unofficial family historian and was very interested in what I was doing. Mark had only met Imogen once or twice, but he was able to put me in touch with a friend of the celebrated illustrator Joan Hassall, Christopher's sister and Imogen's Aunt Joana.

In no time at all, one friend of Joan Hassall grew to many, one of whom knew where to find Imogen's long-lost brother Nicholas. Approaches were made and I was given a mobile telephone number.

Despite a reputation as a reclusive loner, Nicholas Hassall was eager to speak to me. And so in January 1998, almost a year to the day since my research began, I found myself in a caravan park, somewhere on the South Coast.

By the end of the day, I had a taped a 50 page interview, which has been added to regularly over the succeeding months and years via letters and telephone conversations with Nick, who is always on the move and never in one place for too long.

Nick Hassall has been exceptionally helpful and encouraging. He has provided me with a wealth of unique insight, and has written letters of introduction that have gained access to documents that would otherwise have been barred to me.

Sitting opposite him at his makeshift table—after all the questions and myths and speculation—I felt almost as if I was privileged to be in the presence of a famous figure from fiction, come to life, this man of mystery about whom everyone was asking—Imogen's brother.

"My crazy brother is back in the country," Imogen used to tell her friends. "And he's living in a van." And I was speaking to him. Physically, I could stand beside her grave. Spiritually, this was as close as I could be. Nicholas gave me Imogen the child, and Imogen the child was Imogen the woman—not childish but child-like. She was a child inflicted with the disturbing chemistry of womanhood.

Nick gave me her broken soul. He is her brother, her flesh and blood; he is part of her. She is part of him.

Above all, he confirmed that my instincts were correct. Imogen was indeed someone I knew well.

One great question remained unanswered, the awful timing of Imogen's final, fatal cry for help: the very eve of a fabulous, much anticipated holiday to the sun, designed to restore her equilibrium and put her world to rights.

Without an answer, the book had no end. I knew who could tell me. It was Suzanna Leigh, the friend, who in November 1980 had been looking forward to sharing that holiday with Imogen. I had already written to her several times without reply, and was warned that Suzanna, like Nicholas Hassall, might be reclusive.

But once again, I was rewarded for rousing myself and showing a spark of my own initiative. I tried a new tack, and received a call from Suzanna's agent.

By another of those many coincidences, Suzanna was writing her autobiography, and Imogen, I was told, had a big part in it. I feared that Suzanna might be uncooperative, wanting to protect her material, but the opposite was true. Suzanna gave me the answer, or an answer—one of the first things that I sensed about Imogen is that there are many answers to every question, as many answers as there are Imogens.

Imogen's story, as it has been told to me, is one of many contradictions, some as extreme as Imogen herself could be. Each has his/her Imogen, and some defend his/her Imogen fiercely against any other Imogen, who is someone they do not recognize.

For all her extremes, it is clear that Imogen was loved by those who really knew her, they knew a warm and caring, generous person who had a huge affection and was capable of tremendous giving.

Despite the storms and disturbing mood swings, for all the demands that Imogen made upon their time and patience, her friends remember the fun—laughter, excitement and *joie de vivre*. She was an adventure.

Her friends, from different times and places, may not recognize another's Imogen, but they are united in one thing—they all miss her.

Imogen's friends are special people—showbiz people. They cannot resist performing, even to an audience of one. Imogen's drama was played out before my eyes. Their trained voices are wonderful. I love listening to actresses; their melody sends a shiver down my spine. Imogen had a marvelous voice, they say—and they speak with her voice, as they become her. It is magical.

Some are names. Most are of the rank and file, serving in the trenches. A few have left the business, disillusioned. Others, being roughly of Imogen's generation, are of an age when the jobs become scarcer. Some are lonely; others fall back on family, other creative interests, or the day job. I might feel sorry for some of them, if I didn't envy them so much. They have all been incredibly kind to me, a complete stranger, an outsider. They have made my life extraordinary.

I feel guilty, because what I have written about Imogen

Imogen was always ready with a pose.

has saddened and disturbed some of them. What I have written has supplanted her old friends' memories of her, of their Imogen. Now, when they think of her, they are recalling not their own Jenny or Imo, but the person—a complete stranger to some of them—described in these pages. I have taken away their memories.

"It just goes to show," said one "how you can never really know someone."

"Her life story wasn't her."

I never met her, but I know her very well. She was someone I recognized, from the very start.

"You have written with remarkable insight, understanding and compassion," wrote Nicholas Hassall. "I am particularly struck by your uncanny ability to bring Jenny's personality to life as if you knew her better than I did."

I have felt her presence, standing by me at her graveside, strolling beside me through her old haunts of Kensington and Chelsea, Fulham, Putney and Wimbledon. I see and hear her, when her friends become her, and after I speak to them she follows me home. When I am occupied by other things, she is waiting for me when I am finished, when I come home. I never dream about her, because she is not stored in my subconscious. She is in my every-day, waking consciousness—she is a living part of my life.

"You must wish that you'd been able to meet her."

There is surprise when I hesitate. I'm not so sure. Which Imogen? Imogen who was an absolute delight at all times or Imogen the nightmare walking?

I've been told that I'm in love with her, that I'm obsessed by her, that I would have been one of her victims.

I doubt if she would have noticed me.

I try and avoid fantasizing about her. I do not indulge in the fan's common delusion that if only *I* had been there for her, none of this would have happened, *I* would have sorted her out. Imogen is not my Marilyn Monroe. Imogen was *not* Marilyn. Nor was she a Judy Garland. She might have wanted to be Vivien Leigh.

If I do let my imagination wander, I put Imogen in *Persuaders*-world, through which she strolls arm-in-arm with Lord Brett Sinclair. Brett might have been Imogen's ideal Mr. Right—handsome, protective, rich and benign.

The strength of her presence is unpredictable, just as she was, and her moods have swung dramatically.

I once lost eight weeks, laid low by a severe chest infection. For eight weeks, I did not visit her grave. In the eighth week, late in the evening, an awful, crushing weight of sadness descended upon me without warning. The force of it was frightening, because I could not recognize it as one of my own familiar moods. This great blackness belonged to someone else.

Pale and sickly as I was, I said, "All right, I'm sorry, I'll come and visit you tomorrow." The tremendous weight dissipated, followed by a strange tranquillity, the calm after the storm, as if someone roused from a terrible nightmare had been gently coaxed back to sleep.

Next morning, coughing and shivering, I stood in the cold rain, beside Imogen's grave. From that day on, I had no more such disturbances. Once, her presence was almost as extreme, but this time it was the very opposite. It was as if the room was glowing, full to bursting with bright sunlight, a happy exuberance.

"When I hear music," Imogen said to a friend. "I want to dance." Imogen was danc-ing.

I have been accused, by my more spiritual acquaintances, of being hopelessly earthbound. There may be many things that we don't yet know of or understand, but I don't hang labels on them. I have never believed in ghosts or little green men.

But I have felt these things, that's all I can say.

"Perhaps she's taking you on a heavenly trip," said Jackie Ingham. My friend Caroline believes that this was meant to be—unfinished business, she suggests.

Imogen does indeed have unfinished business. She deserves better than her dubious immortality as a bikini-clad pin-up.

"Oh yeah, Imogen Hassall," sneered a stallholder at a Film and TV Memorabilia Fair. "She was a mad nymphomaniac."

This is not a traditional showbiz biography. It is not a celebration of a long and il-lustrious career, or the brief but brilliant life of some bright and fleeting comet that blazed unforgettably across the Hollywood firmament. It is the human tragedy of a warm and caring, loving individual, who was broken inside and was lost.

"She would be delighted to know that we're all talking about her."

CHAPTER ONE
WAR BABY

If ever there was an uncertain year, and an uncertain time in which to be born, it was 1942.

All around the world: total war. In Europe the Nazi fist held the occupied countries in an iron grip. To the East, Hitler's legions, despite stiffening Soviet resistance, were still cocky and confident of ultimate victory; while in the desert, Rommel's Afrika Korps was poised to launch a sweeping offensive to Gazala and beyond. In the Far East and the Pacific, the Japanese were unstoppable expanding their Imperial horizons.

But as 1942 developed, Allied fortunes began to show signs of improvement. Montgomery triumphed at the second battle of El Alamein and Anglo-American forces paraded ashore in North Africa, banners waving. On the Eastern Front General Winter had worn a red star, and an entire German army was bleeding to death at Stalingrad. Across the Pacific the United States Navy and Marines were now giving as good as they got at Midway and Guadalcanal. Lancasters and the first B-17s rolled like thunder over Germany, while the unsung heroes of the Merchant Navy were pushing through and turning the tide in the Battle of the Atlantic.

After Alamein Churchill summed up the year of 1942 as not the beginning of the end, but the end of the beginning, defining it as a year of uncertain hopes. In embattled Britain there was the first faint glimmer of light as tired people, haunted by the smoke and darkness of the Blitz, dared to hope that victory just might be possible.

On August 25, 1942, a tiny piece of private history was made. A daughter was born, a small package of uncertain hopes to an actress and a Captain in the Education Corps.

In 1942 the London theatres were never dark—they were still an oasis of escapism and optimism. Bright lights, laughter and wit sparkled like champagne bubbles when *The Dancing Years* was playing at the Adelphi. It was a continuing triumph for Ivor Novello—the darling of those lost inter-war years which were the golden age of glamour and sophistication.

The Dancing Years was but one of many jewels in Novello's glittering crown: *Glamorous Night*, *Careless Rapture*, *Crest of the Wave*, *Arc de Triomphe* and *King's Rhapsody*. Ivor wrote the music for the songs that captured the romantic longings of his times. The words were written by Captain Christopher Hassall of Old Woking, Surrey.

In 1942 30-year-old Christopher Hassall was lauded as a limitlessly gifted man, who had fulfilled the promise of his youth.

As an undergraduate at Oxford, Christopher was a handsome Romeo in a famous production staged in 1932 under the direction of John Gielgud: "Christopher was a charming young man and I much enjoyed working with him at Oxford...he was a very good Romeo with the youth, looks, and energy needed to partner Peggy Ashcroft and Edith Evans."

Christopher was determined to seek a life in the limelight and made his professional debut in the summer of 1933. His career hit the ground running, and he saw out the rest of that year touring Egypt and Australia with Athene Seyler and Nicholas Hannen in a grand repertory of 13 plays.

A young Christopher Hassall painted by his sister Joan (1930/31).

Christopher was also a poet, above all a poet, a man who had an uncanny knack with words. His gifts made him a bright prospect in his day. But it would be the poetry that he wrote to be set to music that would earn him his lasting fame—although he could not have imagined that in 1933.

Hassall's stage career lasted into the late 1930s and included an appearance in a play that he penned himself—another of his many talents. He was a veritable Renaissance Man.

By then he had been distracted by an unexpected and more exciting challenge. In 1934, Christopher Hassall met Ivor Novello. Things were about to change.

Christopher had come to Ivor's attention as a proposed understudy for a Romeo that never saw the light of day. Ivor set eyes on this charming and rather beautiful young man and employed him at once, taking him on tour in *Fresh Fields* and *Proscenium*. In gratitude and as an expression of his admiration, Christopher modestly offered the great one a slim volume of his poems. Ivor actually took the time to read them, and must have been impressed.

In September 1934 Christopher was playing a small part in *Murder in Mayfair* at the Globe in Oxford. One evening Ivor waylaid him as he arrived at the stage door, and mysteriously took him to a nearby café. Ivor told Christopher that he wanted him to write the lyrics for a musical destined for Drury Lane. The startled young actor-poet felt obliged to point out that he had never attempted lyrics before, and he rarely attended musical plays.

Ivor had read Christopher's poems and was backing his instincts. Producing a scrap of paper with a few bits of a tune scribbled on it, he ordered Christopher to take it away to his dressing room and deal with it during the long intervals between his few short scenes. He was told to have a complete lyric prepared by the end of the show.

"See if you can get the words glamorous night into it," was the only advice he had for his bemused protégé. And so was forged the emotional and professional chemistry of one of the most productive and successful partnerships in the history of theatre.

1934 was a doubly momentous year for Christopher Hassall. It was Novello who introduced the aspiring young poet to Sir Edward Marsh—the man who would become his mentor and greatest friend.

They met at a midnight supper in Oxford hosted by Ivor Novello. His relatively low status in Novello's touring company hardly merited his dining out with the management, but Ivor was eager to arrange the encounter—Christopher remarked, "I must meet this old friend of his...and let him see what I had written."

In 1934 Eddie Marsh was aged 61—Christopher's senior by 40 years. The young man must have felt humbled in Marsh's presence. He summed up his patron's achievements in his introduction to *Ambrosia and Small Beer*, an anthology of their lifelong correspondence published some 30 years later: "In 1934, when our paths crossed, Marsh was private secretary to J.H. Thomas at the Dominions Office, and due shortly to retire from the Civil Service after a full career chiefly distinguished by its period of 23 years spent at the right hand of Winston Churchill. Apart from the personal secretary who was known to have accompanied his Chief through so many vicissitudes of his middle life, there was the collector of paintings, among the first to encourage Stanley Spencer, Paul Nash, Mark Gertler, before the first world war, and latterly Ivon Hitchens and Graham Sutherland: the friend and biographer of Rupert Brooke: the mentor of Flecker, D.H. Lawrence, de la Mare, and the rest of those poets who first won public notice in the pages of *Georgian Poetry*, the series of five anthologies which appeared between 1912 and 1923 without clue to their editorship beyond the initials E.M.: the patron of theatrical first nights, and more recently the translator of La Fontaine's Fables."

The midnight supper party began rather stiffly: "We must have made some headway over the meal, for he asked me to lunch with him at the hotel next day. Naturally it was not until long after our first encounter that I began to realize how timely for him had been my first appearance on the scene, or how well qualified I was, by mere chance, to engage his interest. The Georgian enterprise, when poets were his almost daily companions, had come to an end some 10 years before, and he must have been missing the interest of sharing the problems of an author who was as yet only trying to discover himself."

Marsh, like Novello, read Christopher's verse and was inspired. Here began yet another collaboration which would evolve into an abiding and profound friendship.

Christopher would be a frequent visitor to Eddie's apartments in Gray's Inn, where they would sit up into the early hours discussing great things. Christopher might stay the night, sleeping in a portable camp bed that once belonged to Rupert Brooke, a treasure which would become one of his daughter's proudest possessions.

Christopher Hassall's eccentric good fortune was in keeping with his nature. Christopher was an odd mix of the scholarly and the bohemian. An extremely cultured, academic and quite conventional figure, he also had a taste for the glitz and glamour of the footlights and the silver screen.

His working habits were obsessive and had to be. When he first met Ivor Novello it was fortunate that Christopher was unmarried and without commitments, for his new employer had him churning out lyrics at an incredible rate, struggling to keep pace with Novello's creative flow. Christopher would snatch his meals whenever he could and would fortify himself with Guinness while chain-smoking and gulping endless cups of tea. He would cut himself while bleary-eyed and attempting to shave—still distracted by the words whirling in his head. He would bleed all over a Guinness and tea-stained muddle of paper.

"What fun it all was," Novello reminisced to Christopher while he was in the military. "You could bring me a lyric and give it to me and I would say 'No, it stinks.' Then you would clutch your head, alter a word and I would read it again and say 'It's heavenly.' That's the way to work."

"Isn't this heaven?" Ivor would exclaim. "Can there be anything more enjoyable than what we are doing?"

It is generally assumed that Christopher's relationship with Ivor Novello went beyond the bonds of friendship. Many think gay when Christopher's name is mentioned.

The association, of course, was because Ivor and several of Christopher's closest friends were homosexual. Some suggest Ivor was in love with this handsome, cultured, charming young man, but Christopher was anything but gay—the very opposite.

Others concede that, while Christopher may have had a gay side, it would never have found physical expression; that was not his nature. And those were different times: there was no coming out—such impulses would often be repressed by feelings of shame and self-loathing and well-hidden behind a façade of so-called respectability; homosexual activity was subject to criminal charges.

There were levels of deep same-sex friendship which, while profound and emotional, had no physical sexual expression. As for Christopher's set, few people so heavily immersed in the arts can lack gay friends and colleagues.

It seems that there was an element in Christopher's character that causes people to arrive at an obvious conclusion. One thing is certain, Christopher had immense charm, and it is easy to see how some men, as well as many women, fell in love with him.

The same word association games are played with regard to Christopher and Eddie Marsh. With the same lack of foundation.

Those who knew Hassall say Eddie Marsh fell under his spell. Like Ivor Novello and Rupert Brooke before him, Christopher was both beautiful and gifted. Eddie's love was channeled into an urge to adopt his latest protégé as an unofficial son—to support him and nurture his talents. Ever conventional, he was keen to observe all the proprieties, going so far as to meet the young poet's parents. Christopher's son Nicholas remembers: "It was patently obvious that my Father was held by Eddie at the highest level of his affections. By his effusive manner when he visited the house, which at times was somewhat irritating to

Mother, he made that abundantly clear even to me as a small child. There was a tenderness that sometimes I found faintly disturbing—his 'dear boy' instead of 'dear chap' or 'old fellow.' However, it must be said that without Eddie's help we would have gone down the tubes, and anyway affection it was, sex it wasn't."

Nicholas acknowledges that Edward Marsh was an important figure in the history of his family—"of all my father's friends he remains in my memory most clearly. I believe he may have contributed to the purchase of one of the houses that was bought...My father would have been unable to make any progress as a writer, penniless and unknown as he was, without the enormous amount of help from Eddie."

Eve Lynett as a rising young actress in *Children in Uniform* (1932.

Christopher's inclinations would be irrelevant except that, years later, his daughter admitted that such assumptions troubled her.

In 1973 Imogen mentioned how difficult it was to be the daughter of someone *thought* to be bisexual or homosexual. And there will be shocking allegations made about his sexuality and his behavior, all the more shocking because—whether true or not—it is claimed that his daughter made them.

Many assert that the key to Imogen's troubles is to be found in her relationship with her father. It is clear that the issue of Christopher's sexuality preyed on Imogen's mind, and her concern would be expressed by her in a characteristically contradictory and disturbing manner.

Where Christopher Hassall could be scholarly and conventional, his wife was rich and colorful. Eve Lynett was an actress and was everything that an actress was expected to be: vivid, glamorous and temperamental. A chorus girl in the early 1930s, her dark, exotic beauty was sufficient to make her a Hollywood prospect. Tinseltown beckoned and she posed for stills and made screen tests. Unfortunately, the camera did not love her, so she came back to the English theatre.

Imogen inherited her mother's good looks and more. There was Indian blood on her mother's side, which made the baby's beauty even rarer. And her mother gave to her daughter her volatile nature, fragility and extremes.

The marriage was a fractured one and doomed, an ill mix of conflicting chemistry. Christopher wanted a goddess and tried to idealize Eve into a role for which she was utterly unsuited; the wife, who in later years, would torment her blameless sister-in-law with lurid tales of her husband's sexual shortcomings.

The poet by Joan Hassall from the title page of *Penthesperon*

Their daughter would be discovered crying all alone because her parents were always arguing and were about to go their separate ways. And that child would grow into a woman, who privately would sum up her childhood bitterly, darkly, with confused images of fear and rejection.

The baby had an extraordinary pedigree; she was born with a lot to live up to.

It did not begin with Christopher. The baby's grandfather was John Hassall—the successful poster artist. And Aunt Joana, Joan Hassall, was a much-praised illustrator. It was Aunt Joan who won a competition to design the invitations to the Coronation in 1953.

Friends of the family were drawn from the ranks of the great from the arts, the theatre and far beyond. The baby would grow up surrounded by greatness and fame and talent. In her world talent was something that one took for granted.

The extraordinary world of the Hassalls began with grandfather John, the important graphic artist famed for his humorous advertising posters.

John Hassall was a true Edwardian, and he was larger-than-life. Affability radiated from him; a sociable, gregarious man, this doyen of the bohemian Savage Club. There was a certain twinkle in his eye and in his prime he sported a set of handsome mustaches.

"More often than not," says his grandson Nicholas. "He was in a total state of inebriation." But John was ever good-humored. He was never violent or abusive. "His drunkenness was limited to a form of paralysis that rendered him incapable of climbing the steps to his front door in Notting Hill."

Christopher with the aid of Joan would retrieve him and drag him indoors. It was a regular and embarrassing experience that had a profound and lasting effect on them both, driving them to an opposite extreme of conventionality.

Their mother Maude was a stark contrast to her flamboyant husband. She was a supreme Victorian "involved with the church next door [and] had extreme views on people enjoying themselves and...resented deeply her husband's addiction to alcohol."

Her grandson says Maude was a prude. John Hassall was a bohemian, well traveled, sophisticated and given to the enjoyment of his food, his drink and the company of his friends at the Savage Club.

The marriage—a classic disaster and a model of incompatibility—occurred on the rebound, following the death of John's first wife, who was a far more fitting and lively companion. Maude's attitude was imprinted on her offspring. Joan took it philosophically, but Christopher was deeply affected psychologically.

Imogen's brother Nicholas is a year-and-a-half older. The odd one out, he was somehow out of place with the rest of his charismatic family.

Those who do recall Nicholas Hassall remember him as a peripheral figure, not an ugly duckling by any means, but lacking the clan's natural glamour. Nicholas was quiet and reserved, more academic like his father. Those who met him say that he was a nice and polite young man, but kept very much to himself. He was not quite of this world, highly strung, and preoccupied.

To this day Nicholas Hassall appears a mystery man even to his sister's closest friends and even, it seems, to his sister. He soon took off by himself and was a constant traveler. He did have the creative genes; he was musical, and his ambition was to be a composer. He was ingenious, mechanically and electronically, and there are reports of his supporting himself by busking with a home-made organ on the streets of Rome.

Seen through the eyes of Imogen's friends, Nicholas remains a distant, fleeting phantom, re-surfacing occasionally.

His sister let slip other, strangely troubling things, while on tour in 1978, about her childhood, giving disconnected glimpses of pain and rejection.

Imogen died in 1980. Nicholas was at the funeral.

Today Nicholas Hassall is a determined loner, living on the move in a compact mobile home drawn by an old Mercedes. He does not want the world to know where he is and says that he makes a living busking and doing odd jobs including mini-cab driver, petrol pump attendant and even a spell as a bookkeeper. He was a French horn player in an orchestra for a few years—and claims that the musical establishment froze him out—but his ambition remains to be a composer. He is always composing on electronic keyboards, a lap-top computer and a stack of homemade synthesizers: "Six symphonies, tone poems; I don't even know if it's any good, but I go on writing them." There has only ever been one professional commission, which was for the BBC in the 1970s, which he says he owes to the good offices of his sister.

Nicholas has been, and still is, a troubled soul sustained by his yoga and his beliefs in the spiritual and the occult. He speaks with great depth of feeling about his sister and his parents.

Nicholas was born in 1941 although he admits that he could never be the older brother Imogen needed.

He says that his earliest memory of his childhood was of his parents fighting.

It was a shipboard romance, an infatuation between two sophisticated, highly intelligent, clever, but utterly incompatible people.

The name Imogen was significant long before the birth of Christopher's daughter. It was bestowed first upon Eve by Christopher who was inspired by the romantic heroine of Shakespeare's *Cymbeline*.

"I brought to luncheon Evelyn Chapman," wrote Christopher Hassall. "The original Imogen of the Soliloquy, who was soon to become my wife."

The Soliloquy is "Soliloquy to Imogen," published in the anthology *Penthesperon* in 1938; a long love poem recounting their first meeting and the mystic immediacy of their attraction:

> We danced
> Shyly, not speaking, more as partial friends
> Newly remet than as a man and a woman
> Nameless to one another, for there shone
> Within our minds a half-light of acquaintance,
> Distant, vague as though Love were the sunrise
> And we two sleepers drowsily disturbed.
> Perhaps, while yet a little boy, my head
> A world of toys, I'd stoop to pick a flower
> And found the texture of your cheek; the slow
> Murmur of August was your sound, and leaves
> Touch'd me like loving hands. It may have been,
> Turning the pages of an old romance,
> The indistinct phantasma of a face
> Had moved under the print, and peer'd as if
> Through the wire grating of a cage, then vanished
> Before my nails could scratch it free; for here,
> Mortally woven in one shape, were all
> The premonitions of my earliest days,
> Alive, perfected, and attainable,
> New only in compounded loveliness,
> All else familiar

In August 1942 Eddie Marsh harked back to the Soliloquy upon hearing of the birth of his friend's second child: "It was the greatest joy to hear your news—and to welcome Imogen—certainly the slow music of August is her sound."

But this Imogen would never dance to slow music.

Christopher was a young touring actor with ambitions to leave the stage and be a poet and a man of letters. Eve was a strong-minded, professional woman of independent means, who had come from India with little or nothing and made a good living as an actress and coloratura soprano. At one time she even had her own repertory company and under a pseudonym wrote books and magazine articles. She was an intellectual in her own right.

The repertory theatre was not exactly Eve Lynett's, but she was crucial to its survival. The company in question was John Counsell's at the Theatre Royal, Windsor. In 1933-34 the company had failed and—as John Counsell recounts in his autobiography of 1963, *Counsell's Opinion*—it was not going to start up again until he had secured backing to the tune of what was in the 1930s a very large sum of money, calculated at some £2,000.

Three or so years went by before John Counsell felt ready to set himself to the prolonged and arduous task of fund-raising. Then, one morning, he received a telephone call from Eve:

"I see you're opening the Windsor theatre again."

"I'm hoping to, but nothing is settled."

"My name is Eve Lynett. I came to see you when you had the theatre before. You said you couldn't give me a job because you were going bankrupt the next week, but that I'd better have some coffee. I was wondering if..."

The young lady had read something in the papers—"I was obviously about to be bombarded with requests for jobs from every out-of-work actress in London." I replied, "Drop me a line when you see that I'm definitely starting, and I will arrange to see you again."

"I wanted to see you now, because I think I might be able to help you financially."

"I think that is very unlikely. I'm needing a very large sum of money."

He had already turned down "several budding geniuses who had offered to put up £50 if they could be my leading lady with a guarantee in their contracts that they were to play Lady Macbeth and Saint Joan in their first season." His caller was not to be put off. She persuaded him to meet her for a drink—"Besides, she sounded like a nice girl—must have been, or I wouldn't have given her coffee when we met before."

They arranged to meet for lunch at the Café Anglais: "I found a petite, pretty dark-haired girl wearing a pillbox hat with a tassel. She looked about 15. She rose to greet me with a warm, friendly smile. Her piquant personality and obvious sense of style impressed me at once. After the preliminaries were over I said, 'If I ever do get started I should very much like to have you in my company, assuming you have had sufficient experience. What have you in fact done?' " She replied, "We are not here to talk about me, but about your plans for Windsor."

John Counsell had been grinding out the same old tune for months, but Eve's keen attention restored his enthusiasm—"I went further than the usual exposition of facts and figures and held forth at length upon my ideas as to how a theatre should be run, and what one should aim at achieving."

His companion's response overwhelmed him: "Eve leant forward to stub out her cigarette and with almost studied casualness said, 'I had meant to offer you £500, but after hearing about your ideas I propose to make it £1,000.' "

Counsell was overcome by surprise, gratitude, bewilderment, disbelief and a sudden wild upsurge of hope: "She went on to explain that her offer was made without strings, but if I really meant that I would like to have her in the company she would be delighted and honored to play as cast. I must promise, however, that no one in the company should know that she had put any money up. Having written the check, she was going to forget about it and asked me to do the same. Our relationship was to be that of manager and actress, and she would have no more say in how the theatre was run than any other member of the company."

Casting in John Counsell's company followed the principle of making the best possible use of every member of the company, irrespective of salary or professional status. Eve was as good as her word, accepting whatever role was offered her—just an ordinary member of the company. She appeared in Windsor Rep's first production after its revival, *Dear Brutus* by J.M. Barrie, staged in March 1938. Later, she played the lead before King George VI and Queen Elizabeth in *Rose Without A Thorn*, the tragedy of Henry VIII and Katherine Howard.

Eve was obviously thought of very highly at Windsor. "Ivor went on Wednesday to see *Distinguished Gathering* at the Windsor Rep," wrote Eddie Marsh. "Where he said he found everyone speaking with admiration and affection of Eve."

The Windsor management were fulsome in their praise—"The Counsells told Ivor and me how supreme Eve had been in *Dear Brutus*."

Eve had done good work with other companies at other theatres. In October 1934 she was Sombra, one of the leads in the well-known musical comedy *The Arcadians* at the Grand Theatre, Leeds. In May 1936 she was billed to appear in *Fritz*, described as "a new musical play of exceptional merit...a colorful romance of the Paris boulevards," which was about a humble cigarette maker who survives on her dreams of stardom.

Once merely one of the ladies of the chorus, Eve Lynett was now a charming young musical comedy star. With John Counsell, she proved her worth as a dramatic actress.

Eve's generosity could be counted upon on a regular basis. When John Counsell was in urgent need of £250 for re-decorating expenses, he knew that he could call upon Eve. Her constant generosity would be testified to over the years by friends and family and even the most casual acquaintances — it would be a trait inherited by her daughter.

And Eve's bounty extended far beyond the theatre. In 1938 in a chemist's shop in Chelmsford, a base for the British Vitamin Products Company, Ralph Chapman was experimenting with a range of vitamin C enriched fruit juices. Eve Lynett was a Chapman before she was a Hassall and she gave much-needed financial support to brother Ralph, whose endeavors grew eventually into the Britvic Company. Much later, Eve's daughter would be referred to in the tabloids as the Britvic heiress, although her errant behavior, or so Imogen claimed, would forfeit her alleged inheritance.

Christopher and Eve: the slow murmuring music of August was drowned out by the clash of genes and chemistry. Christopher was half Welsh, and he had something of the Welsh temperament. He married a woman who was, effectively, a foreigner — half Indian, brought up in a totally alien environment. Apparently Christopher failed to appreciate this and was somewhat nonplused by it. Looking at his daughter in whom the exotic strain manifested itself for all to see, he used to say, "It's hard for me to understand. Here I am, a so-called Englishman, and I've got a daughter who looks either like a Southern Italian or a Northern Indian."

But Eve fell for Christopher and sacrificed her career for his sake, following him from one temporary home to another during the uncertain war years. Eve not only gave up her career but her freedom for the sake of her children. It was Eve who brought up Nicholas and Imogen as the family migrated, following Christopher's fluctuating fortunes from Highgate to the Vale of Health, then to the Manor House in Old Woking. "Old Woking was the nicest of the houses because it was the quietest and most peaceful — apart from the rows, and the rows were very, very serious at times."

Imogen as a happy baby

Christopher Hassall's life was with his friends and not the family. Nicholas does not blame his father—"he couldn't have been any different." Unmarried, he would have been perfect. He was a genuinely kind man, generous and gentle, but he was useless as a family man.

When his children were in their teens Christopher was able to relate to them as individuals, but in their infancy and early childhood he appeared to show little or no interest in them at all. "If my mother had brought up both of us by herself it would have been a lot better...she would have made a better job of bringing up her children on her own than having to put up with the relationship with my father at the same time."

Eve applied herself to the task of raising her children as professionally as she did with everything else in her life—"she was obviously resentful, but her consolation was that she had us." Christopher was simply unable to adapt to the family scene. He treated the home as an office and a place to have a meal. He was often away and was always attending great functions to which Eve was not invited. Many people actually believed that Christopher was unmarried. This is what hurt Eve the most. "She couldn't stand Father bossing her or just ignoring her, which he did."

The rewards, both emotional and professional, that Christopher reaped from his friendship with Ivor Novello were far more meaningful to him than any marriage could bestow.

Like Eddie Marsh, Ivor loved Christopher for his talent and his beauty and lavished attention and affection upon him. The romantic in Christopher loved to be adored, and he clearly basked in the warmth of such adoration. Ivor's interminable telephone calls were a frequent intrusion in the marital home, and Eddie Marsh also was competing for Christopher's time and emotions. Eve, largely ignored, would recoil at the effusive terms of endearment that embellished her husband's conversations with his friends.

Christopher's friends were his priority, and friendship the very essence of life. "Father indeed required the affection of his friends while being unable to maintain that similar level towards my mother. Indeed deep friendship was so central to his personality that on noticing how seemingly insular I was, maintaining few friends and none close, that I remember him well into my teens berating me for my inability to have close friends."

But there can be no doubt that the force of Eve's character made a great impression on her husband, and in particular, her passion and fortitude as a mother.

In April 1941 Christopher related an extraordinary incident to his friend Eddie Marsh, in which Eve, assailed by the full fury of the Blitz, was an inspiration to all those around her:

> By this time I had managed to rejoin my wife, who on 16 April was about to leave the hospital in Chelsea, where she had given birth to her child, when the whole area was involved in one of the worst air raids...
>
> All that Wednesday night in London she had been up with the baby under one arm, pushing beds to places of safety as the walls shook; and once she washed and changed the clothes of an old woman who had been unable to control herself with fright. On another occasion they had only just wheeled all the beds to the floor below when a patient was killed, so they all had to be moved again, and keeping Nicholas close under her breasts, she ducked low to avoid a piece of flying glass that, only a few feet away, penetrated deep into a nurse's thigh. At another time the

lights were suddenly extinguished, there was a scream, and four white-aproned figures were blown like leaves into a huddle at the end of the passage by a blast that Eve, by stepping back into a doorway, had miraculously avoided. There was no respite, for now the casualties from outside began to come in, and the main hall of the hospital was like a battlefield, while all around, on benches against the wall, sat the old people from the workingmen's houses opposite, hugging their bundles, and palely looking on, while nurses threaded their way to and fro with towels and bandages; and every time Eve passed carrying Nicholas they would smile at each other and nod their mute approval. She stopped to pat the hand of one and suddenly her fingers were crushed in a terrified grip. Just for a second the old crone showed the terror she was trying to hide. By now Nicholas was howling, and Eve found a small room, empty, no furniture; so she sat on the floor against the wall and uncovered her breast. A doctor followed her in, stood and watched a moment. "A woman feeding her child," he said at last. "So life is going on." There was blood on the lapels of his white coat. "You know, we're all very grateful to you," he said, and went out.

Christopher, the old-fashioned intellectual, lacked the practical turn of mind to be the head of a family. He was "a medieval man...He would have liked to work by candlelight if it wouldn't have been too much bother. He only used a ball-point pen because a quill pen was too much bother. He should have studied how to put a nail in a wall—useless he was! He couldn't even put a light bulb in!"

Christopher was most definitely not technologically minded. This was a source of continual exasperation to his son, who had a flair for anything mechanical/electrical.

Nicholas once asked his father to record a music program from the radio. He set everything up in advance and rehearsed his father thoroughly—all he had to do was press the record button. Nicholas then went out for the evening. When the time came Christopher panicked and did not dare touch the machine.

At a time when the television age was dawning, the Hassall household was a TV-free zone. Nicholas does not complain about this—he sees its absence as a positive contribution to his intellectual development. When Christopher did purchase a TV set, it was for the sole purpose of watching the Coronation in 1953. After that, it was banished to a side room where it sat unused, gathering dust. Fascinated, Nicholas could not resist the temptation to dissect it, leaving it in bits scattered all over the floor. Eve did suggest that he might want to re-assemble the set in case Imogen wanted to watch something. Imogen showed no interest. And so, in the Hassall home, the TV languished unwanted.

Exasperation could flare into arguments between father and son. "His irrational rages were a smokescreen for a person under deep psychological strain. I remember the incredible reaction one elicited from him on subjects as diverse as the matter of where I was going to do my laundry, and an encounter with a drunk in the crush bar of the Marlowe Theatre in Canterbury."

In the theatre bar, a man plainly the worse for wear from drink had breathed all over Christopher while complimenting him fulsomely on his many achievements. This trivial incident provoked an extreme reaction. Describing the event to his family, Christopher broke down in tears, reminded traumatically of the embarrassments caused by his bohemian father. "Father's reaction was caused by the tensions in his childhood background."

It would be a row about how Nicholas had chosen to do his laundry that made Nicholas turn his back on his family and begin a solitary life on the road.

Lest it be thought that Christopher Hassall was utterly ineffectual, it should be noted that soon after the outbreak of war he decided to enlist. Nor was his military career confined to the Education Corps. He joined the Royal Artillery and in May 1940 was posted to take

Imogen with a favorite toy dog—as an adult she would have many beloved real dogs.

charge of an anti-aircraft unit at Sevenoaks—"...the jumble of potato-peeling, drill, metal-polish, battle-dress and gun mechanism, which had become my life; and after a while they were following me from airfield to ammo dump, or wherever it might be in Kent that had called for our mobile defense against low-flying attack."

He had a daredevil streak in him, a touch of the T.E. Lawrence, making his tours of inspection on a fast motorbike, rushing, exploding, as he put it, from one gun emplacement to the next. Christopher's adventures "raised my hair," said Eddie Marsh, who reported that Eve had told friends that Christopher had "broken 31 army bicycles by [his] impetuosity."

At home Christopher was far less extroverted. He found it very difficult to show affection—"one would kiss him on the cheek every Christmas." And, although he sired two children, sexually he was a disappointment to a very sensual woman. "His mother was a terrible battle-ax of a woman, something to do with the Church of England, and brought him up in true British fashion—no sex please we're British."

Nicholas acknowledges his father's strong emotional attachment to Ivor Novello—"when he died, he collapsed, practically," but insists that "it wasn't a physical thing, the idea of having physical co-habitation with a man would have appalled him. If he had any sexual relationships at all, he would have had them with the women who were also his closest friends."

Desperate for some kind of life of her own, Eve resorted to purchasing a mobile home as a means of escape. By the end of the War the husband and wife were barely cohabiting. The final split would come when Christopher moved to Tonford Manor, Canterbury, in 1961.

Deep down Christopher and Eve remained fond of each other. After the final separation, they would meet on Victoria Station for what Nicholas describes as sobbing sort of reunions.

Nicholas portrays the Hassalls as the absolute classic example of a dysfunctional family, but he refuses to blame his parents for his own troubles or for his sister's pain and destruction. "I'm not blaming Father, Father couldn't have been any different...they were both lovely people in their own right—I felt sorry for both of them. It was not all doom in my family. The humor and jokes that passed among us, even at our own expense, could be hilarious."

As a young child, Imogen gave no hint of the storms to come. "She was a placid, quiet little individual...a trusting, innocent small child."

The family called her Jenny, and little Jenny idolized her big brother and used to follow him about. She never got in the way and benevolent big brother would tolerate her. "She wanted me to be an older brother all her life, in a way."

Little sisters, of course, rarely understand their big brother's games, but, ever tolerant, Nicholas would allow her to participate.

Once when Nicholas was seven or eight and Jenny was about six, he put his sister in a crate, tied a rope around it, tossed the rope over the roof beams in the barn and proceeded to haul the crate up until Jenny was swaying in mid-air about 20 feet off the ground. He then ran off to call his mother: "Look what I've done Mum, I've pulled Jenny up in a lift!"

Eve came and saw and screamed. But Jenny was blissfully unconcerned. She always trusted her big brother.

It appears that little Jenny caught the acting bug at a very early age. She was, even then, a natural performer. "Jenny's first experience of acting must have been when she was about five. For I loved to build as a child vast constructions out of anything I could lay my hands on, stacking up chairs and tables to the ceiling in a most precarious manner. On occasion I would build a proscenium arch and a stage for Jenny to give a theatrical performance. Apparently it must have been very funny, because I always remember both parents helpless with laughter, Jenny's face slightly perplexed but otherwise pleased that she was so well received. Oh yes. She had the acting bit in her blood from both parents."

An old friend of the Hassall family, Iain Stuart Robertson, on a visit to the Manor House in Old Woking, saw how Jenny's parents indulged her.

Little Jenny, barely out of her toddlerhood, was observed in the garden busily cutting the heads off all the flowers. To Iain's astonishment no one lifted a finger to stop her.

Eve Hassall did her best to be impartial with her children. They always got the same and the best of everything—whatever they wanted. They were spoiled children—"it was always easier to fob us off with toys."

But Nicholas was his mother's favorite. Eve had lost a child and Nicholas was a complicated birth; she had a special place in her heart for him, and Nicholas says that his mother was the only person he was ever really close to. "I took my mother's side and still maintain today that she was the best mother a boy could have had. She sacrificed her own very lucrative career to bring up her children, giving her not inconsiderable wealth away to Father and to her brother for Britvic. What did Father sacrifice in his life? Nothing as far as I can see. He did pay the bills when he could like any family man and for that we had to put up with his double life in which he lived in the house but was not of it. He lived among his friends and gave nothing of his anima, either to his wife or to either of his children."

Imogen with her big brother Nicholas

Jenny grew into a very strong-willed girl and soon asserted herself. "The pecking order in the family eventually became Mum, Dad, Sister and then me at the bottom."

There was the inevitable spark of competition between mother and daughter. "She felt that Mother was trying to upstage her...it was my mother in public that was demonstrating a degree of professional poise that my sister was not yet capable of emulating...she reacted by feeling diminished in my mother's company. My mother could be formidable when she wanted to be!"

Academically Jenny reigned supreme. Nicholas would struggle to achieve his academic goals by a long and painful process of crammers and private tutors. He had trouble at school; Jenny was popular and hard-working and passed all her exams comfortably.

Eddie Marsh had tried to encourage Christopher to think deeply about the upbringing of his children. When son and daughter were still in their infancy Eddie wrote: "I've ploughed through the book I told you I was getting with a view to the education of Nicko and Jenny, *Psychology of Early Childhood*, but I don't think you'd care about it. One good thing is that he drives a coach and horses through the Freudian theories about sex as the chief thing in the lives of babies. You'd never believe the sort of things that psycho-analysts do to children. One woman told a little girl-patient that the reason why she had broken a toy-man was that she wanted to revenge herself on her father's penis. The little girl was delighted—and no wonder, says the author."

According to Iain Stuart Robertson, Christopher stood back and left it up to Eve to direct the children's education. It was plain that Eve's attitude was very un-English, for when Nicholas expressed himself unhappy at his new boarding school Eve let him come home rather than telling him to stay and tough it out.

Little Imogen strikes a serious pose for the

Iain suggests that both of the children suffered from not being made to stand on their own two feet. Nicholas Hassall says that it was not as simple as that: "The fact is that Jenny's schooling was less of a problem than mine, and a problem that could easily be handled by both parents together. She gravitated from one school to the next like a ship at full sail, always with distinction. She could accommodate herself remarkably well to the exigencies of school life. Whereas I was a much more troubled child who needed watching more than she did. My mother therefore did try to do just that, but often with a great deal of opposition from Father. Father insisted that I was brought up in the same mold as he was in the true stoic mold of the stiff upper lip of the English middle classes. You must remember that Mother was not English, not even of the same religion, and was by nature a sympathetically minded person who could see the uselessness of allowing me to continue to be chastised in an environment that was basically alien to my nature. I have never forgiven my father for having insisted, despite my mother's protests, that I was constantly sent to Father's old schools."

Nicholas recalls that on one occasion he acquired a reputation as the most unpopular boy at school. His experiences at school have had an everlasting impact upon him: "In consequence of the nightmare of my extreme youth in boarding school, I have nursed a serious grudge against the English establishment which probably explains why I live as far away as possible as I can from it, either in a caravan or when in a house, among working class people, or if not that, as much abroad as possible."

Jenny changed schools constantly while following her family's frequent migrations. Her stays were usually relatively brief, her comings and goings at odds with regular term times. This constant uprooting may have contributed to her insecurities, but by all accounts she was always happy at school.

Her first recorded school is Dorlands, Hook Heath, near Woking. Then from June 1949 to May 1951 Jenny attended Channing School in Highgate. She was in the junior school Fairseat (the former home of Sir Sydney Waterlow), which overlooks Waterlow Park—a lovely place.

Jenny received glowing reports from all her schools. Her little chums called her Imo, which Nicholas did not like—he can remember them running through the house in pursuit of her, shrieking "Imo! Imo!" She was popular with classmates and teachers alike. Her teachers noted that she relished responsibility and rewarded her accordingly. There was that side to her nature that was highly organized; although she always needed somewhere to let her hair down, to let it all go. "Her ability to turn heads didn't suddenly emerge full blown at some period in her teens but grew from the admiration that her presence far back in her schooldays engendered."

Imogen (far right) with classmates in the dance studio at Elmhurst

Elmhurst Ballet School is a lasting monument to the vision of one woman, Helen Mortimer, who was teaching dance in Camberley, Surrey, in 1922. That vision, and the spirit of the school, would be summed up in the many tributes to her following her death in 1958: "This was one of the first schools to combine education with a dancing tradition; it was certainly the first specifically Church of England theatre school...Students from the school are appearing at the Royal Opera House in the Royal Ballet, in many London and provincial theatres, and teaching all over the world...She instilled into them a sense of loyalty and a sincere belief that in their chosen profession they were doing God's work."

In 1944 Mrs. Mortimer instituted the Manners Prize, which was presented each term. To the first winner she wrote, "It is presented for what I consider one of the most important things in life. Hold on to and develop your good manners and count them as one of your most cherished possessions."

According to one of her former pupils, Helen Mortimer had "a wonderful ability to imbue everything with a sense of fun. But underlying everything—the disciplined training of the dancers, the ups and downs of school life, the frustrations and the fun—was the Christian faith that motivated so much that went on there."

Students in leotards and their colored sashes drill on the tennis court.

Such was the reputation of the school that Mrs. Mortimer never had to employ the services of an agent to place her girls in work. Producers came asking for them. From the beginning, Elmhurst attracted famous parents, well-known in society circles or stars of stage and screen.

The greatest tribute to the school are the fond memories of its graduates. In her book *At Your Service*, published in 1998 to commemorate Elmhurst's 75th anniversary, Jennifer Rice quotes from the reminiscences of one of the most celebrated Old Elms, Merle Park:

> Enjoying the dance and theatre work tremendously...
>
> The fun of summer prize giving on the lawns that doubled up as tennis courts.
>
> The shelter that was an Aladdin's cave filled with costumes.
>
> The gardens and borders kept so beautifully...
>
> Ballroom classes in the big studio or new studio, dancing with each other, living in hopes that perhaps Sandhurst cadets might be invited to join the classes one day.
>
> Piano practice in the hen-house, big studio or new studio before breakfast on cold mornings.
>
> Bowls of strawberries at Confirmation breakfast.
>
> Laying tables, clearing away, washing up, putting away, instructed by Hilda and Evelyn, the maids. Rock cakes, doughnuts, tragedy on the Alps [white blancmange and a spoonful of strawberry jam], powdered egg swimming in water—ugh!
>
> The theatricality of the Chapel...
>
> Being taken to performances at Covent Garden, seeing Fonteyn for the first time.

Jenny and fellow classmates pose in their Victorian costumes complete with parasols.

No computers only occasional television viewing. No
mobile phones, but letters to be written and imagination
used constantly...

Merle Park attended Elmhurst School between 1951 and 1953. Those post-war years were a time of great expansion. When Christopher Hassall joined the roll of celebrated parents in 1952, the School boasted five houses with residential accommodation and classrooms in three of them; and four studios for dancing.

At age 10 Jenny Hassall is an exquisite pixie. In a crowd of pretty girls she is outstanding, her dark complexion singling her out as rare and exotic.

The School photographs show her kitted out for dancing in a short pleated skirt or black leotard with the broad belt that would have been colored according to her grade—and in costume, a Victorian frock with a bow at the back, complete with parasol and dainty feathered hat. She is striking a pose in the studio or dancing on the tennis courts in rehearsal for the 1952 Summer Demonstration, a display of classwork followed by ballet and character numbers presented before the annual Prize Giving.

The name of Imogen Hassall is not in the chronicle of prize winners, but she looks happy and determined. She is in her element.

Looking at the photographs is so terribly poignant when one thinks of all the sadness and turmoil that lay in store for this delightful child.

It was an unforgettable experience, even for a child, meeting that young Imogen. New girl Patricia Fitt arrived at Elmhurst Ballet School in September 1952: "With her dark hair and skin and lively personality she was quite the most beautiful and exotic creature I had ever seen. Imo was already established and accepted as the best actress at Elmhurst. I think

Dress rehearsal on the tennis court

that year of 1952 she co-hosted the annual show with Mrs. Mortimer. The two of them played out little scenes in between the ballets. I was always in awe of her and never really got to run in her set. She was one of the Reds who were the *crème de la crème* of the ballet classes at that time."

As a classmate and a friend at Elmhurst, Andrea Jacobs remembers Jenny as lovely — "I was very fond of her."

Andrea recalls that Jenny's talents were conspicuous in drama. Jenny and Juliet Mills were the two children in *The Tree of Life* in one major Elmhurst production.

Juliet Mills is remembered as one of Jenny's set at Elmhurst; she is one of the group in Jenny's school photographs. However, according to her sister Hayley, another Elmhurst graduate, Juliet has chosen to keep her memories private.

Andrea Jacobs remembers her little friend as generally bright and happy, but there were dark undercurrents.

Andrea saw Jenny unhappy at night and crying. There was one particular occasion when the two of them were obliged by unforeseen circumstances to stay behind at the school for a few days after term had ended and all the other pupils had gone home. In Andrea's case it was simply problems booking passage to take her back to her family. With Jenny, it may have been domestic difficulties. Andrea is not sure but suspects that Jenny's midnight miseries had something to do with her parents failing marriage.

In the photographs, however, she is as bright as a button, dancing or striking a pose.

The ballet was the thing. Jenny would soon be off to White Lodge.

"The most important thing in her life was ballet," says Nicholas Hassall. "There was nothing else."

Nicholas can recall no defining moment which inspired his bright-eyed sister. It seemed that she had always been dancing, her instinct for self-expression taking its purest, most natural, physical form. As a small girl she was forever dancing around and everyone had to stop and watch her.

She was a dancer, body and soul. "She was a ballet dancer, that's all she wanted to be."

With the arrival of puberty the calm waters of the brother-sister relationship became tempest-tossed. "I got on well enough with her until she was in her teens, just before, puberty started, and then we used to have terrible fights...not only word fights, physical fights too—pulling hair out...she did the pulling of the hair out—I think I was more of a gentleman—but we certainly did have scraps, up until the age of 14 or 15—then it got a bit too much because we were semi-adult by then and it would have been too dangerous if we'd had physical fights."

From the age of about 12 onward, there were tantrums and fits that seemed to come from nowhere. Nicholas says that there was a family history of serious mental problems on his mother's side. "It was considered that all these Anglo-Indians were highly strung... it appears a lot in Anglo-Indian families."

His sister was hysterical at times—"it would be put down to the fact that she was part-Indian."

Her hysteria reminded him of the behavior of his mother's temperamental, pedigree pet poodles. Like the dogs, he felt his sister might be picking up subconsciously on the taut family environment.

Her delicate genetic structure, some internal imbalance, combined with the disturbing chemistry of puberty and the strained atmosphere tore her apart. "The effects of a fragmented, broken family on her psyche must have broken this structure that she was born with."

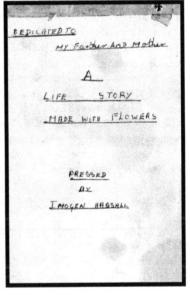

In 1954 a 12-year-old Jenny sat down with paper and pen and scissors and sticky tape to construct a slim, pocket-sized volume dedicated to her father and mother called *A Life Story Made with Flowers*, Pressed by Imogen Hassall.

This self-published work has only that title page and two leaves, which appear to be Basildon Bond letter paper, now yellow and stained. Secured to the pages by little irregular rectangles of decaying brown sticky tape, carefully spaced, is a varied selection of tiny leafy twigs and sprigs of fern and wild flowers. Souvenirs perhaps of a day out rambling in the woods, they are as dry as straw and almost colorless. Some are damaged; one or two are missing.

Page one is headed simply 1954. Each faded specimen has been captioned with blotchy blue ink in block capitals and underlined: MONEY; TIME; WEDDING; JOY; SORROW.

The second and final sheet is titled STAGES 5 and its themes, each one again illustrated by a particular twig or flower, are: DEATH; BIRTH; LIFE; MOTHER; FATHER.

Who knows what youthful enthusiasm sparked this instance of creative self-expression. It has obviously been executed with all the care and consideration that a 12-year-old could muster; all done in pencil first then gone over in ink—the titles and each caption underscored precisely with a ruler.

It may only have been a pleasing commemoration of a jolly day out in the countryside, a school project perhaps. Was it strictly private like a secret diary or for official presentation

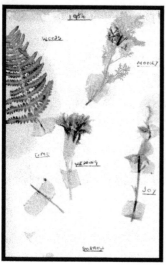

as its dedication suggests? Was it aiming to impress? Jenny was always eager to impress her parents, eager for appreciation.

Or was it profound for a 12-year-old? Was there a symbolism in her mind in the careful matching of specimen to caption that hints at her anxiety?

Was it intended to bring her parents closer together at a time when they were obviously breaking apart?

Jenny's *Life Story* is intriguing and moving. One can imagine the inexpressible, bittersweet sadness with which an older Imogen might have gazed upon its long-lost, ancient pages when it surfaced occasionally at the bottom of a drawer or fell from between the pages of a dusty book.

As she reached her teens Jenny was evolving into a strong-willed, independent individual and brother and sister were growing apart. From the age of 12 or 13 big brother was no more.

At the age of 13 Jenny was well into puberty. She had her own life to lead with her own friends and was less involved with the family. At 15 or 16 brother and sister would often holiday separately, divided between their parents. At home their paths would rarely cross, each leading separate lives, two very distinct personalities: Jenny gregarious and outgoing, Nicholas already a loner.

In their teens the roles of brother and sister were reversed. "Every now and then, I'd try and be the big brother to her, which was totally useless, because she actually behaved more like a big sister to me."

Jenny matured quickly in the ways of the world. Physically she blossomed early and "she grew up very quickly with regard to putting men off or encouraging them."

Aged 16 or perhaps 17 Jenny visited her brother in Aix-en-Provence, where Nicholas was studying. She disappeared with two of his fellow students. Anxious and protective, Nicholas went in search of her. He recalls shouting up at the window of a house only to have Jenny emerge and say, "Calm down, Nick, I can handle myself, I'm perfectly all right, these guys I can handle."

The two lads, meanwhile, were looking very sheepish—"she'd obviously given them a hell of a time."

But beneath the self-willed exterior Jenny was amiss. "Something broken inside," Nicholas agrees. "That's an accurate way of putting it."

The tragedy was that no one recognized her troubles. "She had a psychological problem—it was identifiable, it was there, it was real—the classic symptoms—but nobody suggested she do anything about it."

The family attributed it to the Anglo-Indian chemistry. "Two things—a glandular problem—it all started to go wrong as soon as puberty came on...the Anglo-Indian problem, which seems to exist in our family, of derangement on that level."

The doctors were no use. Nicholas, by the time he was 21, was also deeply troubled—"you can't expect to be anything else because of your parents," said the doctors, and gave him some pills, "a cure worse than the illness."

Nicholas is convinced that the doctors would have said much the same to his sister. "She had an identifiable illness," he insists. "And should have had someone to sort her out psychologically."

Nicholas was able to dig deep and pull himself back from the brink. He took up yoga and meditation and developed the beliefs in spiritualism that have sustained him ever since.

His sister never found such comfort: "She couldn't internalize herself well enough... I have beliefs and a philosophy which helps keep me together. My sister did not have that, she had nothing. It affected my sister more because she didn't find some inner resource."

But young Jenny did have her beloved ballet. At the age of 12 she would be off to fulfill her dreams at White Lodge. That dream, however, would turn sour and some friends say it would become the source of her everlasting, crushing disillusionment.

Those who remember Imogen as a child say simply that she was always dancing. They can identify no defining moment when the ballet set light to her romantic soul.

Was she taken to the ballet by her parents, or went with her school? Or was she, like an entire generation, inspired by *The Red Shoes*? The film was made in 1948, the very year that a family friend saw a delightful pixie-child, dancing on the lawns of the Manor House, Old Woking.

Might she have seen a revival of the wartime romance *Waterloo Bridge* and been entranced by a lovely young ballerina—Vivien Leigh—so exquisite and vivacious? There is a certain resemblance to Vivien Leigh, which was remarked upon throughout Imogen's life, especially when she was young. Imogen would have been flattered. It is said that she identified strongly with Vivien.

They shared the same blood in their Anglo-Indian roots, and it has been rumored that they were related on Eve's side. Young Imogen projected that charm and vivacity which the youthful Vivien Leigh displayed onscreen and both were unusual, exotic beauties.

Did Jenny, subconsciously, consciously even, as young girls do, model herself on Vivien, and enhance her own undeniable charisma with a touch of Scarlett O'Hara? Film critic Alexander Walker observes: "Quite a few people of Imogen's disposition go through a period of close identification with Scarlett O'Hara. I still get a fair number of letters from girls of school age who have seen *Gone With the Wind* and wish to know more about Vivien. The attitude that 'I won't cry today, I'll cry tomorrow—for tomorrow is another day' is one that appeals to those who have very little sense of consequence, which many a girl of that age has."

For most, maturity and the everyday responsibilities of marriage and/or career make the Scarlett phase a thing of dim and distant memory. Imogen retained very little sense of consequence throughout her life.

She resembled not only Scarlett but Blanche Dubois too, the haunted soul of *A Streetcar Named Desire* (1951) so passionate, lonely and desperately seeking kindness. She would also parallel Vivien's later life—her extremes and her agonies. Would Imogen have detected a kindred spirit, someone to identify with and admire—an actress tortured by her demons?

In *Waterloo Bridge*, Vivien's heroine, her dreams corrupted, destroys herself; as, indeed, does Moira Shearer in *The Red Shoes*. Imogen and some of her friends give the impression that her cries for help began—or at least that she was talking about suicide—when she was still quite young, in her late teens.

Young girls, inspired by an Ophelia, a Juliet, and other doomed heroines, have been known to foster romantic notions about suicide. They usually grow out of it, but Imogen was an eternal child. Perhaps a seed was sown in her youth, and it seemed to be a grand, romantic gesture. It became, as she saw it, her only practical means of drawing attention to herself when she felt alone and abandoned, of letting the world know that she wanted someone to come and sort her out.

In 1952 when Jenny was 10 and Nicholas 11, there was a new face at number 8, The Grove, Highgate, N6.

Fresh from college, 22-year-old Gillian Patterson took up the post of secretary to Christopher Hassall. She continued to work for him until his death in 1963. She remembers, "He was very sweet, very funny, very good company. Everybody adored him—you couldn't help it. If he was in the room, it was a happy room."

Gillian recalls Christopher used to cry with laughter, he used to roll about—and he found a lot to laugh about; he loved silly jokes.

Gillian cannot find anything extreme or extraordinary in the family environment—"It was as normal a family life as you would expect, from a theatrical family." There were obvious strains, between husband and wife, and there were rows, but "it was never vicious, they weren't unkind about each other."

The death of Ivor Novello in 1951 was an event that had significant implications for Christopher's income. By 1956 the family had taken a more modest residence in the Old Cottage in the Vale of Health. There, they all tended to live on top of each other, and the strain became more apparent.

Christopher, says Gillian, lived the life of a bachelor with a home to come back to. Eve, meanwhile, for all her good intentions, was not very good at the daily routine of managing a household. She was not a housewife: "She had very high aims which were always beyond her. You never knew when lunch was going to be on the table because she was always cooking something terribly grand. It would take hours to cook. Lunch would come onto the table at about 3-3:30. It was always delicious—whether it ever got there was always a bit of a toss up."

Eve, according to Gillian, was very chaotic. She was forever late and throwing others into a panic. When the family had to leave, it was Eve who would be holding them up.

That Christopher was largely a non-participant in the running of the household, Gillian puts into the context of the times. In those days, she points out, it was more the woman's part; the man was not expected to run the house and bring up the children.

Besides, the family depended on Christopher's career, and he was always working very hard, working all hours. Gillian remarks, "They were no less compatible than a lot of people. Although nowadays they would have broken up a lot quicker."

Eve, says Gillian, was not happy with the Novello lot and was of the opinion that they resented her. Christopher would complain that he had given up seeing many of his friends because Eve did not get on with them. And Eve felt that Christopher's friends thought that she was not good enough for him. "She was resented by a lot of people who thought that they could have done better for him."

There was no obvious manifestation of Indian culture in any way about Eve. Christopher, says Gillian, was unaware of the degree to which Eve's blood was mixed, and when it became apparent to him later—and it most certainly manifested itself in his daughter—"he was not very keen on that."

Eddie Marsh, at least, appears to have thought highly of Eve, judging by his correspondence with Christopher Hassall. Writing to Christopher following Eve's heroics during the bombing of the hospital, Marsh was touched by her coolness and subsequent thoughtfulness with regard to a trivial gift that he had sent to her: "I'm terribly sorry for Eve, but what miraculous escapes she and Nicko had in the blitz—she is a real little heroine. Fancy her writing me that serene letter of thanks for the mug without the slightest hint of what she had been through!"

Marsh was equally appreciative of Eve's contribution to his regular visits to the Hassall home. After spending the New Year of 1941 with the Hassalls in Highgate, he wrote: "Dear Eve, this is to thank you for my perfect visit and for all your delicious hospitality, the festive goose under the festoons, the Pol Roger and Clicqot and all."

Such lavish fare in wartime—the Hassalls were indeed glamorous and well-connected people. Ivor Novello served a term in prison for petrol rationing offenses, which upset Christopher and Eddie dreadfully at the time.

Eve began to take off on her own while the family was living in the cottage in the Vale of Health. Effectively the parents were separated and, his fortunes restored and success assured, Christopher was living in style in Tonford Manor, Canterbury.

He still had the daunting task of maintaining a career, keeping a house going, and sending two children to school. After Eve had left Jenny tended to spend more time with her, but it appears that the children did not take sides, although both stayed with their father. His house was always a home for them. "In that sense, he held the family together more than she did."

According to Gillian, Christopher did his best to support and encourage his two very different children. "Jenny was very outgoing, everybody was very fond of her. Nicholas was rather quiet, and didn't have so many friends."

Gillian remembers Nicholas as by far the more complex child, and not very successful at things. Jenny, meanwhile, sailed through everything; not, perhaps, exceptionally bright, academically, but she got on with everybody and was a great success.

The relationship between father and son, says Gillian, was not an easy one. Nicholas could never make up his mind what he wanted to do. "Whatever he tried to do didn't come off. He had very high standards, great plans that never quite came off."

Christopher tried to support his son, but it was never easy. Nicholas was a withdrawn child—except for his music. He would play loud music all day, "which drove his father mad. But that's what children do."

Looking back, Gillian does not remember the family as being all that dysfunctional, as far as the children were concerned. Nicholas Hassall concedes, "On closer consideration, Gillian's attitude about normalcy with regard to my family is probably right...I would defer to her judgment about such matters." Gillian insists that Christopher doted on his beautiful daughter. "He absolutely adored her, no question."

She also inspired him. Jenny told her school chum Patricia Fitt that she had provided the spark for the song "I Left My Heart in an English Garden" when she came skipping into the house one day singing "I left my hat in the garden" and her father, searching for a lyric, overheard her.

Like any father he was concerned about what was happening to her. They might have rows, but that was simply because Christopher did not approve of what she was doing—just a typical father and daughter.

Once, when Jenny was a well-developed teenager, Gillian was sent along with her to buy a new dress for some special occasion. "She was a very determined young girl," and talked Gillian into coming home with something daring and strapless. Christopher, whom Gillian describes as rather conventional to say the least, was shattered and appalled. Gillian was in big trouble. Jenny, of course, thought it was gorgeous.

Then a young journalist, David Wigg first met Imogen as a teenager, escorted by her father. David had always been interested in theatre. His was a musical education, and he was brought up on Coward and Novello. His family lived near Canterbury; when he discovered that the great Christopher Hassall had a home there, he made an appointment to interview him. Christopher was "absolutely charming...so artistic, clever, brilliant, so good-looking."

A regular visitor to the theatre in Canterbury, David would often encounter father and daughter there. Jenny, then in her late teens, made an immediate impression: "this beautiful young girl with long black hair, the slimmest figure and the longest legs."

"Who's your beautiful date?" David inquired.

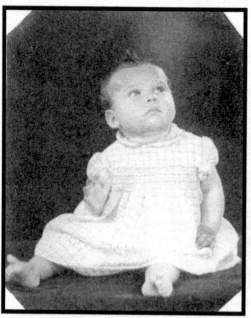

Litlte Imogen would become a Daddy's girl

"My beautiful date is my daughter," Christopher replied.

It was always Jenny who went with Christopher to the theatre. David never saw him with Eve; but by then husband and wife were living separate lives.

And it was clear to David that Jenny was very much a Daddy's girl. Christopher, says David, adored her and there was, it was plain to see, a special bond between them—"it was just like seeing a couple out on a date."

The child that Gillian Patterson remembers was "bright...a strong personality and very popular." Jenny liked being popular, to be the center of attention. "She needed to be responded to—not exactly praised, to be appreciated."

She was "a very pleasant, attractive child, full of life, very funny." Jenny was a natural leader and, at her schools, was an obvious candidate for Head Girl. She was, however, not a goody-goody by any means; she would not have been, says Gillian, one of those prim and proper Head Girls. "She was a leader into mischief as much as anything else. She would have been out there in the front, whatever was going on."

Gillian says that while Jenny had everything going for her, it would be unfair to accuse her of having it all too easy, because she worked so very hard at her ballet: "She was deeply upset at having to give it up...ballet children start so young; it's such a concentrated and devoted sort of career...if you then fail at it maybe that sort of failure stays with you, you feel that nothing else is quite as successful."

Gillian observed that, as Jenny grew into a stunning young woman, Christopher kept a concerned eye on her behavior, but at a distance. There was little he could do to influence her.

He would not have approved of her leaving the Royal Shakespeare Company in 1962, lured, as he would have seen it, by the temptation of film parts and the glamour of being seen on people's yachts. He felt that she was being exploited and he was worried that she was far too young and inexperienced and naïve to be able to handle it.

There was always a welcome waiting for her at Tonford Manor: "Christopher was there for Jenny to come back to. She always had her room—the best room—and was always made to feel that was where she belonged."

Gillian believes that Eve rather enjoyed the jollifications that came with Jenny's escapades, although "she was always picking up the pieces as well." Christopher, says Gillian, might have been a more stable influence. He would say, "if only someone would take her in hand and treat her properly."

Christopher Hassall died of a heart attack in April 1963. His daughter was not yet 21.

Jenny's father, says Gillian Patterson, could not have left her at a worse time.

CHAPTER TWO
THE SWAN

For any small and determined ballerina, there was only one goal—*the School*.

From its inception, as the Vic-Wells Ballet, the Sadlers Wells Ballet Company had a school, which in 1947 became a fully accredited educational institution based in Talgarth Road, Barons Court, London.

1955 was a landmark year, a time of expansion. The elegant White Lodge, the jewel of Richmond Park, was acquired for the Junior School, while the Upper School premises at Talgarth Road, were enlarged and enhanced. 1955 was a year to remember for little Jenny Hassall.

On January 10, 1955, the 12-year-old Imogen Hassall with long dark hair and bewitching big eyes, arrived at the soon-to-be Royal Ballet School, brimming over with enthusiasm.

At 12 for the first time a public Imogen appeared. And here begins the puzzle of the many Imogens, all contradicting each other. Only a child—Imogen, Jenny, Imo—but already a riddle.

The School welcomed the sons and daughters of famous parents. These exotics were sometimes resented by the serious students, the dedicated ones.

A contemporary remembers Imogen as one "who should not really have been there." She recalls the pretty picture of young Jenny sashaying down the corridors—"she used to flounce around"—and noted that her extrovert behavior made her unpopular with the serious crowd, although she was the life and soul of her own set, the daughters of the rich and famous. "You had to be humble."

Already at 12 Imogen did as she felt and spoke her mind. It was not in her nature to assume the humility appropriate for one so low in the pecking order. An exceptional talent might have excused her, but some are sure that Imogen's gifts were very small. To send Imogen to the School, they believe, was most unfair on her. Too much was expected of her, and they did wonder at the time, whether Jenny really wanted to be there.

Yes, Jenny did want to be there! Her family will tell you, the only thing in the whole world that she wanted to be was a dancer. Her friends all say she was a dancer body and soul. Some of them like to believe that she could have gone all the way to the top.

In later years, Imogen recalled her spell at the School as a happy time. In an interview she gave to the *Radio Times* in November 1971, she had one special memory. "I remember entertaining Princess Margaret and pouring tea all over her dress."

The incident made headlines in 1959—perhaps the very first of incident-prone Imogen's many headlines.

"She was a very good student," insists Nicholas Hassall. "Very conscientious, she worked bloody hard at it!"

The current Academic and Pastoral Principal of White Lodge says that when the school accepts a student, it is "recognizing a potential which we are then prepared to explore."

Of Imogen, he observes, "The fact that she stayed and went on to the Upper School meant that she must have had something."

That something is at the outset an inborn talent and desire for dancing—a musicality, made up of a strong sense of rhythm, dramatic ability, imagination and personality.

At her audition, the aspiring ballerina might be asked to skip in time to music and show how high she can jump. She might be asked to attempt some simple ballet movements; and to improvise to music, to show if she was musical, imaginative and artistic; miming the petals of a flower, flying like a bird or a butterfly.

She will be subjected to close physical scrutiny—seeking perfect, straight legs and the correct body shape; testing the elasticity of her calves and hamstrings, and the flexibility of her hips. Her feet will be examined minutely.

Little Jenny would have enjoyed her audition. The children who are accepted into White Lodge tend to be those who performed with a smile on their faces.

Of the hundreds auditioned each year, few are chosen. Jenny was one of that chosen few, although she was not optimistic at the time. Relatives will testify to the importance of the occasion. Imogen's cousin, Rosemary Meredith, remembers, "Imogen came in with her mother rather downcast as they both thought she had failed in her entrance trials for the Ballet School."

It is not hard to picture the scenes of wild excitement, when the good news arrived.

A second audition would be more in the form of a straightforward ballet class, accompanied by a stringent medical test; and an opportunity for the School to meet the proud and anxious parents to ensure that they too had the right attitude.

By this time, the School will be looking beyond the appropriate physical attributes to the child's character—the right personality, someone eager to work, who truly loves to dance, willing to dedicate their entire youth to the single goal of becoming a member of the Company. The School does not want children who have been pushed into auditions by starry-eyed parents. It wants children who are there because it is the only thing in the world they want to do.

Even after passing a second audition, the prospective swan remains on trial. And the student is expected to work, not just at dance; White Lodge is a real school, its pupils must be very attentive to their normal lessons, and succeed in their exams.

When it comes to the dancing, absolute dedication is the order of the day. The teachers, as patient and sensitive as they are to the needs of each and every individual, will not tolerate anyone who fails to try their hardest.

There are regular assessments; only about one-third of the pupils go through at the end of the first trial year.

At the end of five years' dedicated training—and a lot of fun and excitement too—a privileged few are selected to go on to the Upper School in Talgarth Road.

Jenny was selected to go on to the Upper School. She must, therefore, have been one of those who showed "outstanding promise and proof of absolute dedication."

And the School must have recognized Jenny's other qualities; the force of her personality. In her final year of 1959/60, she was Head Girl.

Alfreda Thorogood, now Artistic Director of Dance at Elmhurst Ballet School, was Imogen's best friend at the Royal Ballet School, despite the fact that Alfreda was a day girl while Jenny was a boarder at White Lodge.

From the very first, Imogen stood out from the crowd—"a very different, a very individual person." Physically, she did not fit the mold; at a young age, she was already developing an outline shapelier than that stereotypical of a classical dancer: "She wasn't as similar in the way that the rest of us were. She had this marvelous background with this very famous father...we were all quite surprised that this girl was coming to a dance school, because she was so physically different to the rest of us."

It was obvious from the beginning that Jenny's talents lay in drama. Drama, as such, was not studied at the School, but Arnold Haskell would make the pupils recite and read out loud and encourage them to speak properly. Jenny was in her element, totally confident.

She became a star in the classroom. "She had that lovely voice. It was really quite a rich voice for a very young girl."

She was a star, but never a show-off. Jenny was popular, she wanted to integrate and fitted in very well. "She didn't dominate the group," says Alfreda. "She was just one of the class."

Her classmates nicknamed her Jenny Wren.

It was important to Jenny to be the star; when it came to standing up and reciting poetry she knew she was the best. But dance was the great leveler. "She wasn't one of the high flyers, neither was she one of the worst, because she gave it her all. She wanted to do it and she put a lot of effort into it."

However hard she worked, says Alfreda, one knew that Jenny, purely on a physical level, would never get into a classical ballet company. She could not, at that time, have been accepted by a ballet company because her physique was all wrong. "They wanted girls with flat chests, and her costumes would never have fitted her with her 18-inch waist and very large bosom, so completely different to everyone else."

Nevertheless, while Jenny was not suited to the ballet, she was good enough, suggests Alfreda, to have excelled in other aspects of the dance, had the opportunity been afforded to her. "We literally specialized in ballet. We didn't do jazz or contemporary, it was unheard of. Had she done those things, she might have been a marvelous jazz dancer, she probably would have been wonderful in films and shows, a star."

Alfreda does not know whether Jenny recognized her own shortcomings—she was so keen—"she always worked hard; we didn't have a choice. But she wanted to, we all wanted to."

Besides, failure was not to be contemplated. "We were all too frightened to discuss it, the possibility that we wouldn't get into a company."

So how did this unusual child come to be at a ballet school? Alfreda speculates that Jenny's parents probably wanted her to be in a boarding school. Because of their lifestyle, it would be more convenient to have her in a boarding school, and at first Elmhurst and then the Royal Ballet School were among the very few vocational boarding schools available at that time.

Jenny was capable but generally average academically, recalls Alfreda. Therefore, the priority might not have been to send her to a proper, academic school first and then let her study drama and/or dance later. Her gifts took precedence, this child of gifted parents, and so, first of all to Elmhurst.

At that time, it appears that drama and ballet were equal at Elmhurst, with the balance tilted perhaps in favor of drama. It might have been drama, suggests Alfreda, that attracted the Hassalls to Elmhurst. Was it there that little Jenny—who was always dancing—lost her heart to the ballet?

Christopher Hassall's name, and Jenny's powers of self-expression, her natural ability to project her vibrant personality, would have opened the doors of White Lodge to her.

Alfreda says that Jenny was very aware of being the child of a famous father. "He was kind of like a god. One felt that. When Jenny talked about him it was as if he was a god."

Alfreda remembers Jenny talking about her father in a very respectful way. "Her father was very important to her. That's not to say that she threw him at you all the time. He was very important in her life."

Alfreda was taken home to meet the Hassall family when they were all living in Hampstead—"I found them very sophisticated, very much the actor's family. Everybody spoke with command."

It was obvious that Jenny adored her brother. "It was quite special if she did something that involved her brother. She'd always talk about that, she'd make a point of   it."

Jenny's arrival at White Lodge coincided, roughly with the time in her life when, according to Nicholas Hassall, her fractured nature first became apparent. Alfreda saw none of this.

Jenny, Alfreda recalls, could be a bit low when her back was playing up, but never depressed. "She was effervescent, an energy person, not a dull person, ever. She had all the ingredients of somebody that should have been terribly happy in her make-up."

Imogen went to the Upper School in August 1958, during her third year, two days before her 16th birthday. Now would follow the thrills of learning repertoire and covering *corps de ballet* rehearsals, just in case of injury or illness—before the ultimate selection of the very best students for the Company.

The climax would be the School's annual Gala at the Royal Opera House, Covent Garden. Jenny performed in her Gala on that hallowed stage.

"She went out of White Lodge with flying colors," says her brother Nicholas.

But Jenny's dreams were shattered.

Significantly, she appeared but did not dance in the School's Gala Matinee of 1960. She was the Princess Mother, a non-dancing role, normally taken by the elder members of a company.

Some say that Imogen was forced to quit the ballet because her breasts were too big; as simple as that. Strapping them down was a losing battle—she thought about having an operation, but it was all too much.

Others believe that Jenny was having problems with her foot; water on the heel.

Nicholas Hassall says that it was much more complicated, and dramatic. "She was told by a doctor that she must stop being a ballet dancer because it would kill her."

It appears that Imogen was broken inside not just psychologically, but physically. "She had a malformed back; in other words, she was a cripple."

For the time being, says Nicholas, she took walk-on parts, hence the Princess Mother. "And even then she got notices for her ability—she was using her acting talents then, which were innate in her, from her mother."

She had her moment, though. Alfreda Thorogood says that Jenny had danced in at least one School production, as the lead Mazurka Girl in *Coppelia*.

At that moment, at least, Jenny was a ballet dancer.

But her world had fallen to pieces. Her brother saw how she bore the burden of her disillusionment for the rest of her life.

With the stage in her blood, acting was a natural alternative, but never a real substitute. "Acting wasn't her first love, but as she said to me: 'It's all I can do...there's nothing else I can do anyway...'"

So many if onlys and what might have beens...

In public, Imogen dismissed her dancing years lightly, and talked herself down, as always, laughing at herself, when she told the *Evening Standard* in 1970. "I was never more than 26th or 28th swan...so I thought 'Blimey, I'm never going to be a prima ballerina' and I left and went to LAMDA."

Imogen's talents as a dancer are debatable, much like her abilities as an actress. She never did herself justice; she never gave herself the chance; she was never given the chance. But if you watch her on your TV screen you will see how she moves like a dancer.

Many, however, tend to agree with Imogen's own, typically throwaway estimation of her potential—26th or 28th swan.

"She was never going to be a dancer of any significance," suggests Gillian Patterson. "She might have been in the chorus, no more than that."

But all agree that the dance was the one great dream in Jenny's life; and they all insist that she worked very hard at it.

From an early age she had a personality that was so full of life and expression.

"I would guess that she was an intelligent dancer," says Gillian. "A dramatic rather than a romantic dancer. She would put a lot of feeling into it, which would come across."

Imogen could project a lively, entrancing personality, from the stage, and make an immediate and considerable impact on those who watched her. That force of life must have been apparent when, as a child, she attended the trials at White Lodge. It would now serve her well in her auditions for the London Academy of Music and Dramatic Art, and then the Royal Shakespeare Company.

It may have been a second choice, but the acting bug bit Jenny in her early childhood; and it persisted in her adolescence. It punctuated her studies at ballet school, over one very special Christmas.

The Little Theatre, Bristol, has earned a place as a footnote in the history of many who went on to see their names in West End lights, or shimmering on the silver screen.

If Manchester was good enough to have its own repertory theatre, then so was Bristol. So said A.E. Stanley Hill in 1923. He appealed directly to the vanity and civic pride of Bristol Rotary, who agreed to finance the project. It was full steam ahead: Sir Arthur Pinero did the honors, and the curtain rose on the first of countless opening nights.

Bristol Rotary persevered for six years, and then withdrew its sponsorship, just in time for the great slump of the early 1930s. The tale of the Little became that of the old familiar struggle in hard times to maintain a high standard of weekly rep.

Then, in 1935, came a savior, Ronald Russell, a former student at the Little. What had been Bristol Little Theatre Ltd. handed over all responsibility and risk for management and production to an enthusiastic new company with the swashbuckling name of The Rapier Players. Within a year, the Little was boasting an unprecedented profit, a grand total of £3.

In 1937, Ronald Russell wed a young actress in his company, Peggy Ann Wood, taking on not just a wife but a business partner. As the storm clouds burst and war engulfed Europe, it was Peggy who took charge at the Little, while Ronald did his bit as a police reservist. During and after the War, and into the 1950s, it was effectively Peggy Ann Wood's Rapier Players.

The Rapier Players would bow out in June 1963 when the Little linked with the Bristol Old Vic—but not before becoming a footnote in the history of Imogen Hassall.

Before joining the Rapier Players, Peggy Ann Wood had been on the London Stage in musical comedies with wonderful, evocative titles such as *Damask Rose*, *El Dorado*, *Lavender* and *The Geisha*. One of Peggy's best friends in the chorus, was none other than Eve Lynett, and Peggy and Eve Lynett/Hassall remained firm friends and colleagues into the 1950s.

In December 1958, during the Christmas break, Eve brought a 16-year-old Imogen, still a Royal Ballet schoolgirl, to take the stage with the Rapier Players.

The occasion was *The Amazing Adventures of Miss Brown* adapted by Peggy Ann Wood from a farce of the Gay Nineties by Robert Buchanan and Charles Marlowe with music and lyrics of the period. The play was set in a select academy for young ladies and chronicled the hero's endeavors to gain access to his beloved, disguising himself as Miss Brown. The production ran for a prodigious six weeks, from December 23, 1958; and Imogen portrayed Victoria Bowman, one of the young ladies of the Cicero House Academy.

Sweet 16—Scarlett O'Hassall and the Rapier Players in _The Amazing Adventure of Miss Brown_

John Baddeley played the part of Miss Brown. He was somewhat reluctant when, at all of 25, Peggy Ann Wood asked him if he would keep a paternal eye on a young newcomer.

He was not enthusiastic, but he was in for a very pleasant surprise. "I was taken aback when I met her. She was without doubt one of the most beautiful girls I have ever seen."

Imogen's beauty made John's responsibilities both a pleasure and a strain, but he carried out his duties impeccably. They went to the pictures once or twice, and chatted a lot. Imogen, says John, was sweet and charming. He remembers her for her sense of fun and vitality.

At 18 Jennifer Lessimore was two years older than Imogen and an experienced member of the company. But she took a shine to the new arrival and they became great friends for the duration of the production; the two Jennys.

Jennifer can still picture Imogen's entrance backstage at the Little, "a beautiful little thing with huge eyes, long dark hair and a great big smile."

Imogen made a pretty picture in a bright red coat, nipped in at the waist to accentuate her hourglass figure. Her eyes were sparkling; she was very excited to be in a real theatre:

"Oh, I can't wait, you're so lucky," she told the other young ladies of the academy. "It's all going to be such wonderful fun!"

The other girls, veterans all, shared a knowing glance. But Imogen's enthusiasm went undimmed. As if she could not quite believe that she was in a proper theatre, in a proper play, she had a habit of looking at herself in all the dressing room mirrors, peeping over everyone's shoulder. The others thought this rather vain.

But the other girls were also mightily impressed by her, by this lovely daughter of the famous Christopher Hassall. They were especially impressed when they learned that, at barely 16, she was already ordering custom-made bras.

The girls nicknamed her Hassallbug, although no one remembers why.

Vanessa Hill was one of the young ladies of the Cicero House Academy. Her first impression of the new girl was of "the most amazing figure and the smallest waist I had ever seen."

Imogen was "a nice lass," says Vanessa. With hindsight, she observes that, even at such a young age, "she had this feeling of being different." Imogen possessed a quality that distinguished her from the rest of the company, from the other girls, who were very much a gang.

She was different in other ways. Imogen was "very physically aware," says Vanessa, of her habit of peering at herself in the mirror; as many young girls are, only more so. Physically, she was quite balletic.

Jennifer Lessimore says that Imogen was a sweet kid, young and ingenuous. She felt sorry for her, and recalls finding Imogen standing all on her own in tears. "Mummy and Daddy are fighting all the time. It makes me unhappy when they're so unhappy."

Her parents, it seemed, were in the throes of separating. Imogen, says Jennifer, "sobbed on my shoulder" on more than one occasion. She doted on her father and Jennifer observed that he had a kind of Svengali effect.

There was this underlying sadness, but most of the time Imogen was bouncy and bubbly and full of life.

"She was a wonderful dancer," says Jennifer. "She was ostensibly a dancer; she was never an actress."

And young Imogen was working hard. At an after show party, Jennifer recalls, Imogen was so tired that she curled up in a big armchair and went to sleep.

Jennifer can still see her, "like a little kitten."

In Jennifer's scrapbooks, there are pictures from the production. Imogen is exquisite, and full of joy. There is no suggestion of a certain sullenness that would cloud her features in years to come.

"Her face hardened from the face I knew," says Jennifer. "The eyes became heavier, her mouth had a downward turn."

Imogen's face in Jennifer's photographs is all smiles, a silent laughter that, some say she inherited from her father. She looks like a young Scarlett O'Hara, a compliment that would have pleased her immensely.

Anthony Collin, an established Rapier Player and member of the cast of *Miss Brown*, was enchanted by Imogen. He remembers "a sweet young girl, charming and very shy."

The girls had a communal dressing room and Jenny, out of sight of her elders and betters, no doubt had a lot more to say for herself. In her peer group she would have shone. If ever there was a face with mischief in it, it was Jenny's; she was always great fun, an adventure, and laughter followed her everywhere.

For Anthony, Imogen was the prettiest girl in the chorus. No one ever looked quite like Imogen, except—and Anthony also noticed this—Vivien. Anthony Collin thought Imogen was ravishing and a beautiful mover. Imogen was still at the Royal Ballet School and according to Anthony was "very much enamored of her dancing."

Imogen was by nature enthusiastic to an extreme, at times a self-destructive extreme. But this was 1958 and Jenny was sweet 16. To be young is to be keen but that youthful enthusiasm, however sincere, has to be driven by concentration, dedication and sheer bloody hard work. This is the difference, between the young who want to act or dance, and those who actually make it. And, of course, enthusiasm is rarely a substitute for real talent.

But, Jenny was in her first real play. And she was "always on top of the choreography," however modest in *Miss Brown*. She was dancing.

Eve Hassall was there supporting her daughter during the entire run of *Miss Brown*. There are several Eves, just as there are many Imogens. Some say that Eve was always supportive over the years and was always there when Imogen needed her—for morale or money. Others claim that their relationship was distant and strained—or say that Imogen got

...*Miss Brown* was set in a select academy for young ladies and chronicled the hero's (John Baddeley) endeavors to gain access to his beloved by disguising himself as Miss Brown.

the worst of Eve, her fractured temperament; that Eve incited her daughter's slow, agonizing downfall by starting her on the pills to which she became addicted, the pills that killed her. If you want to see where it all went wrong, they say, just look at the parents.

Eve Hassall comes and goes, like her daughter she is elusive.

Anthony Collin remembers Eve as volatile, very funny and very nice. Like mother like daughter. So much of Eve went into Imogen.

Eve appeared in four plays in repertory with the Rapier Players during 1958. She arrived in her own grand style, traveling in a custom-built motorized trailer. In rehearsal she seemed edgy and unsure of herself, leaning heavily on her director. Years later colleagues were to make similar observations about her daughter.

Jennifer Lessimore also remembers Eve as being very nervy. It had been a long time since she had appeared regularly on stage, and she had a horror of fluffing her lines.

Jennifer, however, remembers Eve chiefly for her kindness. When young Jennifer was enduring the pangs of a broken romance Eve was very sympathetic and even invited her to come and stay with the family.

Imogen too, would be remembered for her generosity and her many small kindnesses.

And so, we say farewell to Christmas 1958, and to the Imogens of John Baddeley, Jennifer Lessimore, Vanessa Hill and Anthony Collin.

How could Jennifer Lessimore and Anthony Collin possibly recognize in that sweet child of 1958 the turbulent, troubled woman who took her own life in 1980?

CHAPTER THREE
STROLLING PLAYERS

Nostalgia isn't what it used to be.

The world was a better place in the good old days. The streets were safer, the girls prettier; cars were works of art; and footballers were true heroes. Pop records were instant classics, not like the rubbish they churn out nowadays! It was *The Theatre* with real stars and genuine talent. Actors had the pedigree, the training and the mileage in those days. They paid their dues in rep—the school of hard knocks.

Things just ain't what they used to be. The graduates of the London Academy of Music and Dramatic Art will tell you that. In 1960 LAMDA was basking in its Golden Age when the caliber of its teaching and its intake was unsurpassable.

London was getting ready to swing and much of that energy was generated in its art and drama schools.

From age 18 in 1960 to 28 in 1970. The peak of Imogen Hassall's youth and beauty would span the Swinging Sixties.

On October 5, 1960, a fresh-faced batch of first-year students arrived at LAMDA and were herded into Room 3 to await the ritual introductory oration by the Principal. Room 3 was the largest space in LAMDA, the Movement Room, equipped with bars, mirrors and a grand piano. It would have looked reassuringly familiar to young Imogen who was fresh from the Royal Ballet School. It would have given her confidence which, coupled with her friendly nature, would have impacted immediately upon her fellow newcomers.

The atmosphere in Room 3 would be familiar to any fresher. The air charged with nervous excitement: some trying to appear blasé, cool and aloof; others over-compensating by being extroverted, laughing loudly. Those gripped by a sudden, sinking feeling of total inferiority would be casting glum sideways glances at the attractive ones, who already seemed to be popular and so sure of themselves. Already, tentative friendships would be taking shape, the first in-jokes attempted.

Imogen stood out from the crowd. John Samson noticed her immediately. "A strikingly attractive girl with a dancer's figure, pretty face and the most beautiful long hair."

Janet Suzman, a year ahead of Imogen, still recalls her dark hair, her large eyes, her enviable waist. With those looks, she says, Imogen was expected to sail forth to a career in films rather than the stage.

John Samson agrees. It soon became obvious that, as an actress, Imogen was not going to set the Thames on fire, but all were convinced that her charisma and beauty would guarantee her success in the movies and on TV.

John, a lad fresh up from the provinces, was in awe of anyone related to someone famous, and there were plenty of those at LAMDA. But he liked Jenny; noting she was a sweet girl with an innocent quality, a vulnerability.

John Samson's Jenny was neither outgoing or gregarious. She was not quite fitting in. According to John, there was something about Imogen that distanced her from the rest. She was somewhat enigmatic, a quality which some of the other girls misinterpreted.

"She's so bloody shallow," he heard them say.

That lovely long dark hair was the envy of the other female students. And Jenny could afford to have it done sometimes twice a week.

Drama school is an intense place. Students are exhorted by their tutors to take themselves and their craft seriously. They work hard at being very serious. That was not Imogen who could make a joke out of her darkest terrors, who would speak her mind and not endure any pretension. Imogen was deep, but in her own way. She could talk about poetry and Chekhov, but she would do it her way. The intellectual, however, was something from which she jokingly backed away.

Imogen's wariness of the intellectual may have had something to do with the stark contrast between her academic, ever so English, middle class father and her more colorful mother. There was much of Eve in her beautiful daughter.

Or it might have been her distrust of the many academic men she attracted: among them some of her father's colleagues and friends — who, she was convinced, were interested only in her body. With good reason, many believe Imogen's claims that these intellectuals made passes at her when she was barely in her teens.

She was something of a disappointment to her father in not being serious. It was observed that she shared few of her father's interests.

Imogen, however, always had a lot to say for herself. She was well-spoken, articulate and witty, conveying an impression of a mature intelligence that disguised the child within. And as she grew older, she could be commanding, which created an illusion of strength. At times the overpowering impression Imogen made on people masked her true fragility. Her behavior too was deceptive — Imogen was promiscuous, but one can be falling into bed and still be innocent. Imogen's innocence was the child within her.

Like a child she would often say whatever came into her head, however outrageous, in order to make an impression or provoke a reaction.

Alan Whitehead, the drummer from the pop group The Marmalade, was entangled romantically with Imogen for about a year in the mid-1970s. When her demons were upon her, Imogen could appear monstrous and cruel — she could be crude in her sexual poison — or that is how it seemed to him.

Imogen's friends, however, warn against taking anything she said too seriously. The joke was always lurking in there somewhere — she was trying to provoke or to shock to get a reaction. She was ripe, of course, for the tabloids, who would flavor her quotes to suit their agenda. Her friends say the press never saw the joke.

Whether in jest or lashing out in real or imagined pain there are as many contradictions in Imogen's own words as there are in what others say about her.

Catch her if you can!

According to John Samson the teachers at LAMDA were tough on Jenny Hassall. She was not applying herself. She was not proving herself and they wanted her to work harder. One has to do more than aspire, one has to perspire. But John Samson's Imogen just got on with it as best she could.

Everyone took it for granted that she would simply stroll into the movies.

Jenny was serious about drama school, but she was going to have fun.

John Samson could already detect a darkness in her — the mark of doom, but to others Imogen was about fun. There was always laughter wherever Jenny went.

And if she did appear at times to be a little distant from the rest she was still in her heart a dancer. Some think her parents had stars in their eyes — the kind that twinkle on Hollywood Boulevard.

Norman Ayrton, the Vice-Principal of LAMDA, was an old friend of Christopher Hassall. According to *Who's Who*, along with many other prestigious directorships and fellowships, Christopher was at one time a Governor of LAMDA.

LAMDA was the obvious choice.

Jenny may have had the heart and soul of a dancer but in 1958 the Royal Ballet School teenager had been very excited to be in a proper play.

Whatever doubts she may have had, Imogen's natural enthusiasm would have soon taken over. For the rest of her life she would crave recognition as an actress—and get in her own way by taking ill-judged short cuts to stardom—she so desperately wanted to be a star—her enthusiasm was often taken to self-defeating extremes.

Young Jenny would never have harbored any delusions about her skills as an actress. Imogen was always cruelly honest about herself, too hard on herself; the joke was always on her. When she arrived at LAMDA she was still every bit a dancer. She delivered her lines like a dancer, over the top, but she did work at it, and she did improve.

And if Jenny was ever shy she would soon come out of her shell. She had the looks and the resources. She was never going to struggle; she had her own car, a rarity among the young in those days. She was direct, and friendly, and she had her infectious enthusiasm and sense of fun.

Imogen Hassall was the girl who had everything. The world was hers for the taking as she stood at 18 on the threshold of the Swinging Sixties.

The essential Jenny is remembered by friends at LAMDA as a straightforward person, happiest just to sit around and chat. But she could be impulsive, spontaneous.

"Whenever I hear music," she said. "I want to dance." And she would, right there and then.

She acquired a certain reputation. Her outgoing nature and those exotic looks made everyone, especially men, assume the obvious. Jenny tried very hard to come across as a woman of the world. And such a sophisticated woman of the world would not have been satisfied with the company of mere boys. Young men in 1960, even the gilded youth of LAMDA, would have had relatively little to offer in the way of wit, wisdom, status or, in purely material terms, entertainment and excitement—although, among the students in the senior year there were some who were older than the average intake and more experienced—better able to respond to Jenny's "sophistication."

But for all her airs and graces Jenny was still very much a child which could surface at any time without warning.

As for sex, this teenage sophisticate was still relatively innocent. Sex for Imogen could be a troubling complication. Her exotic looks cried Sex! and the public's expectations of her would be as a pin-up and sex symbol, but for all her promiscuity the reality was quite different.

Among the other girls there was some resentment and jealousy. Some said she was superficial, a spoiled rich girl. As an actress she was quite unfashionable. Imogen was an old-fashioned personality, a throwback to a larger-than-life, flamboyant, theatrical generation who, in the late 1950s and early 1960s, were being displaced by a new breed of intellectual Method actors with their social awareness. A new vogue for social realism was simply not Imogen's style.

Jenny may have presented a superficial and shallow front to some of her contemporaries at LAMDA, but she had great depths; and they were very dark. At barely 18, Imogen was already talking about suicide.

While many of her contemporaries shared modest digs, Jenny was established in relative splendor in a flat of her own in Aunt Joan's house at 88 Kensington Park Road, which was once the studio of her grandfather John Hassall. There were always men and boys and parties, but Jenny was obviously lonely and envious of her friends, who were sharing lodging in good companionship. She would come knocking on their door, anxious to escape the solitude of her ivory tower.

Jenny also had her midnight miseries. In 1980, while on tour together Maggie Guess watched a 38-year-old Imo take pills to make her sleep and pills to wake her up. Imogen told Amanda Richardson that the pills began when she was about 18 with sleeping tablets prescribed on her mother's advice.

From 18 to 38, friends would get the phone calls in the early hours of the morning. Imogen had the miseries — please come on over!

Nicholas Hassall cannot recall when his sister started taking the pills, but says that she would have had a good store of sleeping pills. "She'd go and renew her prescription when what she needed was treatment."

Nicholas says that Imogen loved going to sleep. Her sleep was more important to her than anything else.

Sleep was her refuge. On one of many holidays with her mother Jenny was driving Eve across France when they knocked down an old man, who had stepped off the pavement in front of them. The gendarmes said that the victim was a well-known reckless drunk. It was bound to happen sooner or later; he was asking for it they said, and then let the handsome Hassall women go.

Jenny's reaction to this calamity was to sleep for 24 hours. After that the incident was never mentioned. She never told Nicholas about it; he eventually found out from his mother.

Sleep was also her strength to face the day. "It didn't matter what happened during the day if she could get a good night's sleep."

If she could sleep, she could recover her equilibrium. "She was scared of not sleeping."

For the rest of her life, long-suffering but patient and caring friends would sit up with Imogen time after time. Her routine complaint: No one ever looked beneath the skin. People — meaning men — only wanted her for one thing.

Many men no doubt wanted her for only one thing — this rare beauty with the extraordinary body. The seeds of Imogen's deep and dark distrust of men and their ulterior motives were sown early in the advances made upon her by some of her father's intellectual associates.

She was notoriously promiscuous; but in her promiscuity was there an expression of her fears? Sex can work like a sleeping drug, a tranquilizer. Did Imogen sometimes consent to or even demand sex because she hoped that afterward she might be able to sleep?

Meanwhile, on the floor below, Aunt Joan would stoically endure the tread of heavy feet and the sound of loud voices.

Joan Hassall is remembered with affection by a cousin of Imogen's, Mark Hassall, as a lump of Turkish Delight. She has been described as an old-fashioned English gentlewoman, having a lovely naiveté and innocence, dedicated to a quiet life of music, art and literature.

Joan was devoted to her brother, whom she called Topher, with a love that, while pure and sisterly, was unusually intense. They would communicate in a private, almost child-like language, which was full of words of their own invention.

"I went a long walk over the hill with Joan," wrote Christopher Hassall. "She brought her flute with her and played country dances to the sheep in the hope they would gambol — but they only stared in dumb alarm."

Bernard Palmer, a close friend of Joan remarks that the brother and sister were highly conventional. They were always immaculately turned out and their manners were impeccable. Bernard Palmer believes that they were careful not to resemble their father, the Bohemian John Hassall — an Edwardian rake, says Bernard, a very rackety man.

Iain Stuart Robertson, another old and close friend, remembers Joan's intellect, the joy of her company and her sense of humor. He recalls the stories that Joan would tell about John

Hassall's eccentric household—the tipsy Irish serving woman who would frighten away the devout Maude's church circle by shouting "bugger off!" through the letter slot.

For some time Joan lived with her brother and kept house for him. When Christopher married Eve, Joan moved only a few doors away. This, she later admitted, was a great mistake, for Eve resented her presence and was clearly jealous of Christopher's affection for his sister.

In later years Eve would vent her spleen by regaling Joan with all kinds of unpleasantness. Eve was a sensual woman in a way that Joan, the happy innocent, was not. Eve would taunt Joan by giving her scathing reports on her brother and would provide graphic details of their unsatisfactory love life over the telephone, which Joan found painful and horrid.

Joan's correspondence tells a different story.

Christopher Hassall's papers are catalogued and kept by Cambridge University Library. In one box from that collection is a bulging file of Joan's letters to her beloved brother. A great many of these letters are actually addressed to Eve Hassall. The tone of them is always warm and caring—which is so very typical of Joan, say all those who knew her.

Joan's warmth and concern shine through, particularly during Eve's confinement with her eldest, Nicholas; Eve had lost a previous baby. Joan's joy and excitement after the birth of Eve's son leaps off the page. Referring to what appears to have been a visit from the baby's famous grandfather, she exclaims. "I hear Nicholas is a most extraordinary baby and gave Dads a searching and profound look when he came to see him! How wonderful if you have hatched a prodigy."

From Joan's letters it is clear that she was at times in dire straits financially and that Christopher would bail her out with substantial loans that he never expected to be repaid. However, it is plain that Eve was also sending Joan money, smaller but equally appreciated donations for which she was effusively grateful.

"I met Joan at *The Tempest*," wrote Eddie Marsh. "She gave such a good account of Eve."

In 1956 Joan was thrilled to receive the gift of an antique harp from Eve, which was restored and restrung. And yet, it is alleged, that this same Eve would later torment Joan with lurid tales of Christopher's sexual shortcomings.

Eve's generosity was inherited by her daughter—as were her contradictions.To give Eve her due, she did tell her daughter to be careful and delicate with Aunt Joan.

There is no doubt that Imogen regarded her Aunt as a very important person, but Eve's instructions went in one ear and out the other. In 1960-62, Jenny was brimming over with the new excitements of LAMDA and living in the heart of London. Her flat was directly above Aunt Joan and she would often invite her girlfriends over late at night—"like a herd of elephants," Aunt Joan would protest, mildly.

Joan was continually perplexed by her niece's behavior. Like her mother, Imogen was the sensual creature that Joan most definitely was not. Years later, not long before Imogen's death, Joan wrote, sadly: "...the girl is so wanton...." In 1960-62 it was the little things that were a cause for confusion and conflict. Aunt Joan would note how even being asked to take responsibility for the simplest of chores such as putting out the empty milk bottles would throw Jenny into a kind of panic.

Jenny was making waves even before she had actually taken up residence at 88 Kensington Park Road. She had declared an intention to keep pets, which threatened to cause ructions with some of Joan's other lodgers.

Christopher was very keen that Jenny, who was all alone in the big city, should live with her Aunt. And it was he who was going to be paying the rent which was precious income for Joan. Joan was therefore anxious not to upset her brother, so Jenny got her way.

Imogen's long-suffering Aunt Joan, whose patience was severely tested by her niece.

"I have quite decided in my mind now about the cat problem and the flat," Joan wrote to Christopher. "And am *very sorry* I ever raised the point at all to worry you, because obviously if it is made quite clear at the beginning that cats and dogs are never to wander about the public stairs, Jenny could keep 10 cats behind her own front door if she wanted to."

It was so like Joan—she was ever the peacemaker.

And Jenny was established in style at Number 88. The flat had a separate bathroom, bedroom, kitchen and front room complete with fireplace, all freshly decorated and furnished to her taste.

Bernard Palmer was another of Joan's lodgers and a close friend for many years. He witnessed Jenny's behavior towards her Aunt and describes her as wayward, capricious, thoughtless—and very, very beautiful.

Bernard says that he regarded Imogen with awe and tended to steer clear of her. "There was something of the witch in her."

As Bernard puts it there was no love lost between Jenny and Joan. Joan Hassall was worldly wise but also saintly and Jenny embodied everything that could offend her. "Imogen represented a principle of disorder and Joan needed order to survive."

Bernard recalls Aunt Joan's regular reports of Jenny's latest household horror. One of her more distasteful habits was to regard the loo as a convenient waste disposal unit and it was often blocked by her intimate feminine gunk. Joan was forever cleaning up after her.

Imogen was a constant source of puzzlement to her Aunt. They were worlds apart. Once, referring to the gentlemen of the press, Imogen told Iain Stuart Robertson, "Of course, they're only interested in me because of my boobs." When Iain happened to repeat this statement to Joan, she was mystified. "They're only interested in her because of her mistakes?" Iain had to explain boobs to Joan, who thought it was hilarious.

Imogen also had something of her mother's capacity to hurt and shock. This was evident in 1971 when the BBC made a television documentary purporting to celebrate all the famous and talented Hassalls. The program had a stellar cast. Taking part alongside Joan, Eve and Imogen were Sir William Walton, Dame Edith Evans, Dame Peggy Ashcroft and Olive Gilbert. The soundtrack included excerpts from Walton's *Troilus and Cressida* and Ivor Novello's *King's Rhapsody*. Other incidental music was provided by Joan Hassall playing traditional airs on the harp and accompanying Olive Gilbert.

The documentary, *Celluloid Love*, was sub-titled *The Hassall Family*, but, according to Iain Stuart Robertson, Imogen stole the show. There are those who believe that the whole thing was engineered by someone who was infatuated with her. "Somehow or other the family approach seemed to fade and the subject and star and original participants were rather reduced to the status of extras...Imogen was not a person to be ignored."

Representing the now and with it generation, Imogen raised a few family eyebrows when she appeared onscreen as the living canvas for a body painter—bullseyes on her bottom as her cousin Mark recalls. The artist was none other than Peter Blake, creator of the *Sergeant Pepper* LP cover.

Joan Hassall watched the show with a friend and was astonished to hear Imogen tell the world that her Aunt Joan was jealous of her because she was so beautiful and her Aunt was so plain. Joan told her friend that it was simply not true and never had been.

Bernard Palmer confirms that Joan was a person who was completely above jealousy. Imogen had no reason to be so vindictive. Perhaps it was the child in her seeking attention, a reaction.

According to Susana, Lady Walton, Imogen would go even to greater extremes when she accused her Aunt Joan of seducing her when she was a very young girl—an allegation which would provoke only incredulity and outrage.

With such stories Imogen succeeded only in alienating the bulk of her family and their friends and acquaintances, including people who might have helped her in her life and career.

Speaking of his mother's behavior towards Aunt Joan, Nicholas Hassall says that Eve was a spontaneous person, implying that she spoke without cold and calculated malice or cruelty. It was surely much the same with Imogen. She could be baffling, exasperating when she spoke out seeking to make an impression—she could appear monstrous when her unbalanced chemistry brought on her dark moods—but no one who really knew her says that she was ever cold-bloodedly malicious.

Nicholas Hassall is amused by the suggestion that his sister was setting the cat among the family pigeons. "That was in fact her intention. A bit of black humor?"

Mischief then, not malice?

Inevitably Jenny exceeded the limits of even Aunt Joan's considerable endurance. Joan told Christopher that his daughter would have to leave Number 88.

The new tenant was Norman Painting, who, like Bernard Palmer, would also enjoy a deep and lasting friendship with Joan Hassall. Norman recalls that when moving out Jenny wanted to take all the furniture in the flat with her. The only item that she was willing to sell to him was a Victorian bureau, the only piece that she did not own.

"She was totally unprincipled," says Norman Painting.

Although impervious to Jenny's obvious charms, Norman's overwhelming impression was one of sex, sex, sex—the sensual being so opposite to Joan. According to Aunt Joan it was not only female friends that Jenny brought back to her flat. Her bedroom was directly above Joan's and on occasion the sounds of lovemaking emanating from overhead would drive Jenny's Aunt to seek refuge in the basement.

The worst that Jenny did was to cause a great deal of pain to her father and her Aunt. Joan Hassall once described her close bond with her brother as being like William and Dorothy Wordsworth, but Jenny succeeded in causing friction between them. Christopher was not happy when Joan told him that she could not put up with his daughter any longer.

"A great black cloud has come between Christopher and me," Joan told Norman Painting. "And it's called Jenny."

Norman Painting says the pain that Jenny caused her Aunt was a deep hurt that was rarely talked about and would occasionally surface but seemed almost too much for her to bear.

Jenny, however, would go on about her own troubles at length. Norman wanted to tell her "think how lucky you are—there are worse things!"

Speaking more in sorrow than in anger, Norman Painting says that Jenny had an over-inflated notion of her own importance. She had no depth of emotional feeling for anyone but herself and was ruthless at exploiting her family connections.

"She was totally egocentric," says Norman Painting, although he concedes that she was probably encouraged to be that way by her parents. She was "a pretty, talented, charming little girl."

Iain Stuart Robertson describes Joan Hassall as "amazingly broadminded with everybody provided they weren't nasty and didn't hurt anyone."

Jenny was more than Joan could bear.

Clive Graham knew Jenny at LAMDA. He saw no evidence of troubles and pills.

Clive was one of the second year students, a year ahead of Imogen. The A's, the new arrivals, would staff the student shows in which the B's appeared—handling props, sets and lights, sometimes even understudying. That way, everyone got to know each other.

To Clive it was a vintage year. They were an exceptionally experienced and academic lot, a mix of university and National Service; perfect material for the new science in drama, new attitudes that sought to affirm acting's place in the real world.

The Grand Manner was on its way out. Clive notes: "French windows were being replaced by the kitchen sink." The theatres were taking their lead from the new writers. With *Look Back in Anger*, staged at the Royal Court in 1959, drama was becoming more socially aware. It was a time of issue plays and growing protest; a politicizing of drama coming from left of center.

LAMDA caught the mood of the times. Other schools still concentrated very much on technique. LAMDA set out to equip its students for the type of theatre that was emerging from the new authors. Influences at LAMDA went back to the teachers at the Bristol Old Vic School in the late 1940s and early 50s. Many former students from Bristol were now teaching at LAMDA.

"Stanislavski was the fount of all wisdom," Clive recalls, but at LAMDA it was never the Method in the strict sense of the Actor's Studio. "There was a nod towards Lee Strasberg, but we were also interested in the little old deaf lady in the sixpenny's—it was not a scratch and mumble school."

The quest was for a personal truth in characterization rather than the more obvious entertainment of anyone-for-tennis—the visceral qualities of the character rather than the extrovert and superficial.

The extrovert and superficial—for some of her fellow students, those words might sum up Jenny Hassall—she's so shallow. But not for Clive Graham.

Clive Graham's Jenny was a very serious-minded young actress. She would not have been allowed into LAMDA purely on the strength of her father's connections with the powers-that-be. She would have had to convince them not just of her potential but her absolute commitment.

Clive is convinced that Imogen was not making a frivolous entry into showbiz. Had she simply wanted the glamour and razzmatazz, she could have bypassed drama school altogether and found quick and easy ways into the movies and TV.

No, by going to drama school, and LAMDA in particular, Imogen was making a statement of her intent to be a serious actress.

And Clive's Jenny did not waste her time at LAMDA. She would not have been allowed to, it would not have been tolerated by her teachers.

Clive recalls that very few students were ever asked to leave LAMDA. Their skill and judgment in selecting their intake was too finely tuned to allow for a significant failure rate. Just as Imogen would not have been permitted to stroll in simply because her father was Christopher Hassall, she would not have been suffered to remain had she been deemed to be inadequate.

Jenny, Clive agrees, was honest enough to realize that she was never going to be one of those modern visceral actresses. Clive detected a certain awe on Jenny's part and a realization that she would never attain the necessary skills and knowledge to embrace that approach to the work. But if she felt any resentment she channeled it into humor by sending them up. Never, says Clive, did she go to the extent of saying that she would prefer to do rubbish.

"She was a damn good actress," Clive insists. Imogen, whose public would remember her best for *Carry On Loving* and *When Dinosaurs Ruled the Earth*, could have risen to the challenge and played parts with real substance. With her glamorous looks and large personality, however, she found it hard to be taken seriously.

Norman Ayrton was Vice-Principal and Head of Movement at LAMDA in 1960, a coincidence of some significance for Jenny Hassall.

Norman, an old friend of the Hassall family, first encountered Christopher in 1948 when he lectured at the Bristol Old Vic School. The Hassalls were enchanting, brilliant people and Norman Ayrton was charmed by Christopher's wit, humor and erudition—although he did notice that Christopher and Eve appeared to live quite separate lives and that there were certain tensions between them.

Norman Ayrton asserts, Christopher and Imogen were very devoted and adored each other. Where some see a lot of Eve in Imogen, Norman sees much of Christopher. Her father was also dark and beautiful in his youth. Imogen had his eyes and smile.

The Jenny that Norman Ayrton remembers was born to be a dancer. He can still see the six-year-old Imogen, pirouetting in the garden of the Manor House, Old Woking. She was an exquisite child with her big bright eyes and her long dark hair floating behind her as she turned and turned about—a fairy child skipping across the green grass.

According to Ayrton, Imogen was forced to give up dancing because she was having back pain. However, she remained a natural performer with an urge to express herself.

Norman was an old friend and LAMDA was the obvious choice. He was very keen for her to go there. With Jenny's instinct to perform it was an obvious step to be an actress. Norman Ayrton can still picture Jenny's audition for LAMDA—kneeling center stage, an intense and striking Juliet:

> Gallop apace, you fiery-footed steeds,
> Towards Phoebus' lodging! Such a waggoner
> As Phaeton would whip you to the west
> And bring in cloudy night immediately.
> Spread thy close curtain, love-performing night,
> That runaways' eyes may wink, and Romeo
> Leap into these arms untalked of and unseen...

"We were knocked out," he says. It was not so much an impression of some great gift, but her presence. "...An instinctive feeling for acting and a lovely personality...great animation and charm."

It was agreed that there was something to work with, that she had something in herself to give.

Jenny duly enrolled and was soon settling into her flat above Aunt Joan at 88 Kensington Park Road. Norman Ayrton would get off at the nearest tube, knock on the door and Jenny would drive him in her car to LAMDA.

On reflection Norman Ayrton soon realized that she really should have been a dancer.

Her intensive training at the Royal Ballet School—her dancer's instincts—were now major obstacles. Being a dancer does not make for being a good actress. This is confirmed by Jenny's teacher of Movement at LAMDA, Patricia Arnold—ballet is much too special-ized, too concerned with a form.

The ballet is not seeking the naturalness and spontaneity of the theatre. Its emotions are reflected in a face lit up by an expressive pair of eyes, expression amplified through the angles of the body, as the body moves from one pattern to the next.

Jenny moved like a dancer; her gestures, her expressions and body language, belonged to the ballet and not the theatre. And like many dancers, observes Norman Ayrton, she had terrible, sloppy speech.

Jenny's teachers had their work cut out, to take her to pieces and reconstruct her; to get her to be spontaneous. "Knocking it out of her, trying to uncover more."

Norman and his colleagues were fighting an uphill battle. It seemed to be impossible for her to achieve that spontaneity, that subtlety and truth. Jenny was a frustrating student—lazy and rather silly. She lacked the necessary fire or commitment and though her teachers tried, it appeared that there was little to be uncovered. "She had so much difficulty relinquishing her dancing and there was not enough there to replace it."

Clive Graham says that very little work was done at LAMDA on light comedy, which might, in retrospect, have been Imogen's forte. The emphasis tended to be on important plays. And there was that lack of emphasis on technique, which was essential in light com-edy and farce.

Norman Ayrton can remember Jenny appearing in a choral part as a washerwoman in a student production of a play by Lorca. Otherwise, as a student she left no real impression on him.

He remembers her vividly as a lovely person: not very bright but adorable, funny and charming. There was not a shred of malice in her and like so many who knew Jenny he speaks of her innocence.

And so, innocently, Jenny pursued these new excitements of acting; if not measuring up to the prescribed standards of discipline and dedication, then serious in her own way.

Many say that Imogen's gifts, as an actress were minimal. But others insist she had unlimited potential.

Some at LAMDA dismissed her as being too shallow, not serious enough, lacking the necessary strength and depth. But on at least one occasion she looked deep into herself and found powers which have left an indelible impression on fellow student David Calderisi: "It would have been sometime during the winter/spring of 1962. I was in my third year of studying at LAMDA. Imogen was in her second. She had asked me to help her with her interpretation of Irina for a production of *Three Sisters* her class was working on. I gladly agreed. On the evening I remember we were working on a speech in which a sobbing Irina expresses her longing to see Moscow, to be in Moscow—Moscow having become for her a mythological place where all her thwarted dreams might be realized. In those days the

Imogen, front and center, strums her lute in the Royal Shakespeare Company's *Curtmantle* (1962) by Christopher Fry.

teaching of Stanislavski was never far from mind and I suggested that Imogen reach into herself for a memory/sensation of something comparable to the intensity of Irina's yearning to be in Moscow, something wanted deeply and never achieved, something which in some deep sense she knew she would never have. The result was more eerie than I could possibly have anticipated. I can still hear the strange, haunting, heart-curdling moan that erupted from her, 'Ohhhhh!...M-M-M ooooo ssssk ohhhhhhhhhhhhhh.' The power of it disconcerted us both. Clearly some well-spring of emotion unfulfilled had been touched. I don't remember whether she managed to incorporate that feeling into the production, but to me it indicated that she had the potential to be an exceptional actor."

More than just the intellect was being exercised at LAMDA in those heady early 1960s with the first whiff of liberation in the air.

Drama school is an emotionally disruptive place with young and sensitive minds being set continually to the task of exploring and testing one's emotions.

"Hormones were absolutely screaming about the place," says Clive Graham.

Jenny's extraordinary charms soon impacted on Clive's hormones. She was quite stunningly attractive and exotic.

Clive's Jenny, or Jen, was lively and full of humor, full of sparkle but not in any boring extrovert way; Jenny didn't want to be the center of attention.

There were family connections of a sort. Clive had gone to King's Canterbury. Although he did not know the Hassalls when they lived in Canterbury, he and Jenny would later go together to see a plaque unveiled for Christopher Hassall.

Clive's parents were both actors, his mother as a gifted amateur. He is sure that his father had worked with Eve Hassall or at least knew her socially. When his parents traveled to London from South Wales he would take Jenny to meet them. They adored her and Jenny had a great empathy with Clive's mother, who was a strong, extroverted lady.

Clive's friendship with Jenny was very special to him—in a way she was almost like family.

But Clive and Jenny were more than friends. They were lovers for a while, merrily and fondly.

Jenny was still an innocent in so many ways but not in every way. She brought a boyfriend with her when she came to LAMDA, a handsome dancer. He would come to visit and Jenny's fellow students would see his camper van parked outside the school.

Years later an older and sadder Imogen would reminisce fondly about being blissfully in love with her beautiful dancer. He was her first great love she said. She gave up her virginity to him she claimed at age 17 in "a most appalling bed-sitter in Baron's Court...every time a train went by on the Tube line dust and plaster blew off the ceiling..."

But this relationship did not survive Jenny's transition to acting and the dancer left the picture.

Meanwhile, two B's, Clive Graham and Janet Suzman, were entering the first, formative stages of a relationship. It was early in that tentative prelude to a relationship, which ebbs and flows, where there can be hesitations and even long lulls.

It was during one of those lulls that Clive and Jenny discovered each other. "It was not a solid affair," remembers Clive, "we picked up when we could." It was not an *affaire de coeur* but intense and passionate, mutual fun.

There was no conflict, no contest; this was not any love triangle. "It was not that big a deal," Clive says, for either of them—not for him and not for Jenny. Jenny might have wanted Clive to go with her and not off with that older crowd, but she was never trying to steal him from Janet. And Clive is sure that had he chosen to stick with Jenny, Janet would have simply moved on.

Janet Suzman recalls Jenny with kindness and sadness—friendly waves and the odd student joke. Her "jealousy" was confined to Jenny's enviable 18-inch waist.

For Jenny, Janet and her peers must have embodied the kind of actress she knew in her heart of hearts she could never be. But Clive's Jenny was too honest for envy. Jenny would have felt only admiration.

It is a tribute to these three young people that this brief triangle was resolved without complication—with no ill-will and no damage done. Clive Graham and Janet Suzman did form a relationship and remain close friends to this day and have only kind things to say about Jenny Hassall.

Clive says of Jenny that their lovemaking was warm and wonderful, a sharing, a kind of loving fun.

His Jenny was not the troubled, turbulent Imo that other people talk about.

Clive would see Imogen again on and off as the years wore on. During the late 1970s for one brief and shining moment he would believe that he had found his Jen again, but she would vanish abruptly behind a twisted mask.

Upon graduating from LAMDA Jenny did not do what her fellow students expected of her. She did not sally forth glamorously onto the silver screen. Instead the young actress went to Stratford.

Imogen would join the Royal Shakespeare Company in interesting times, just like the Royal Ballet School. It was equally typical that she would not hang around.

Peter Hall took the helm at the soon to be Royal Shakespeare Company in 1960 and unleashed the winds of change. He secured a foothold for the Company in London at the Aldwych and determined to create a true company of loyal players. He introduced a system

Imogen as a possessed nun in *The Devils*

of long-term contracts, thus forging a new generation whose aspirations, talent and acclaim would transcend old-fashioned notions of stardom. The productions staged by the RSC during the early to mid-'60s have become landmarks, still talked about and celebrated in the history books.

1962 was a significant year for the RSC. Peter Hall finally succeeded in his struggle to pry a modest grant out of the Arts Council. Making her mark as an equally modest footnote in the Company's casting archives, Imogen Hassall would appear for just one season.

As Imogen told it, her audition for the RSC moved abruptly from the classics into farce, from high to lowbrow in one split second.

As Jenny launched into her prepared party piece—a reprise, perhaps, of her LAMDA audition—pins magically unpinned and her skirt descended.

One might suspect that this was a cunning ploy; young and ambitious actresses have been known to pull the most unlikely stunts to ensure that they were not lost in the crowd. But Imogen did not have to do it deliberately—this was just the sort of thing that happened to her. She was more than accident prone—or rather incident prone—she was positively gifted.

But Jenny was not the type to turn scarlet with shame or babble with embarrassment or burst into tears.

There would have been peals and peals of laughter.

In her solitary season with the RSC—glossed up in her resume and in interviews in the years to come—Imogen was little more than a walk-on carrying a spear in three productions on tour and at the Aldwych: *Curtmantle*, *The Devils* and *Troilus and Cressida*. The last was directed by Peter Hall himself—its anti-war message particularly powerful coming at the height of the Cuban Missile Crisis.

Sir Peter Hall remembers Imogen although she was a mere walk-on as a very vibrant personality and as a good member of the company. Once again Jenny was making a statement of her serious intent by going to the RSC. But had she done the right thing?

Clive Graham suggests that carrying a spear with the RSC was like an extension of drama school. Would Imogen have been better off going into rep with its broad base and depth of experience and its greater opportunities to play the meatier roles? Did she consider it or was the RSC the obvious choice—aiming for the top?

Was the decision all hers? Might her father have had a hand in it? He was certainly unhappy when she left.

Clive wonders would rep have known what to do with Imogen? With her exotic looks and vibrant personality, a repertory company of that time with its seasonally permanent company and wide variety of plays might not have found Imogen to be versatile enough so as to make good use of her. Imogen was never seen as an actress with a potential for range—agents and producers would take the easy way out in placing Imogen, going for the obvious and casting her as a series of sexpots and exotics.

Whether or not Jenny had made the right choices, and even if she seemed too light-hearted, there was no doubting her sincerity. She wanted to be a serious actress.

Curtmantle, written by Christopher Fry, dealt with the reign of Henry II and was, according to the program notes, about the man and "...the interplay of different laws: civil, canon, moral, aesthetic and the laws of God..."

Christopher Fry had come to know Imogen's father well over the years—as far back as 1934 when Christopher Hassall read a prologue to one of his plays. The rehearsals of *Curtmantle* brought the playwright and the aspiring young actress together. Imogen made a good impression, "Delightful and friendly and beautiful—I had a very nice letter from her after the opening night."

Dorothy Tutin, who was in *The Devils*, remembers how beautiful Jenny was and exotic. She says that Jenny seemed to be popular and was always professional. But Dorothy was one of Peter Hall's rising new talents, far above lowly Jenny, and their paths rarely crossed.

In *Troilus and Cressida* Jenny had to sit in the sand pit, a stage buried in real sand, as a member of the court of Queen Helen of Troy. She was also cast in *The Devils* where she was told off for wearing her make-up to play a nun. A nun in full war paint. It must have taken a voice of great authority to separate Imogen from her make-up. Even at appropriate times Imogen always wore just that little bit too much.

"Why do you wear so much make-up?" her father would complain again and again.

In *Troilus and Cressida* Imogen was a mere observer as a handmaiden of Helen of Troy.

Doubtless his daughter would have treated him to that look of pity and resignation, which says that men just don't understand. It seemed odd to some: Christopher Hassall, who was so tasteful in everything, so utterly English and middle class, surrounded by two exotic almost gaudy women.

Jenny's friends would visit the Hassall family home, Tonford Manor outside Canterbury, and all were struck by the contrast between Christopher and Eve. Jenny, all agree, was very much like her mother. The Hassall estate was impressive. In October 1963 the *Kent Messenger* would report the sale of the Manor following Christopher's untimely death:

> Tonford Manor, near Canterbury, where Henry VIII changed his clothes on the way to France in 1512, has been sold to a local doctor for £10,000...
>
> The dwelling, as it at present exists, consists of two totally different houses—15th century and Queen Anne. There is a Kent tile roof on the latter part and one charming white paneled room of the period. The other part of an original fortified building remains intact...the whole property, including the ancient walls, was restored with infinite care by Mr. Hassall. It was sold with over six acres of land...

The interior of this fine old house was furnished appropriately—17th and 18th century paintings of the English, Flemish and Italian Schools hung in the hall beside a Houdevin landscape. Charles II chairs accompanied an old oak table.

The drawing room boasted a Persian rug, paintings and Majolica; its dominant feature a marquetry chest of drawers.

The Italian School was represented in the dining room along with an ancient oak coffer and a Flemish tapestry. Carved wooden putti and several Flemish tapestries were mounted on the stairs and landing; an Aubusson hanging graced the guest room.

This was the home that was always there for Jenny to come back to.

Some felt Jenny's taste, like that of her mother, was terrible and greatly out of place. Her concept of décor has been described variously as like an Indian restaurant or a whore's boudoir.

Jenny's exuberantly inappropriate taste extended to her wardrobe. Her coloring, she was advised, was best suited to the more muted end of the spectrum but Jenny would most likely show up in shocking yellow or electric turquoise, tight as could be and cut low and short.

She was a little girl dressing to please herself and to prompt a reaction.

"That looks really tarty," her friends would protest. "Take it off!"

Jenny would be the picture of innocence. "Does it...? Do you really think so...?"

Whatever the time and place, Imogen would always wear her war paint. It was expected of a star she told everyone—the furs and the high heels. Imo was always willing to give them what they wanted, what they expected, her public—the paparazzi and the tabloid hacks, who, scarcely believing their luck, crowned her Queen of the Premieres and the Countess of Cleavage. After all, as Imogen would tell you, what else did she have to offer?

The cliché is that women who wear a lot of make-up do it to hide their insecurities. Jenny or Imo disguised her insecurities more with laughter than with make-up. The make-up was just her style.

According to the photographs, whether pretty party frock, perilously plunging spangles or elaborate stage costume, there was always close at hand a copious handbag, which was big and deep enough to carry all that make-up—the emergency repair kit. An obvious favorite was a black beaded affair, 1930s by the look of it. Perhaps it was a hand-me-down—a souvenir of her mother's faded glamour or maybe it took Imogen's fancy in a King's Road boutique—the flapper look was popular in the Swinging Sixties.

That handbag might also contain Imogen's expanding diet of pills; her pills to take her up and pills to bring her down, all clanking around in there with her make-up. A concoction of chemicals would fuse with her already uncertain structure and send a delicate balance teetering wildly, as her dependency grew ever more desperate. The explosive, unstable chemistry that was meant to be soothed was ultimately exaggerated by the little bottles that she carried in her handbag.

The pills were never a dark secret, she never tried to hide them. They would emerge quite openly from the depths of her handbag. She even made jokes about them and would make a black comedy out of her desperate attempts to escape them.

She was not unusual. Her generation used a pill for every problem—"Mother's Little Helper." Suburban housewives survived on Valium while reading tabloids that screamed about their pot-smoking sons and daughters. Those were the good old days of solutions out of a bottle, prescribed by Doctor Robert—come back for more when the bottle is empty; solutions that only created new and bigger problems, a potentially lethal, legal drug addiction.

Some say Jenny was already taking pills and talking about suicide at 18. Whether she really meant it then or when she was 38, she carried with her the tools to do the job.

Cherry Morris was also in *The Devils* in 1962. She was able to take a close look at the new arrival. "A lovely person who was her own worst enemy." Cherry believes that Imogen was sincere in her work and wanted to do well but was all too easily tempted by the lure of an aftershow party and too often late for rehearsals, the morning after. "But I liked her and chided her gently when she put a foot wrong. She never took offense."

Imo would pay mere lip service to good counsel and then go her own way regardless, while all too often following bad advice to the letter. And, however distracting and exasperating it might be, her long-suffering colleagues would go on and on listening to her pour out her troubles; and offer sage counsel even though they had no doubt that she would go and do the opposite. They liked her, and loved her, because at heart she was a kind and loving person.

Cherry Morris saw that men were attracted to Jenny like moths to a flame. "She was physically breathtaking and, consequently found it difficult, I believe, to be taken seriously."

The primary males of the troupe must have preened and strutted for her. Rumor has it a certain higher-ranking actor was the first great infatuation of Imogen's life.

At those after show parties Jenny would invariably draw a crowd. All that attention must have flattered her but being such a target for the male ego would also have diminished her already fragile self-esteem.

Throughout her life Imogen was always ready to see the joke against herself, to laugh at herself and make light of her terrors and her disappointments. Those who knew her well thought that she was compulsively doing herself down, and saw in this self-mockery an expression of her low self-worth.

Imogen, as soon as she was developed enough to attract the attention of the opposite sex — and she developed early and spectacularly — began to believe that her beauty was also her great failing, that people saw nothing in her beyond it.

In Imogen's teenage years, Nicholas Hassall detects a source of this significant flaw in her nature, noted by many who knew her when she was older — her very low self-worth. "It started as a teenager...at least I've got looks...people will employ me for my looks."

Nicholas defines his sister's low self-esteem as almost masochistic — a part of her despised herself, wanted to be punished. He describes it as one of the many conflicting contradictions in her complex nature. "There were two sides to her — one incredibly perspicacious — another side to her that was totally unaware."

Imogen, says Nicholas, was incredibly astute when it came to other people. Very few people ever managed to get one over on her.

And she could be quite commanding. "She could order people around physically, but the things inside herself she could not deal with."

Nicholas was able to help himself through newfound spiritual beliefs. His sister had nothing to fall back on, neither family nor ballet. She was seriously ill but "was too involved in her life to stop and get off this treadmill and think: I need something to sort me out. The insubstantial things, the shadows in her life, she could not get at."

There were moments in her life when she was reflective, when she was aware that something was very wrong, that she seemed to be causing a mayhem: "But she could not analyze herself — to say perhaps I was wrong there — she didn't dare do that. She daren't find herself in the wrong — she was too frightened of what she would find. She was under terrible psychological pressure — it was very, very serious and nobody was aware of it enough, least of all herself, to be able to help her."

The 1960s were about to start swinging and liberation was in the air. A sexual revolution was storming the old moral barricades, heralded by the introduction of the birth control pill. It was not just a revolution, but a revelation: "It meant that sex could be spontaneous, carefree and relaxed...It was almost as if Britain discovered sex for the first time. It was no longer something to be coy or embarrassed about, but a pleasure, a joy—almost a sport. You could talk about it, read about it in books and magazines and see it in films. Above all you could *have* it, without fear or worry, and without feeling you had to get married...For many women, their newfound freedom was a cause for celebration. The Pill gave us freedom from fear, fear of pregnancy and backstreet abortions. For the first time ever, sex was fun for women. Bliss!"

But not all women were so carefree and relaxed. For some the old social and moral repressions merely gave way to opposite but equal pressures. Previously casual sex had been furtive and forbidden or sex was attainable only on promise of lifelong commitment, signed, sealed and delivered. Now, sex was a throwaway bit of fun. Many women took it all in stride and were in the vanguard, toppling those old moral barricades. But for an uncertain young woman the Swinging Sixties could be troubling times.

Imogen herself suggested this in an interview that she gave to the *News of the World* in July 1971. In her case the new social forces at work in the Swinging Sixties were destructive.

She had a definition for the root of her troubles "A double image—like those distorting mirrors in a fairground sideshow—in my personality..."

This fracture was wrought, Imogen explained, by the loss of innocence, the release of her sexuality and the shock of the new:

> As a little girl I was always surrounded by the famous and the intellectual members of the worlds of art and society...patting me affectionately on the head and declaring: "What a pretty, sweet little girl!"
>
> ...an Alice in Wonderland world full of enchantment...
>
> ...a few brief years later the Alice in Wonderland vanished...
>
> ...its famous masculine figures were still there, but any contact with them was of a far more intimate nature...
>
> ...the pretty, sweet girl had grown up...
>
> ...the contrast between the two worlds had a deep psychological effect on me...
>
> ...the kind of sheltered and Victorian opulence which my father brought me up contrasted so strongly with the orgy of wealth, sexual permissiveness and high living of my early 20s that my body and brain just could not take it...

Throughout her short life Imogen always needed a man. Occasionally, there would be more than one at a time; often they would come and go so quickly it was impossible to keep up. These needs were something deep and insoluble. She was desperately seeking something that she could not define. But the girl, who would be dubbed Miss Sexpot, once confided in a friend, "I don't really like sex much, but I feel I ought to, because what else do I have to offer?"

Amanda Richardson, who knew Imo in 1980, looked back at the Swinging Sixties and wished: "Oh, I hope she did enjoy herself!" because her Imogen deserved happiness—her Imogen was a good friend and tremendous fun.

Once, in a rage—Imogen did like to row—she drove her car at her lover Christopher Long. But he insists that his Imogen be remembered for her *joie de vivre*, energy, laughter and excitement.

The memory of her voice is the sound of laughter.

CHAPTER FOUR
THE BIRD SPREADS HER WINGS

Jenny only stayed for a solitary season with the RSC, not even a year—a mere eight months. Someone once said that she started at the top and worked her way down, but it was not quite like that. Eight months can seem like an awfully long time to a young person in a hurry, who was expecting to go far and fast. And Jenny was barely 20 in 1962, the year she carried a spear with the Royal Shakespeare Company.

Patience was not one of Imogen's virtues, certainly not the patience that is the foundation of dedication and hard work. Jenny wanted it all and she wanted it quickly, which is natural in the young. She wanted recognition as a serious actress, but she also wanted to be a star.

Perhaps she was making what, in her eyes, was a carefully thought-out career decision for a 20 to 21-year-old. She must have been uninspired by the prospect of paying her dues indefinitely as a mere walk-on, while she saw others around her rising in the ranks of Peter Hall's exciting new company and watched her contemporaries from LAMDA getting on with their careers. She might have felt that she was still at college, while her old school chums were out in the real world, getting real jobs.

By 1970 it would be apparent to Imogen that her career had taken a seemingly irreversible wrong turn. She admitted that she might have made a bad mistake leaving the RSC so quickly. "If I'd stayed I would probably have worked my way up like Di Rigg, but I was too impatient."

Diana Rigg was also with the RSC in the early '60s, but she rose to dizzy heights far above lowly Jenny. Diana rose so high so quickly that she was once quoted as saying that she had decided to do *The Avengers* partly to avoid being taken too seriously. Poor Imogen, how she would have loved to have had Diana's problems!

They would appear together in one episode of *The Avengers*. Imogen is one of the familiar faces of cult TV of the 1960s and 70s. And like Janet Suzman at LAMDA, Diana Rigg is there in the background, the kind of actress that Imogen wanted to be.

In 1962/63 Jenny had it all going for her. She had the world at her feet.

Her fellow students at LAMDA took it for granted that she would just stroll onto the silver screen. There must have been a few eyebrows raised when Jenny went to the Royal Shakespeare Company.

In the summer of 1962, soon after they left LAMDA, John Samson was not the least bit surprised to learn that Jenny had already appeared on television. He was, however, shocked to hear that she had been booked to perform a speech from *Romeo and Juliet* on the popular magazine program *Tonight*, hosted by Cliff Michelmore.

"Wherever Jenny's talents lay," John explains. "They did not lie in Shakespeare."

Be that as it may, John had no doubts that Jenny would succeed. "Nevertheless, she was clearly forging ahead, and the next thing I heard she was starring in a film with Yul Brynner."

That would be *The Long Duel* in 1967. John Samson would meet Imo at the tail-end of the '60s. He would be severely disillusioned.

In 1962/63, however, Jenny's future looked rosy. She was the girl who had everything. After all, London Artists, at that time one of the most powerful theatrical agencies in the world, had the name of Imogen Hassall on their books.

But even London Artists could not get her moving in the right direction. Agents, casting directors and producers look for the obvious, or so many frustrated actors complain.

Type casting, however, is not necessarily a bad thing. Many actors desperate for work would be delighted to learn that there are types in demand. But part identification can be a real problem when an actor with range and versatility becomes so associated with a particular role as to become fused with it and assume its persona and be overlooked for other parts.

Examining a list of Imogen's TV and film credits, one finds a procession of sultry, smoldering exotics: Sophia, Tara, Anjali, Ayak, Dolores, Chriseis, Maria and Gina. And if she was not in Mediterranean make-up, Imogen would usually play the Chelsea Girl: the sexpot; the dolly-bird, the deb. As one reviewer unkindly put it, she would play Imogen Hassall.

Imogen's troubles lay somewhere in between type casting and part identification. Her range and versatility might be questionable, but in any event, she was cast so consistently as the exotic or the deb as to be. in effect, either typecast or identified with a particular role, that of herself.

Put crudely, the obvious place for Imogen was not onstage but in film—and with as few clothes on as possible.

Imogen did not get much help from people who saw their task as fulfilling the obvious. But even when she found someone willing to believe that she had more to offer and who was prepared to put some effort into getting her career back on the rails, Imogen would frustrate them. They would give up the struggle. She could be her own worst enemy professionally as well as privately.

In 1963 Jenny Hassall was in search of fulfillment, on her terms, as an actress. She was making a statement of her serious intent by leaving the RSC in search of greater challenges.

Her obituary in *Screen International* in November 1980 said that Imogen "Will sadly be better remembered as the perennial starlet than the busy actress."

Jenny would never be the serious actress or the star that she wanted to be. But she was going to be a busy young actress.

While his beautiful daughter was testing her wings, first at the Royal Ballet School, then at LAMDA and on to the RSC, Christopher Hassall was incredibly busy, enhancing his reputation as a modern Renaissance Man.

His entry in *Who Was Who* is spectacular in its sheer variety:

> ...Played Romeo in John Gielgud's production for the O.U.D.S., 1932; toured Egypt and Australia with Nicholas Hannen, 1933; played in Henry VIII, Old Vic, and joined Ivor Novello's company, 1934; left stage; wrote lyrics for Ivor Novello, 1935-49; "Glamorous Night," "Careless Rapture," "Crest Of The Wave," "The Dancing Years," "Arc de Triomphe," "King's Rhapsody;" produced and acted in his own *Devil's Dyke* at Oxford Festival, 1937; composed music for production of his *Christ's Comet*, Canterbury Festival, 1938; Radio Series in Five Parts, *The Story of George Frideric Handel*, 1949; adapted Barrie's *Quality Street*, as a musical play (*Dear Miss Phoebe*), Phoenix, 1950; *The Great Endeavour*, drama for the Empire Day Movement, Drury Lane, 1948; *The Player King* (verse drama), Edinburgh Festival, 1952; Director of Voice, Old Vic Theatre School, 1947-49; Poetry Editor, B.B.C. Third Program, 1950; played Ishak in *Hassan*, 1947; Antonio in *The Duchess of Malfi*, 1941, for the B.B.C.; Poetry Reader for the Apollo Society, 1946; A.C. Benson Medal and Hawthornden Prize, 1939; Councillor and Fellow R.S.L.; Director of the Performing Right Society; Governor of The London Academy of Music and Dramatic Art; Mem. Arts Council Poetry Panel, 1951-53. Joined

R.A., June 1940; commissioned March 1941; trans. Army Educational Corps, 1942; demobilised as Staff Major War Office, 1946. Founded Stratford Annual Poetry Festival, 1954. original librettos for Opera: (for Anthony Hopkins) *The Man From Tuscany*, Canterbury Festival, 1951; (for Franz Reizenstein) *Anna Kraus* (Radio Opera), 1952; (for William Walton) *Troilus and Cressida*, 1954; (for Arthur Bliss) *Tobias and the Angel*, 1960. Original texts for Cantatas: *The Rainbow* (for Festival of Britain), 1951; (with Thomas Wood) *Yggdrasil*, Bryanston Summer School, 1951; (with Wilfred Mellers) *Voices of Night*, 1952; *Genesis*, 1958. English versions of Opera: Dvorak's *Rusalka*, Rimsky-Korsakov's *Kitesh*, Donizetti's *Il Campanello*, Bartok's *Bluebeard's Castle*, Lehar's *The Merry Widow*, *The Land of Smiles*, and Johann Strauss' *Fledermaus* (these last three for the Sadler's Wells Opera Company). Publications: *Poems of Two Years*, 1935; *Devil's Dyke*, 1936; *Christ's Comet*, 1937; *Penthesperon*, 1938; *Crisis*, 1939; *S.O.S. Ludlow*, 1941; *The Timeless Quest*, 1948; *The Slow Night*, 1949; *Words By Request*, 1952; *Out of the Whirlwind*, *The Player King*, 1953; *The Red Leaf* (poems), 1957. Edited the ABCA Song Book for the War Office, 1944; (Ed. With Introd.) *The Prose of Rupert Brooke*, 1956; *Edward Marsh, Patron of the Arts, A Biography*, 1959. Posthumous publications: *Rupert Brooke*, 1964; *Ambrosia* and *Small Beer*, 1964...

Christopher's best known collaboration was with Ivor Novello. Perhaps his most ambitious was with William Walton.

In the winter of 1947 the BBC invited Walton to write a new opera. The suggested theme was the doomed romance of Troilus and Cressida, and the proposed librettist was Christopher Hassall.

The wheels were set in motion. They were to turn very slowly over a period of some eight-and-a-half years.

With William Walton came a Hassall family association with the Isle of Ischia, where Imogen would often holiday at the Waltons' home. Sometimes she would bring friends.

"We used to call her Jenny," says Lady Walton. "And thought she was a darling and so very beautiful."

Imogen would say proudly that William Walton was her godfather, but Susana Walton believes that this was an invention. And Imogen, eventually, ruined this relationship also. "We followed her career with interest and then anxiety, she finally mucked-up when she sold her life to the *News of the World* as she chose to embarrass our friends on Ischia with invented spicy stories."

Christopher's collaboration with Walton was not always as harmonious as that which he had enjoyed with Ivor Novello. Walton detected what he regarded as Novello's bad influence in everything that Christopher wrote. He felt that Christopher had been ruined by Novello. According to Lady Walton. "He came to believe that Ivor Novello had taken possession of Christopher's soul."

Christopher did not take kindly to Walton's repeated suggestion that he subdue Ivor's influence, particularly as Walton had a habit of dotting the initials I.N. in the margins of Christopher's libretto, thus indicating the passages of which he did not approve.

Walton could be tactless; Christopher was deeply hurt when the composer wrote: "It evokes the worst type of music for me, real neo-Novelloismo, which I fear cannot be tolerated on the operatic stage..."

Christopher Hassall on his way to La Scala, Milan, is seen off by his wife Eve and daughter Imogen.

However, on the occasions that Christopher came to visit Ischia, his charm ensured that all was forgiven. Despite the friction that persisted between them professionally, their personal relations were usually amicable.

Laurence Olivier was invited to express an opinion on Hassall's work-in-progress. At one time Olivier was to produce *Troilus*. Sets were to be designed by Henry Moore.

Olivier and Christopher were well-acquainted. Such glittering names and famous faces would have been a matter of daily routine for Imogen. In her environment talent was taken for granted, success assured. How could she possibly grow up not knowing that she would be talented and successful? And how deep was her disappointment when she knew that she was not as talented as she ought to be given her pedigree?

After ages of blood, sweat and tears *Troilus and Cressida* was ready. Critical reaction was lukewarm.

The Continental premiere was to be given at La Scala, Milan. Christopher was seen off at Victoria Station by his admiring family and recorded by an *Evening Standard* photographer.

It is an oddly unconvincing picture. Squeezed tight between her parents, a 13-year-old Jenny stands on tip-toe to kiss her father on the cheek. Christopher, with a faint smile, looks slightly embarrassed. Eve Hassall is beaming at her husband over Jenny's shoulder. Almost shyly, Christopher appears to be looking past them both.

This might be reading too much into an obviously posed picture, a tableau contrived for the benefit of the camera.

There was an accident-prone performance at La Scala with booing and hissing from sections of the audience and scorn in the Italian press. The opera was to drop out of sight for several years.

Walton was never satisfied with the libretto and was still describing it as being Novello-ish shortly before the premiere. Christopher Hassall's work was criticized in some quarters as being too flowery and obscure but was also praised as being nicely balanced between straightforward communication and poetic utterance.

His libretto followed Chaucer's tale of Troilus and Cressida, not Shakespeare's, and his summary of the heroine is interesting:

> ...Fear—fear of loneliness, of old age, of death, of love and of hostil-
> ity—And from this Fear springs the only positive passion which can be
> permanent in such a nature, the pitiable longing, more childlike than
> womanly, for protection.

With his many achievements how much time did Christopher Hassall have to be a father?

The Hassalls, Christopher and Eve, are described by Anthony Collin as exceedingly Bohemian. But Anthony admits that he was a simple provincial actor and, to him, folk such as the Hassalls seemed creatures from another planet.

John Samson as a lad fresh from the provinces, was in awe of strange and exotic beings like Jenny Hassall. When he got to know her, he found that she was just a nice, straightforward and friendly girl.

Such gifted, artistic people can be self-obsessed, preoccupied, often at the expense of their children.

Some say that the Hassalls were a dysfunctional family. But others saw Christopher and Jenny as just like any father and daughter.

Christopher, according to Imogen, could be eccentric and if not self-obsessed certainly preoccupied. There are those who claim that he pushed his daughter in the wrong direction, and those that say that he was always sensible and constructive; and supportive at all times, always there for her.

Eve was volatile, and, some say, self-destructive, and there is no doubt that much of Eve's chemistry went into Imogen. It was Eve who introduced Jenny to sleeping pills that escalated into the heavy tranquilizers. But many mothers and doctors did the same in those days with only the best intentions.

Although Eve seemed turbulent and troubled, she was also very nice, kind and very funny.

From Imogen there would be some startling and disturbing revelations—fantasies, some say—about her childhood and her father's behavior. But it is much too easy to blame the parents. There are as many Christophers and Eves as there are Imogens.

Imogen was obviously very proud of her famous father. She was always keen to speak about him and praise his achievements.

In April 1963, while 21-year-old Jenny was a hopeful young actress, *Troilus and Cressida* was revived at Covent Garden.

Christopher Hassall, in a hurry for a performance of *Troilus* suffered a heart attack after running to catch a train and died on April 26.

He was found dead when the train reached the end of the line. There had been no one sharing the carriage with him, no one to help him. He died alone. Jenny once told a friend that she did not want to die all alone.

Gillian Patterson says that Christopher had been getting rather overweight. He was a great one for sticky buns and bars of Turkish Delight. His first words on emerging from incarceration on a health farm were "bring a bag of buns." There was always a bar of Turkish Delight hidden behind the books; he would telephone Gillian and demand to know where it was.

"Everyone was weeping all over the place," says Gillian.

Despite exaggerated tales told by Imogen to the tabloids, the news of her father's death was conveyed by Gary Hope.

In the early 1960s Gary was a young actor on the books of London Management. As was the norm, he was encouraged to be seen at all the important events — "so I squired lots of girls, including Imogen at various things."

Imogen was already emerging as a familiar face on the swinging scene. There were first nights and premieres; new bistros and boutiques opening; so many opportunities to mingle with and be seen by the right people. Imogen was always there, with some beau or other. "It was a joyous time, lots of fun and laughter." And a carefree, careless time. "Abortions galore."

Imogen had at least one abortion. Terminating a pregnancy was not the routine, efficient operation that it is now. Imogen's carelessness would come back to haunt her in later years when she was desperate to have children.

In 1963 Gary Hope had his own television series, *Moonstrike*, based on the true-life exploits of the Special Operations Executive aiding the Resistance in Occupied France during W.W.II.

Imogen and Gary would never share any screen time but they would be cast together in several popular TV shows such as *The Avengers* and *The Saint*. Imogen was booked to appear as a French girl in just one episode of *Moonstrike*.

Rehearsals for the show were held in the Memorial Hall on Parsons Green. On that particular morning, the cast, having read the news of Christopher Hassall's death, had assumed that Imogen would not be joining them.

However, Imogen duly arrived late as usual accompanied by her two little dogs. It was obvious to her colleagues that she knew nothing about her father's death. It later transpired that Imogen had spent the previous night with a certain prominent actor. That actor had seen the news in the morning papers and had packed Imogen off to her rehearsals in blissful ignorance.

Knowing that Gary was friendly with Imogen, the director of *Moonstrike* took him aside and asked him to deal with the situation. Gary led Imogen out onto the Green and broke the terrible news to her. "It was a massive drama. We walked round the Green, and she went through shock initially, and of course the tears began, then the shaking started. It was a massive upset."

It was clear to Gary that Imogen worshipped her father. In the meantime, a car had been arranged and Imogen was sent home.

That was the way it happened insists Gary Hope. But it was not what Imogen told the tabloids.

Imogen gave her version to the *News of the World* in July 1971. She had just returned to England after a sojourn with the Italian *dolce vita* set on the Isle of Ischia. But before she could devote herself to her film career, there was a matter that demanded her immediate attention. "I had to tell my father, Christopher Hassall the famous poet, that I was no longer a virgin. That I had already lived with two men and slept with several more..."

Imogen was planning to go to a party with several film world friends and afterward she would go and spend a few days with her father and break the news of the loss of her virginity. She was always a great name-dropper and cited as protagonists in this drama two of the hottest young male stars of the 1960s.

It all got rather complicated. For some reason Imogen swapped cars with the first of her male leads on the way to the party. As the youthful screen star drove through the night, he switched on Imogen's car radio. His car did not have one, so Imogen drove in silence. The actor arrived at the party shortly after her. He was grim-faced. "Imo—your father is dead. They just gave it out on the news bulletin."

Imogen's reaction was unexpected:

"I was totally numbed. And yet I felt absolutely no emotion. Nothing. No choking feeling, no heartbreak. The people at the party must have thought me a really cold bitch."

Imogen stayed at the party and was introduced to another rising young heartthrob—"this is Christopher Hassall's daughter." "My instinctive reaction was to shout gaily: 'Oh yes, he's dead—ha, ha.'"

Shocked, he slapped her hard across the face. Later, Imogen said, he understood that "...My outburst was merely a nervous reaction to stop myself from crying."

Later Imogen claimed the actor became "my very best friend in the film world."

Gary was very hurt by this; he could not fathom why she had felt it necessary to tell such ridiculous tall-tales.

"Oh well," said Imogen excusing her many fabrications, "I needed the money...I told them what I thought they wanted to hear..."

The simple truth, Gary argued, might have made a more meaningful story; but not, of course, a more glamorous and exciting one.

Was her frequent embellishment and romancing done not just to provoke and to get a reaction but also a means of getting a grip on things when events—as they so often did—were piling on top of her?

Gary Hope would settle down into a new life with a wife and three children, and would not get close to Imogen again until the very end of her life. But whatever she told the newspapers, he says, Imogen recognized a bond forged between them by the death of her father and in 1980 they would be friends again.

In 1963 Jenny was still very much a child—and a child she remained until the end of her life.

As devastating as it must have been, it would be too simple to say this one event shaped the rest of her life. But in 1969 she told the *Daily Sketch*, "I was very influenced by my father...I've wanted to be with a man who had his qualities but I haven't found him...I can't shake him off as an idol. I suppose I need a father and a lover all in one."

Iain Stuart Robertson says that Nicholas was overcome with guilt after his father's death. Iain felt it necessary to accompany Nicholas to the hospital in Rochester to identify the body and then on to Canterbury to make the funeral arrangements.

The funeral service was held in the crypt at Canterbury with the reception at Tonford Manor. Iain recalls that Nicholas wanted a great thing for the funeral. He wanted the music to be played by a full orchestra.

"There's no money to waste on that," said the lawyers.

Iain was able to observe Imogen at her father's funeral. "She was remarkably quiet."

Imogen, says Iain, behaved beautifully, dressed elegantly and appropriately in black. There was no display, no theatre.

Imogen was fully capable of behaving appropriately when the occasion demanded. Her outward serenity might have been a manifestation of the lingering shock which often follows such a sudden and devastating bereavement. She may even have been propped up by sedatives.

A portrait of the young actress with the world at her feet

Her subdued manner may have been attributable to other shocks that, she claimed, were in store for her. According to Susana Walton, Imogen would later assert that her mother had barred her from entering Tonford Manor after Christopher's death—"declaring that he had been interested in men and there were things in the house the loving and bereaved daughter should not see!"

"I am quite certain," says Nicholas Hassall, "that Mother gave no injunction to Jenny to stay away from Tonford."

Christopher Hassall died intestate. Letters of administration were granted to Eve and to Nicholas Hassall.

The gross value of Christopher's estate was estimated at £24,416. There would also be royalties, principally from his collaboration with Ivor Novello.

"With regard to the royalties from my father's estate," says Nicholas Hassall. "I would say that on the whole, as was to be expected, they were on a steady but gradual decline and taking into account that Jenny, like me, only received a quarter, it was very likely that when she was not working she most certainly would have felt the pinch."

By the end of the 1960s, Imogen appeared to be living in style, financially independent, able to afford to buy her own trendy pad, which she proudly showed off to visiting journalists. And Eve was always there to support her, just as Christopher had been.

Eve's brother Ralph had laid the foundations for the hugely profitable Britvic label, and was later able to sell off his interests and retire to tropical climes. Friends recall seeing Imogen referred to in a newspaper as the Britvic heiress, although her behavior would eventually alienate her from her family and, she claimed, put her inheritance in jeopardy.

Other friends will say that Imogen had a lucrative sideline. She had an enthusiasm for interior design. Some claim that she made good money renovating a succession of apartments and houses and selling them at a healthy profit.

In later years as Imogen's career stuttered and stumbled, the tabloids would be regaled by pleas of dire poverty. She did everything in style her friends say—careful with the pennies but careless with the pounds; and always generous, ever eager to pay for lunch and dinner.

At the inquest in 1980 Imogen's solicitor said that she was secure financially. She had no worries on that score, he said.

Within a month of her father's death Imogen was working. Having left the nest of LAMDA and the RSC, she spread her wings and was flying.

She was back on television where everyone expected her to be. On May 5, 1963, she appeared in "A Sunday Morning," the episode of *Moonstrike*. And in September 1963 it was "Position of Trust," an installment of the TV crime series *Scales of Justice*.

The theatre was the serious actress' goal. On June 10 Imogen was onstage at the New Theatre, Bromley, in *Strike Me Lucky*, an Australian play with a cast of mainly Australian and New Zealand actors.

Written by Jon Cleary, author of the best-seller *The Sundowners*, the play took as its theme the disruptive effect—the stirrings of passion and greed—that the discovery of gold has upon the inhabitants of a sleepy New South Wales township. Imogen was cast as Teresa Da Vinci. Barely into her career Imogen was falling prey to the obvious. Certain parts were being identified with her. With her exotic looks and vibrant personality, she was ready-made for those whose job it was to fulfill the obvious.

Again we see more than one side of Imogen.

Roy Patrick was in the cast of *Strike Me Lucky*. His Imogen was delightful, great fun with a delicious sense of humor, although he acknowledges that "there was a slightly highly-strung side to her character. ...Beautiful, talented with everything to live for..."

Another Roy, Roy Purcell, says, "we certainly had a lot of fun with *Strike Me Lucky*, I remember Imogen as a very beautiful girl, but a fairly unreliable actress. One never knew whether she would turn up," he explains.

Roy Purcell says that Imogen might have had a potential as an actress but no discipline. However, setting aside his doubts about her as a professional, he concedes that she had an attractive personality, great effervescence—on a good day.

Roy Purcell says that he observed Imogen's subsequent career from afar and mentions "the gossip that surrounded her. It seems to me that sadly she always carried the seeds of her own destruction."

Imogen Hassall received a mention in dispatches for her first featured role on the professional stage—singled out from an unusually large cast as one of several effective performances.

In the *Bromley Times*, however, Imogen was merely "lovely"—her performance went unnoticed. The play itself was given generous coverage. It was not every week that a new play had its World Premiere in Bromley; and it was reported that the film rights had already been acquired by none other than Marlon Brando.

Sensing the disturbance underneath, agent Peter Charlesworth was never inclined to become involved with Imogen professionally, but he did regard her as a friend.

Peter first encountered Imogen in the early 1960s when she was one of the fresh young faces making the scene. "There were a lot of young starlets like that around then. As a young agent, I was handling several of them; it was a common thing to go out for a date."

Peter never represented Imogen, but it was inevitable that they would meet. They all had a common rendezvous, the White Elephant in Curzon Street. Imogen was young and on top of the world. This Imogen was uncomplicated. "I never had an affair with her—she wasn't my cup of tea—I just enjoyed her company. She was great fun."

Peter would stay in touch with Imogen through the 1970s and right up to the end of her life. He would witness the alarming disintegration, the conflicts and extreme contradictions as her demons took hold.

Peter Bowles found no faults with his Imogen.

The Afternoon Men opened at the New Arts Theatre on August 22, 1963: it was a dramatization of the novel by Anthony Powell, updated from the 1920s to the '60s.

As always, the first impression that Imogen made was one of astonishing and unusual beauty. Peter Bowles says that Imogen was a charismatically beautiful girl and he observed that all sorts of people wanted to date her.

Peter says that he was very close with her. His Imogen was happy and hard-working and trouble-free. He is keen to defend his Imogen against the darker, volatile and disturbed person depicted by others. He is emphatic that he saw no evidence whatsoever of any mental problems and that Imogen was thoroughly professional and showed no signs of strain during intensive rehearsals.

Another "Afternoon Man," James Fox, saw the same Imogen as Peter Bowles—"I remember her as a delightful colleague." He would like her to be remembered with affection and respect.

Imogen played a very English Harriet in *The Afternoon Men*. Her part identification problems embraced two opposite but equally rarefied extremes, the exotic temptress and the cut-glass debutante—the latter type dismissed by one critic reviewing another play as Imogen simply playing Imogen.

Peter Bowles says that it was a very good part and she was very good in it. There were no flaws in his Imogen. She was, he insists, a delight at all times.

Peter is not alone in noting Imogen's childlike innocence. And his Imogen did not carry within her the seeds of her own destruction. "...She was taken advantage of once too often..."

CHAPTER FIVE
LOVE LOVE LOVE

Between 1964 and 1967 Imogen was covering all the bases. She was in demand making film, stage and TV appearances.

In 1964 Imogen played the title role in "Sophia," an episode of *The Saint*. She was cast as a Mediterranean maiden—a Greek innkeeper's daughter embroiled in archaeological skullduggery.

That same year Imogen was Miss Cartwright, a stereotypical secretary in *The Early Bird*, a Norman Wisdom comedy about a milkman. Imogen is second to last in the billing, followed only by Nellie, the milkman's horse. Her screen time amounts to 30 seconds and her dialogue is confined to "Good morning, Mr. Grimsdale? Would you come this way...Sir Roger, Mr. Grimsdale and Mr. Pitkin, and you have a board meeting in 10 minutes, Sir." Although she comes and goes in the blink of an eye, it is well worth catching the moment; she is so chic.

This is not what LAMDA and the RSC prepared her for, but it probably did not worry Imogen at the time.

She was where she was expected to be, on the big screen making the most of her vivacity and spectacular looks.

She was already attracting the attention of the tabloids. An enormous, pretty portrait of a pert and kitten-like starlet dominated the TV page of the *Daily Mirror* in 1963/64:

> The slinky, smoldering looks of 20-year-old Imogen Hassall may explain why this dark-eyed beauty has played a series of Latin and Oriental parts on TV since she left drama school a year ago.
>
> Tonight she turns up as a Middle Eastern beauty, mixed up in an insurance racket in *The Sentimental Agent* on ITV...
>
> But since she filmed this, Imogen has finally won the role of an English girl. Not only an English girl, but the Beatnik daughter of a prospective Prime Minister in the new stage play by William Douglas-Home...

On January 15, 1964 *The Reluctant Peer* opened for a long run of 475 performances at the Duchess Theatre, starring first Sybil Thorndike and later Athene Seyler. Written by William Douglas Home, the brother of the then Prime Minister, the play concerned a peer who renounces his title in order to become P.M., much to the consternation of his family.

Imogen appeared as Lady Rosalind, the reluctant peer's daughter, who has a communist boyfriend. The play represented the kind of light comedy that might have been Imogen's forte, the genre to which her personality and acting style were best suited.

"Imogen Hassall suggests far too youthful a Lady Rosalind to have just served a sentence in Holloway for sitting on an airstrip in aid of nuclear disarmament," said one critic. "But she looked fetching, if improbably clean in her Carnaby-Street-style sweaters and jeans."

Elsewhere, Imogen rated a mention in dispatches. Once more she was singled out as "effective."

Another critic, having written his entire review as a hymn of praise to the great Sybil Thorndike, finished with, "And there must be a welcome for Imogen Hassall."

In August 1965 Imogen was The Honourable Muriel Pym for two weeks at the Yvonne Arnaud Theatre in Guildford in a revival of *Milestones*. The play was an family saga set in a drawing room in Kensington Gore.

For Brian Poyser the highlight of the run was during a performance when he accidentally set light to the colored gel of a false fireplace and brought the "Iron Curtain" down.

Imogen did not appear until the third act; it was a small part. She looked lovely, Brian remembers, in a long white dress, tiara and jeweled necklaces. "She'd obviously learned quite a lot at drama school; she was very good."

And there were no problems at all. Brian's brief working life with Imogen was entirely trouble free—"she was perfectly normal while we were doing the play."

She was an extremely nice girl says John Standing. "A very, very nice girl."

John says that it was he and Imogen who stopped in the middle of a scene to put out Brian Poyser's unintentionally real fire as the stage slowly filled with smoke. They then stood back and watched and giggled recalls Brian—as the safety curtain descended and the firemen arrived.

Once order had been restored in the true tradition of the theatre, the show went on from where they had left off. When Brian, at his second attempt, succeeded in pretending to light the fake fire, he was rewarded with a ripple of applause. Remarkably, there had been no panic in the audience. They were merely bemused to see smoke coming down rather than going up the fireplace.

"We were absolutely thrilled by the whole operation," says John Standing.

Imogen was Bunty Mainwaring in November 1965 in Noel Coward's *The Vortex*, again

Imogen in distinguished company with Sybil Thorndike in *The Reluctant Peer*

at the Yvonne Arnaud. Coincidentally, and happily for Imogen, the play had been a favorite exercise piece at LAMDA.

On film and TV, Imogen may have been letting herself down, but she was being seen in the right places, onstage.

Imogen did not rate a biography in the *Vortex* program. In one copy, however, there is a printed slip "Owing to the indisposition of Imogen Hassall..."

She may quite simply have been indisposed. Some of Imogen's friends say that she was often ill. Or maybe it was less real than imagined; she woke up on the wrong side of the bed that morning and just could not face it. Idle speculation comes all too easy with Imogen: a failed pregnancy—there would be several—another cry for help or just Imo being incident-prone?

Whatever the cause of Imogen's absence on that particular night, the critics had taken notice of her performance, "Imogen Hassall was fascinatingly hard and brittle as the bright young thing engaged to Florence's son..." Some vindication for Imogen's defenders against those who say that she had no talent.

To be cast in *The Reluctant Peer* and *The Vortex* must have gratified Clive Graham's serious young actress. And she would do more good stage work over the years between being dragged back to do cheap, throwaway films and TV fare that did no favors for her public image.

Film and TV must still have appeared to be the more obvious avenue for Imogen, and it is plain to see that there was an open door for her. The 1960s were swinging and there was a new kind of girl in town. The real Imogen Hassall was no "dolly bird" but "obviously" she fit the bill. And if she is remembered at all today, it is as just another of those bikini-clad starlets.

In September 1998, 18 years after her death, Imogen would be a character in a play at the Royal National Theatre. Alongside Sid, Kenneth and Barbara in Terry Johnson's Olivier award-winning homage to the Carry On team, *Cleo, Camping, Emmanuelle and Dick*.

Terry Johnson's play is confined to Sid James's on-set caravan and with sadness and wit, chronicles his inexorable decline from *Carry On Cleo* in 1964 to *Carry On Emmanuelle* in 1978. The script takes dramatic liberties with Imogen's resume — and she was described by one critic as "a clawless clueless sex kitten." But there are many Imogens and Terry Johnson's version is one of them.

The character of Imogen first enters on the set of *Cleo* as a wide-eyed starlet, made up to be a Nubian slave girl, who is lured by the modern shower facilities in Sid's caravan. Off stage "Imogen starts to sing 'For All We Know.' Sid listens until the phone rings."

SID: (Phone) Yeh? Hello Bernie. What? Why not? No, no, I told you: I want to get a little present for Val. No, she's got the wrong end of the stick, mate. Freddie's got some winnings for me. Now Bernie, would I lie to you? All right, but listen mate; it's a dead cert and when it comes in I'm gonna get Val something really special. What do you mean, a divorce? Bernie...!

He puts the phone down and drinks. He seems pressured. Imogen finishes singing and emerges.

IMOGEN: Hello. Everyone gone?
SID: Yep. That was a very nice song.
IMOGEN: Daddy's favorite.
SID: You get on well with your father?
IMOGEN: He's dead.
SID: Oh, I'm sorry. Did you love him?
IMOGEN: I loved him very much.
SID: That's nice. Do you like fruit?
IMOGEN: Yes.
SID: Want some?
IMOGEN: Um....
SID: Have some.

He offers her a different exotic fruit.

IMOGEN: Thank you.

SID: That's a passion fruit.

IMOGEN: Is it?

SID: That's right.

IMOGEN: Why?

SID: I've no idea. Try it.

IMOGEN: I've never...

SID: You can't just bite into it because the skin is very bitter. The flesh on the other hand is very sweet. So before you can eat you have to pull back the skin like so, and there's the flesh, look.

IMOGEN: Wow.

SID: Those taste buds tingling?

IMOGEN: It's beautiful inside.

SID: Isn't it? In you go.

IMOGEN: Mmm. Wow.

SID: Use your tongue.

IMOGEN: I am.

SID: How's that?

IMOGEN: It's....

SID: Mmm?

IMOGEN: Delicious. Mmph; I'm all wet.

SID: Stay that way; it gets better. Move over.

IMOGEN: Do you want some?

SID: No, you enjoy yourself.

IMOGEN: Here.

SID: You temptress. Cor.

IMOGEN: Good?

SID: That's good, isn't it?

IMOGEN: That's very good.

SID: Here; let me.

IMOGEN: No, no; you.

SID: You and me together.

They feed each other. He wipes the corner of her mouth with his finger and tastes her.

IMOGEN: Ooh. I'm all sticky.

SID: You taste good.

IMOGEN: Have you got a tissue?

SID: Who needs tissues? Here.

He turns her head towards him and leans towards her. Barbara enters.

BARBARA: Are you decent? I suddenly remembered I'd forgotten something.

SID: What was that then?

BARBARA: I can't remember. Oh, hello.

IMOGEN: Hello.

BARBARA: Are you Imogen?

IMOGEN: Yes, hello.

BARBARA: There's a runner looking for you.

IMOGEN: Oh heavens. I'm late.

BARBARA: If you're going to hang out with this lot you're going to have to improve your timing.

IMOGEN: I'm all sticky.

BARBARA: Whoops.

IMOGEN: Thanks for the shower and the thingy.

SID: Any time.

IMOGEN: Bye then.

BARBARA: Bye, love.

IMOGEN: Bye, Sid.

SID: Bye Bye.

IMOGEN: Byyye.

Exit Imogen...

Between 1964 and 1967 Imogen was becoming a TV regular.

Scenes from *The Reluctant Peer* were shown on BBC 1 on January 17, 1964.

In 1965, according to the British Film Institute archives, Imogen was a cast member in "The Reunion," an episode of *No Hiding Place*. 1966 saw her in an adaptation of Evelyn Waugh's *Sword of Honour* on the BBC's *Theatre 625*.

Three years go by but it is clear that Imogen is making no progress.

In 1967 she was back in *The Saint*. In an episode entitled "Flight Plan" she portrays Nadya, a Middle Eastern bad girl involved in the theft of a top secret military aircraft.

Imogen's screen time runs to barely 10 minutes. She has little dialogue and mostly hovers in the background, smoldering. Disguised as a nun, she wields a tranquilizing hypodermic as an accomplice in a kidnapping.

She looks startling, stained dark brown, her long hair straightened and almost jet black, wearing a scarlet PVC coat over a bright yellow mini-dress. You can tell that she is a bad girl because she is forever smoking.

Although she is playing an Arab, Imogen does not appear to be making much of an attempt at an accent. Overall, her stabs at foreign accents in her film and TV work are somewhat variable—and she was sometimes dubbed. But those were the days of all-purpose accents, when more or less the same thing would do for several continents, and actors were not as obsessively accurate as they are now.

Imogen's appearance with Charles Gray in *The Moon and Sixpence* for BBC TV is not included in any list of her credits.

The Avengers **"Escape in Time" featured Diana Rigg as Mrs. Emma Peel and Imogen as Anjali.**

That same year Imogen went from Arabia to India as Anjali, in "Escape in Time," an episode of *The Avengers*; a bad girl once again, a small cog in an organization engaged in smuggling wanted criminals to safety.

Swathed in a sari, she seems more natural and this time does the accent. She plays separate scenes opposite both Patrick Macnee and Diana Rigg in an incidental role.

Diana Rigg remembers a very beautiful girl but, otherwise, Imogen left no lasting impression. How did Imogen feel, playing opposite someone who, it appears, represented something to her? Was she thinking, wishfully, "I could have been you—if only," casting her mind back to her premature departure from the RSC in 1962; or was she just thrilled to be seen on such a successful show in such respected company, working with someone she admired?

Imogen left a lasting and vivid impression on Patrick Macnee. "She certainly was very, very attractive. Glowing, full of bubbling amusement—her physical look was astonishing."

In Imogen, Patrick saw someone whose gifts had been both wasted and overlooked. "A very good actress...underrated, because she was such a great First Night escort."

Patrick Macnee as John Steed with Imogen in *The Avengers* "Escape in Time"

He was well aware of the many complications and contradictions that made Imogen so compelling. "She was totally beguiling and very dangerous. You didn't ever know which way she would go!"

She was inherently self-destructive and Patrick Macnee's Imogen sounds entrancing, intriguing and exciting. As to her mystery, he would look to her relationship with her father. "Probably one of the most important aspects of Imogen's life."

Imogen liked Patrick Macnee, once remarking: "I adore him—he's so gentle." There are nice stills of the two of them chatting off camera, Imogen in her sari with a fag in her hand and a big black handbag close by her side looks very relaxed. That's how her friends like to remember her, relaxed and natural, happy just to sit around and chat.

There were other men, whom Imogen leaned on and was plainly comfortable with. Some of them wonder if perhaps they represented some kind of father figure.

Perhaps, but Imogen also had her many lovers.

Peter Fenton first saw Imogen striding down Kensington High Street.

Picture the scene: Swinging London. Handsome young cabaret singer Peter Fenton is cruising Kensington and Chelsea in his red sports car. Sweeping by, along the sunny pavement, he spies a vision of startling loveliness.

Imogen—the very image of a London swinging—stepping out in a low-cut, outrageous mini-dress and kinky boots. A rare beauty: the devil in those exotic eyes; but it's a friendly face. Her extraordinary and commanding profile; long, dark, heavy hair flowing down over her trim shoulders, halfway down her back, swaying lush and glossy in the sunlight. A slim and supple body and impossible waist, emphasizing those joyous, jouncing, bouncing, spectacular breasts. Flashing thighs: Imogen in full sail; a wonderful mover; striding out along the sunny, brightly peopled streets of London. Imogen in sharp focus, every eye upon her, the world a blur of colors revolving around her.

Peter Fenton was astonished. He had never seen anything like her. "Who is that?"

Imogen's attention is attracted and introductions are made; smiling, she leans into the red sports car.

In bed together. A Chelsea morning.

Imogen touches Peter's bare shoulder. "Isn't it tragic," she sighs. "That this is not going to last, that it's going to fade?"

Barely into her 20s, Imogen was already afraid of growing old.

According to Peter Fenton there was no such thing as straight sex with Imo.

It was not that she was into rough sex. But there had to be a battle first, loud arguments, screaming and shouting before making up and falling into bed. Imo's friends report her capacity to argue, with her lovers, friends, strangers often—without warning, without rhyme or reason. And then abruptly the sun would shine again.

Some took it in their stride; some lost patience and gave up trying. Others found Imogen's mood swings deeply disturbing, even frightening.

When she did become difficult or impossible or nasty, her brother says, you could see it coming—"you were quite aware that she was going to have a turn. A lot of her friends were prepared to forgive her, because they knew that once she got over it she would be her sweet self again."

Charlotte Rampling was drawn to Imogen, liked her and enjoyed her company but was ultimately compelled to retreat.

It was inevitable that their paths would intertwine, two beautiful young actresses seen in all the trendy bistros, boutiques and clubs. In 1966/67 they were both cast in *The Long Duel*, which took them on location to Spain.

Although they shared no screen time, Charlotte and Imogen were brought together for promotional purposes, bright smiles and short skirts—the natives watched and wondered, experiencing culture-shock.

They shared a trendy pad for a while in Swinging London. Charlotte's Imogen was fun and lovely. They were so young, she says, and never really talked about the deeper, darker, complicated things.

But it was obvious that Imogen was incredibly unstable and Charlotte believes that she can recall one suicide attempt in the brief time that she knew her. People like that, she says, can have a strong magnetism and they pull you in. They can be very attractive, which makes the manifestation of their inner demons all the more powerful and disturbing. She was never frightened by Imogen's extremes, more alarmed. The worst of it was that she simply did not know what to do, what to say. She herself was far too inexperienced to hand out advice.

Imogen was someone who didn't seem to hear or want to hear. It was a sense of utter helplessness that made Charlotte back away.

Charlotte Rampling, Imogen and Virginia North promoting *The Long Duel*.

"Seeming not to want to hear," says Nicholas Hassall, "was, of course, Jenny's way of getting her own way." The voice of reason might have "attacked her inviolable position. Her slightly upturned nose betrayed her intrinsically, natural and graceful (mostly) arrogance. An arrogance which a lot of people found charming."

Gillian Patterson would encounter Imogen again, occasionally, after the death of her father. "In later years she was a rather posturing, beautiful young woman."

It was very obvious, says Gillian, that there were two distinct personalities—public and private. When Imogen was with people she trusted she would let the veneer go.

Gillian can recall an occasion seated with Imogen for a concert at the Albert Hall. In the company of an old friend Imogen was clearly at ease. "She was the ordinary child, a person with no airs, no performance going on. She would relax completely and she was back to being the old Jenny again."

The old Jenny, says Gillian, "was very sweet, and very affectionate. You would get hugs and kisses, she was always pleased to see you—and laughing—relaxed."

But with Imogen there was always the feeling any time a storm might break. "You had this feeling it was kind of a knife edge."

Peter Fenton's relationship with Imogen foundered on the day she came to visit him in Bristol.

He met her at the station in a chauffeur-driven car. Within minutes, Imo ignited a row. It was the last straw. Peter told the chauffeur to turn around and frog-marched Imo onto the first train back to London.

Peter told her that he could not take any more. As far as he was concerned, their relationship was over.

One week later, Peter was back in his flat in London.

It was past midnight, and he was fast asleep. He woke up suddenly when the bedroom lights went on.

Imo was standing in front of him. Peter had forgotten to reclaim her spare set of keys. She was calmly undressing, intent on climbing into bed with him.

Peter reminded her that they had broken up. There was a pantomime row:

"I'm staying!"

"No you're not!"

"Yes I am!"

This went on for some time, until Peter scooped up Imo's clothes and escorted her, half-naked, out of the door and into the corridor.

All was quiet. Peter went back to bed.

After a while, there was a knock on the door. Imo's voice came faintly through the woodwork: "Can I have my dog back?"

Peter was mystified. Eventually he found Imo's tiny terrier cowering under the bed. The beast had evidently crept in with Imo when she made her midnight entrance. But Peter had no intention of letting its owner back in again.

Imo was still demanding the return of her pet from the other side of the locked door.

Peter had a flash of inspiration. The door to his flat had a box mounted on it for his letters and parcels. Its flap was large enough for the dog. Keeping his door firmly locked, he posted Imo's dog back to her.

Imogen was too much for Peter to take, but he wants only good things said about her.

Two years after he had evicted Imo, Peter was a broke struggling singer. Imogen invited him to stay with her for a while until he was back on his feet again. She even had a welcoming bottle of Scotch waiting for him when he arrived—a kindness typical of her.

On another occasion, out of the blue she called him. Her reward for doing a celebrity spot at Butlins was a luxury weekend in Paris and she invited Peter. "She was very good, very supportive."

That was Imogen. She had a great heart. Imogen's friends recall her many rows, but they want her to be remembered for her everyday kindness and generosity.

She had a great sense of fun, says David Wigg, and was great fun to be with. A social animal, she enjoyed going out, entertaining at home and giving dinner parties, even if at times her boyfriends did all the cooking while Imo played the hostess and poured the wine.

"She loved to laugh," David recalls. "She loved to drink, she loved wine. In a way she was very Italian—she had a great sense of living."

Jackie Ingham, also an actress, says that she met Jenny/Imo—she knew her as both—in the early 1960s, and they remained friends.

According to Peter, they all came together when Jackie, who lived downstairs, in protest against the loud party sounds coming from Peter's flat, pulled the fuses for the house plunging it into darkness.

Jackie says that Imogen had a silver spoon but messed it up, Imogen's family was dysfunctional, her mother suffered from similar depressions and was, like her daughter, promiscuous. And, of course, her father died when she was barely out of her teens.

According to Jackie, she always had to have a man—some were the serious ones, the ones who mattered. Otherwise, Imogen's lovers just came and went; although, as Jackie points out, it worked both ways—Imogen also came and went.

Jackie's Imo was educated, well-read, very witty and amusing. She was crazy in a lovable way.

Imo adored children, or kiddywinks as she called them and was a willing but unreliable baby-sitter. One would have to disconnect the telephone—if Imogen got wind of a party parents would come home to find the children tucked in bed and Imo gone.

There was a holiday in Venice. Imo went out on the town alone one evening. Next morning the beach boys were laying siege to the hotel, while Imo hid inside denying everything.

And there should have been another holiday to the South of France with her current boyfriend, a successful restaurateur. Prior to their departure he asked Imo to look after his pair of prized pedigree parrots.

Inevitably disaster struck. Imo let one of the parrots escape from its cage and her dog—an Afghan hound called Sylvia—promptly devoured it.

Jackie received a frantic phone call. Imo was having a fit and was flat on her back. She ordered Jackie to rush out and buy a substitute parrot.

Parrots, it transpired, were not only hard to match but were also prohibitively expensive. Imo's boyfriend arrived home to a solitary, mourning parrot, one empty cage and a few feathers. There was the predictable explosion. All plans for the South of France were canceled.

Like all those who were close to Imogen, Jackie bore the brunt of her moods. She could be enormously demanding.

Jackie believes that the trigger for Imogen's instability, her chemical imbalances, lay somewhere in the confusions of puberty. She remembers hysterical outbursts and lows on a kind of monthly cycle. Imogen was totally emotional and wrecked things for herself.

Like her career, Imogen's relationships self-destructed. Imo was forever complaining about the men in her life. Jackie recalls hours spent on the telephone, patiently dishing out reassurance and advice. When asked if Imo ever listened, she just smiles and rolls her eyes.

Jackie says that she knew Imogen as early as 1961 and denies vehemently that her young friend had any problems with pills and the midnight miseries, at least not until much later.

No one claims that Imogen ever became involved with the recreational drugs of the 1960s and 70s. But Jackie also insists that, while she may have been taking sleeping pills, Jenny had no chemical addictions of any kind, certainly not while she was at LAMDA and not for many years after. "She was no Judy Garland."

Jackie denies the reports that Jenny was already talking about suicide before she was 20. She is suspicious of the accounts of her addiction to pills; suspicious too of Imogen quoted as saying that her mother had started her on the pills when she was only 18.

If there was a definable turning point, it came with the failure of her first marriage and the loss of her baby in 1974.

Christopher Long, or so it seemed, might have been Imogen's Mr. Right.

She was, says Christopher, a real catalyst, someone who touched the lives of a great many people.

Their attraction was immediate and their on and off relationship would span seven or eight years into the early 1970s. They met when Christopher was an agent. Former clients have testified to his kindness and consideration. He later became disillusioned with the business and left it.

Christopher's Imo was a flitting butterfly. Twice they took out a special marriage license only to call it off at the very last minute. "She would do the classic 'get married and have children' one minute...next minute she wanted to be a serious actress...five minutes later... posing for pictures and going to openings..."

Imogen, says Christopher, had no substantial base. She was intelligent enough to realize what she was doing wrong but did not have the will or the discipline to do anything about it.

For Imo, meanwhile, life was all about love rather than commitment. In 1969, she pronounced: "I fall in love all the time. Every six months. What is more splendid than that? But I have a man called Chris Long...he's very dishy. So why don't we get married? Because when the crunch comes, I don't know whether I want the burden of it... I like the excitement of love, rather than the thought of maintaining it for years and years..."

Imogen would marry twice—both would be disasters. At the end of her life she would still be grasping desperately at the shreds of her second marriage.

For all her bold words about the excitement of love, a great part of her wanted so much to settle down. She wanted her Mr. Right to come along while, it seems, mistrusting the motives of all men; the rare men she might have trusted driven away by her behavior.

Christopher Long sums up Imogen as "a real mixture of being seduced by the possibility of recognition, and desperately craving normality."

Imogen so very much wanted a settled, secure and normal life, a cure for her uncertainties, the solid and reliable companionship of a decent man. She longed for the fulfillment of motherhood, but her volatile nature and fate would conspire against her.

She was, says Christopher, an explosive mix.

With Imo, whatever her mood, up or down, it was always at full throttle. Her moods swung widely and wildly; either everything was all fine or everything was all wrong, there was no in between. And she could be impossible whether she was up or down.

Sometimes, Christopher would almost believe that Imo really did want a quiet, normal life, but her behavior would say the opposite. She just would not listen. She would pay lip service for five minutes to common sense, and then go her own way. She just would not bother.

Her natural enthusiasm would make her take things beyond the limits of acceptable behavior. Christopher likens Imogen to a spinning roulette wheel with the ball always stopping somewhere else. He observed that people often felt eclipsed by her behavior. It was boring after a while; or they just could not take any more. "She would want to do something wild and it would end in tears."

And, of course, there were the rows. Imo, on the spur of the moment, might launch into an argument with the people at the next table in a restaurant for no apparent reason.

Their love life was punctuated by arguments. Imo would throw Christopher's clothes out of the window and slice up his ties. Once, she drove her car at him. She missed and hit the garden wall and kept on ramming the car into the wall over and over until the engine died.

Christopher watched as Imogen's cries for help became more extreme. He rode with her in the ambulance after she had made an attempt to slash her wrists.

Inevitably, his endurance faltered. He brought the relationship to an end. Her behavior was too disturbing, and he couldn't go on living on a perpetual razor's edge.

In 1970 in a more reflective mood the Countess of Cleavage said: "I think he wanted a quiet wife not a boisterous one. My enormous publicity has brought me more problems than success."

Christopher remembers Imogen with obvious affection; there was also love and many good times. He speaks for all who loved her when he insists that his Imogen be remembered for *joie de vivre*, energy, laughter and excitement.

Imo was making the scene, as depicted by Virginia Ironside—half intrigued and half objectively cynical—in her autobiographical novel *Chelsea Bird* published in 1964:

...The sun was shining and London smelt of dusty plane trees and hot exhaust pipes. All the blacks were out in the Portobello Road in very nice clothes, the sun reflecting off their plastic leather coats and the Salvation Army playing on the corner in a sad attempt to catch the beatniks by setting up a band called 'The Salvation Army Skiffle Group'. They played unheard, junk was changing hands, Americans, beatniks, locals and Jews milled around and the shrieks of the model girls and actresses could be heard from the garden of the pub...

...The bar was full of get-ahead young things, new photographers chatting about nothing with their arms around stupid but pretty model girls, journalists and pop artists all talking and looking for better photographers and prettier model girls to talk to...

...Features editors drifted in droves accompanied by their model girl wives, and a few advertising men who modeled in their spare time patted their hair at each other. Men in fur hats, girls in dark glasses, women in Bazaar dresses, art students in jeans, advertising men...they all wore badges of their profession...

Imo gave her own account of life among the Swingers to the *News of the World* in July 1971 — beneath the lurid headline: "A Little Girl In London's Orgy Set." "Although I was a well-developed girl I was still very naïve. Often I would go off to the Ad Lib Club or The Establishment, which were in vogue among the acting set..."

Imogen claimed to have been a mere spectator in what was Swinging London's great spectator sport, the Sex Game. She "used to sit fascinated at the dirty old men chatting up the young debby types who, had they but known it, went there solely in the hope of walking off to bed with some handsome young actor." She saw it all — Naked London

I was introduced in other places to the London sex-orgy set.

The wealthy young business men types and playboys who had made good early in life, had money to burn and insatiable appetites for the kind of way-out sex which was usually portrayed only in under-the-counter magazines...

Everything was calculated to get you into bed as soon as possible.

To them it didn't really matter how many people were already between the sheets making love...

Imogen, however, insisted that she remained purely a spectator. She was an old-fashioned girl at heart:

I always refused to enter into mass love-ins and whenever I encountered a pile of naked bodies writhing about on a bed I would exclaim: "Oh, sorry," and quickly close the door...

I was no prude. But I had always believed the sex act should be something important and delicate between two people...

I must admit that I don't mind watching such scenes. In a way it appeals to my sense of humor...

Imogen was adopted by the tabloids as the embodiment of a new glamour and lifestyle, and she was living the good life. On April 25, 1966, she appeared in the *Daily Mirror*

Swinging London comes to Monte Carlo

reclining decoratively in a tight top and short skirt on a ledge overlooking the harbor at Monte Carlo:

> Monte Carlo 1966 reeled slightly when London 1966 in the shape of Imogen Hassall appeared on the scene.
>
> The confrontation was momentous. But mutual adjustment occurred.
>
> Monte Carlo eventually accepted Miss Hassall's above-the-knee skirt (London '66). And Miss Hassall accepted the old world offerings of Monte Carlo (circa 1906).
>
> She is twenty-two, the actress daughter of the late Christopher Hassall, the poet and playwright, and has been holidaying at the Hotel de Paris with her mother.

"I love London" she admitted. "But it's so tense and frantic—often three parties a night—and it's wonderful to have a change.

"Here in Monte Carlo everything is easy and relaxed.

"I've even been able to sunbathe in the nude because we've got a private terrace at the hotel swimming pool."

Imogen was in her prime with the world at her feet. The world was her playground; she was one of the Jet Set. "I went to several orgies on the lovely Isle of Ischia, off Naples," she told the *News of the World* in July 1971. "Which was attended by many of Rome's *dolce vita* set. All the parties were organized on a grand scale and started off banquet style. The women wore elegant dresses made by some of the most famous fashion houses in Europe; the men were correctly dinner-jacketed; the servants white-gloved and immaculate. The tables were weighed down with the most exotic dishes and expensive wines. As the guests who had been brought together became merry the servants would retire. And then the men and women would pair off and disappear..."

"Ironically," said Imo, her brush with *la dolce vita* came about on a visit to Sir William and Lady Walton: "They are both terribly sweet people and were very protective towards me after my father's death. But as I walked along the beaches in my bikini I was an obvious target for the fun-loving Italian set, who have no other objectives in life than eating, drinking and making love."

To Imogen, it was all a great game: "One evening after the usual type of dinner party I broke up an orgy in which over 20 people were involved. I rushed into the huge room, climbed on top of a cupboard, leapt onto the bed and kept jumping up and down as if it were a trampoline. Nobody, but nobody, can perform adequately in those circumstances..."

It was interviews like this, in which Imogen told all, that would alienate her from important friends such as the Waltons.

Imogen often went on holiday with her mother. Nicholas Hassall says that his mother looked after her to a great extent. They were similar people on a certain level.

Nicholas observed that his mother seemed to enjoy the jollifications that came with Imogen's escapades, although she often had to be there to pick up the pieces. He says that his mother was envious of all the attention that Imogen was getting, although she did her best to hide it.

Eve, according to Nicholas, always encouraged her daughter in everything she tried to do. Others agree that Eve was always supportive and was always there for her when Imogen was down and needed comforting. "My sister would put on her little girl's voice and say 'Mummy, can I come home?' She would stay with my mother for days, even weeks, convalescing in a way."

In later years Imogen told Susana Walton that Eve used to call Jenny at all hours of the night claiming to be about to kill herself—distressing behavior mirrored by Eve's daughter.

Imogen's brother suspects that she was telling tales or at least exaggerating. "Mother was an old trouper. I am absolutely certain that she never tried to blackmail Jenny by declaring that she would top herself for one reason or another. True, they both appeared to be close and would confide in each other over the phone and it is barely conceivable that Mother was at times distraught over something but it would not be until years later, when accelerating senility exacerbated by alcoholism took her, that such a possible situation would have arisen."

When Imogen died, says Nicholas, his mother started drinking heavily. It was the beginning of the end for her. "She blamed herself for Jenny's symptoms and her death."

CHAPTER SIX
THE RISE AND FALL
OF THE COUNTESS OF CLEAVAGE

Imogen's obituary in *Screen International* would say that she "...Will sadly be better remembered as the perennial starlet rather than the busy actress..."

At the tail end of the Swinging Sixties Imogen was very busy consolidating her position as a familiar face and figure on the nation's TV and movie screens.

In 1967 as well as appearing in *The Saint* and *The Avengers*, she was in two films — *Bedtime* and *The Long Duel*.

The Long Duel — somewhere on the North West Frontier...

Imogen is Tara, an odd name for the wife of a Dacoit tribal chieftain — Yul Brynner — at war with British Imperialism, personified by Harry Andrews and Trevor Howard.

Pregnant Tara flees into the hills with her lord and master only to die offscreen in childbirth, 20 minutes into the film.

Imogen has only a small part in the movie, but she does get to play opposite the star. Considering the limitations of the role, she does as well as can be expected. Her face and body language are so expressive — "she was an awful ham," says Peter Fenton.

Star billing was something that would always elude Imogen on the silver screen. In truth she was only treading water. Her film and TV career would remain static with Imogen frozen in small parts, either the exotic or the dolly bird. And if she did rise occasionally into co-starring roles, it would be in very cheap fare.

1967 saw a definitive Imogen Hassall television appearance in "Reply Box 666," an episode of *The Champions*. She comes and goes even before the opening credits as an anonymous temptress of uncertain but definitely exotic stock. Her character, a one-dimensional sexpot, does not even have a name.

She is 25 years old, gorgeous, brown as a berry with wonderful long, dark hair, with mobile features and suggestive body language. She still moves like a dancer. It is five years since she left the Royal Shakespeare Company and she appears to be moving backward.

That same year she was back in *The Saint* in "The People Importers" as Malia Gupta, a lovely Asian girl.

Malia is the sister of an illegal immigrant, assisting the Saint in his crusade against evil. She is a thoroughly modern Chelsea girl, a model — and the script soon contrives to get her into a bikini. It is another bit part, only a few minutes of screen time, but Imogen gives it 110 percent.

Her expressiveness — those large, emphatic eyes — and her vivid body language are reminiscent of the Bollywood school of screen acting. Some have noted that the camera does not flatter her in close-up. It makes her face look broad; the Hassall face remarked upon by family friends, inherited from her father, who grew broader as he aged.

Imogen wanted so much to be a star; but she also craved recognition as a serious actress. This conflict combined with her deeper, darker uncertainties would pull her career apart.

If Imogen was looking to television and the movies to make her a big star, she was achieving nothing except generating a perception of her as a bit of fluff.

But she was getting work and a lot of it, and that would have made her feel successful.

Tara (Imogen) flees into the hills with Sultan (Yul Brynner) in *The Long Duel*.

She played the ambitious starlet to the hilt by courting the press, who were only too eager to wine and dine and discover her. She was young and excited and full of herself; and the tabloids lapped her up. "She has the chameleon character that fits showbiz success. She surveys you—and that means me—as if you are a passport to the heavenly kingdom, leaning forward in a way that makes a waiter miss his aim with the minestrone..."

For the benefit of the press, Imogen was radiating confidence, and the hacks, for the moment, were happy to go along. "Now I hate recommending blatant girls for stardom. I don't really like girls who thrust their contours at you like they are inaccessible bait. But I will say this about Imogen Hassall. That she should make it on talent."

The bright and breezy starlet sought instant fame in the glare of the flashbulbs and became a hot favorite with the tabloids, who knew that they could always rely on Imo for a saucy picture or an outrageous aside.

Imogen's finest hour: *The Italian Girl*

Her good nature was easy prey for a keen reporter. Once in the wee small hours, she phoned her friend, Fleet Street photographer Larry Ellis. She couldn't sleep, she said. There was a man from the *Sun* camped out on her doorstep. He'd been there all night. What shall I do?

Ignore him, said Larry. Just close your curtains and go to bed. Whatever you do, don't let him in!

But the next day there was Imogen, giving good copy as ever and doing herself no favors.

"Oh, I couldn't help myself," she sighed. "I felt so sorry for him."

She was doing nothing unusual or even wrong. The business of show is keeping one's face in the frame, one's name in all the columns. But she went over the top, until publicity became an end in itself and defeated its purpose. The tabloids could not believe their luck when Imogen came along. She would be her own worst enemy and the tabloids' best friend. Over the years, friends and colleagues would try to restrain and shield her, but, again and again, like a moth to the flame, she would succumb to the lure of the flashbulbs, open her mouth and put her foot in it.

But while the starlet was little more than a popular pin-up, the serious actress was soldiering on.

In 1968 Imogen had what she would cite as her finest hour.

Staged in the West End at Wyndham's Theatre, *The Italian Girl* was a dramatization of an Iris Murdoch novel by James Saunders and Iris Murdoch. A complex, sometimes bizarre and often comic family drama, the play gained plaudits most especially for its performances.

Imogen played Elsa Levkin, described in *The Stage* as a character who with her brother David, belong to the race who are hunted all over the world and must either hide themselves or die. Imogen's depiction of this doomed young girl was praised as "quite haunting."

In the production stills Imogen is spectacular and ravishing, clad in a peasant blouse and skirt, her arms and shoulders bare, cleavage tumbling perilously, her astounding breasts impossible on such a lithe and slender body.

She is electric.

Imogen's potential as an actress will remain an unknown quantity. But there appears to be little doubt that she did have potential. As Clive Graham suggests, given the opportunity, she could rise to a real challenge.

Jane Wenham at the time was preoccupied with bringing up a small son and did not have the time to get to know Imogen well. But she remembers her from rehearsals as warm and friendly. "I liked her a lot."

Timothy West got to know Imogen well. "During rehearsals and the initial run at Bristol, she stuck to me quite closely, feeling, I think, a bit lonely and aimless..."

Imogen was often in need of a sympathetic ear, reassurance, someone to lean on. She always had to have someone willing to listen to her troubles, real and/or imagined. "When we got to London, Imogen was clearly in the middle of an unhappy relationship with her current boyfriend and used to come into my dressing room at Wyndham's and complain about it. This became rather difficult to cope with sympathetically, particularly as she was letting the situation interfere with her performance more and more."

The Italian Girl: **tragedy befell Imogen in art as well as life.**

When Imogen complained, she complained long and loud. It could be tedious and distracting for those around her. But, by and large, people tolerated her complaining for as long as they could, and did their best to reassure and counsel her. They knew that, at heart, she was a kind and caring person, and they sensed a genuine unhappiness.

All agree that ordinarily Imogen was good company.

Prunella Scales taught at LAMDA while Imogen was there. She would see Imogen socially and always found her very warm and charming.

Deborah Grant, then a lowly A.S.M., testifies to Imogen's kindness and generosity.

Deborah was starving (and frozen) in a small room during the play's preliminary run at Bristol. Imogen came to the rescue and let Deborah take refuge in her warm hotel room.

It was a typical instance of thoughtfulness. "To me she was a generous, fun-loving friend."

Timothy West, trapped in his dressing room, was made all too aware of the conflicts and contradictions that made up Imogen, but he remembers her with great sympathy: "She wanted to be a star and to be taken seriously as an actress, but she wrecked her career with her thirst for publicity. I don't think she was ever prepared to give the thought and consideration needed to achieve this. She was, nevertheless, a kind and loving person and all of us in the show were sad when she had to leave it."

"Bed-hopping extravaganza" *The Time*

ELIZABETH SELLARS   RICHARD PASCO
JANE WENHAM   TIMOTHY WEST
IMOGEN   CHRISTOPHER   DEBORAH
HASSALL   GUINEE   GRANT

THE
ITALIAN GIRL
A play by JAMES SAUNDERS & IRIS MURDOCH

Based on the novel by
IRIS MURDOCH
Directed by
VAL MAY   Designed by Robin Archer

"A GOOD STORY told by a first-class mind. It has a
HUMOUR which is EXHILARATINGLY RABELAISIAN"
Harold Hobson, Sunday Times.
"A series of climaxes of LECHEROUS MAYHEM.
I ENJOYED IT. It is also VERY FUNNY"   Daily Mail.
"SUPERBLY SUCCESSFUL in liberating its audience
of guilt. WE LAUGH FREELY without inhibition"
Daily Express.
"I ENJOYED IT ENORMOUSLY" The Observer.

OPENS
FEB 1st   WYNDHAM'S   THEATRE
Tel: TEM 3028

There is no doubt that those who knew Jenny in the early 1960s saw a very different person when they met her again years later. They were disturbed by the changes.

Clive Graham could hardly recognize his Jen.

Neither would John Samson: "The end of the 1960s found me living in Chelsea, out-of-work and fed up. Those were the days when Chelsea was swinging—and on Saturday afternoon the world and his wife seemed to descend on the King's Road—to swing and to be seen swinging. On one of those Saturday afternoons, toward the end of the '60s—I can't now remember the year—I was walking towards Sloane Square when a voice hailed me from the other side of the road. I turned and saw a posse of modishly dressed film-type people—and standing slightly apart from them was Jenny. She was clearly part of this group—and yet I had the instant impression that she was somehow distanced from it. I waved, crossed the road, we hugged and kissed and chatted about those things stage-people do talk about when they meet again after a long absence. I was aware of the group she was with—who stood regarding me, obviously wondering who I was. They were obviously growing impatient and anxious to continue their showy promenade down the King's Road and did not appreciate being held up by this nobody talking to Jenny and who was clearly not one of their set. We only spoke for a few minutes, but I noticed what a change the film world had wrought in Jenny. Gone was the lovely complexion—replaced by a pocky shop-worn look. The hair had lost its luster and her eyes had a dark haunted look. At that moment, I recalled a comment made by a fellow student from LAMDA days: 'You know, Jenny is really vulnerable. If success comes, I'm not sure she'll be able to cope with it. Not in this business.' Anyway, we spoke for a few minutes more and then—reluctantly, I thought—we bade each other good-bye. I never saw her again."

Other LAMDA friends invited to Imogen's pad would arrive to find her in glamorous company—a very starry atmosphere, not at all Jenny, the domestic person, happy just to sit around and chat. They did not know this person and had little to say to her.

But Imogen was popular and gregarious and living the high life. Her comings and goings were noted in the public prints:

> The delightful Miss Imogen Hassall, who has been such an attraction in Iris Murdoch's play *The Italian Girl* at Wyndham's Theatre, is leaving the cast at the end of this week. She is going to Rome on holiday...She has also been offered several parts in films and while she is in Rome she hopes to reach a decision about her future plans.

Whatever old friends may have thought of her, Imogen, for public consumption at least, was sitting on top of the world.

As the 1960s made way for the 1970s, the movie starlet was working, working, working.

In 1969 she made the film for which she is best remembered—*When Dinosaurs Ruled the Earth*. Clad in a stone-age bikini, Imogen carried a spear as Ayak, a Jurassic bad girl, pitted against a motley crew of cavemen and monsters.

Dinosaurs, a Hammer follow up to *One Million Years B.C.*, tells the epic tale of tribal tensions in a fanciful, very unscientific Stone Age. It follows the perilous adventures of blonde beauty Victoria Vetri, who escapes from a human sacrifice intended for her and is pursued by the chief of the Rock Tribe, Patrick Allen—who, incidentally, played Achilles in the 1962 RSC production *Troilus and Cressida*.

Sexy cave girls from *When Dinosaurs Ruled the Earth*: Imogen, Victoria Vetri and Magda Konopka

Hammer's primarily male audience liked nothing better than a prehistoric cat fight in this publicity shot for *When Dinosaurs Ruled the Earth*.

Although she has a prominent role in the film, Imogen is billed in the middle. Her Ayak is a jealous lover, a member of the Sand Tribe who shelter Victoria after her escape. Ayak is replaced in her handsome boyfriend's affections by the new, excitingly blonde, refugee.

Ayak is not really a bad person, but, forlorn and confused, she seeks revenge on the blonde interloper and her former lover. Conveniently, she is eliminated from the competition at the end of the film when she drowns in quicksand.

It may appear to be an absurd exercise to analyze Imogen's performance in the context of such lightweight entertainment, but she gives it her all, showing to advantage the dancers expressiveness of face and body.

Clad in a primitive bikini, Imogen is a sensual feast with her mass of long, dark hair and exotic eyes. Her body is extraordinary, bronzed and supple. Sadly, her rare moments onscreen as a dancer — a Stone Age boogie around the campfire in *Dinosaurs* and a disco-dolly bop by the pool in the '60s horror flick *Incense For The Damned* — are embarrassing.

Dinosaurs has a sort of dialogue. Not content with mere grunts and groans, the script delivers a language of primeval gibberish with a somewhat limited vocabulary. What is required of the actors, essentially, is a form of mime. Imogen actually does it very well, conveying vividly with her face and body not just the extremes of Ayak's jealous fury but the subtleties of her hurt and confusion, making her sympathetic. It may be daft to suggest it in the context of *When Dinosaurs Ruled the Earth*, but she knows her craft.

With its bevy of skimpily-clad starlets, *Dinosaurs* generated a generous selection of pin-up publicity stills. Imogen's unusual beauty stands out from the crowd. The photographs

A stunning studio portrait of a very glamorous cave girl

are still in demand today among cult movie and period pin-up buffs, one of Imogen's few remaining claims to fame.

Her friends cringe, but it has guaranteed her a certain immortality.

When Dinosaurs Ruled the Earth reunited Imogen with a very close friend. These busy times saw them work together on three films in quick succession: *Dinosaurs*, *Tomorrow* and *Mumsy, Nanny, Sonny and Girly*.

In all his years in the business, "very few people made a distinct impression on me," says assistant director John Stoneman, but Imogen made a huge impression on him—a lasting and loving impression.

They had first met years before on the set of *The Saint* and their paths would cross frequently at the studios. Both were going through very difficult times in their lives and relationships, and a natural sympathy drew them together. They were looking for the same thing, a permanent, secure relationship. While both acknowledged that they could never find this with each other, their shared needs bonded them in an intense friendship. Onlookers assumed the

John Stoneman still treasures this autographed photo.

obvious, that they were having an affair, but this was not the case. They were friends.

The intensity of their friendship manifested itself strongly when the *Dinosaurs* crew were on location in the Canary Islands. They were all having a relaxed dinner and perfectly normal conversation. But John became aware that Imogen was gripping his hand so tightly that her knuckles turned white. "She needed someone to hang on to." They often sat holding hands and gossips would often make incorrect assumptions.

John bore witness to Imogen's changing moods, to the sunshine and shadow and the sadness below the surface. They shared a lot of happiness and many good times, a lot of laughs. But the next day she would be very sad.

In the early hours of one particular morning, John heard the door of his hotel room opening quietly. There had recently been two robberies at the hotel and he steeled himself to leap out of bed and defend his property.

He saw an unmistakable silhouette. It was Imogen, letting herself in with a key she had obtained from the front desk.

She slept in John's arms that night. She cried and he comforted her until she fell asleep in his arms in the early light of dawn. "She looked so peaceful."

John would see Imogen for the last time in 1974 when he invited her to lunch at Pinewood before setting off for Canada and a successful career as a documentary filmmaker. She was still beautiful but John saw the changes, the great weight of sadness that she bore, the luster that had gone out of her. "She would laugh and there was nothing behind the laugh."

At times she was nearly in tears. She told him that her greatest wish was to find someone who really cared about her and would treat her with respect, and how she desperately wanted to have a baby. "She needed gentility and she needed caring."

They stayed in touch after John went to Canada. In 1979 Imogen was talking about moving to the United States in the hope of kick-starting her career. She promised to stay in touch.

Imogen puts the bite on Patrick Mower in *Incense for the Damned*.

But then there was silence. John kept writing to her in the U.K. but his letters were returned. Imogen was gone. "I believe that the world is a far lesser place as a result of her passing. She was a truly wonderful person."

She was before the cameras again in *Mumsy, Nanny, Sonny and Girly* (1970), a thriller in which Michael Bryant is terrorized for the apparent murder of his girlfriend—Imogen in flashback.

1970 was a breathless year for the busy starlet. She was back on the small screen with Roger Moore and Tony Curtis in "Overture," the pilot episode of *The Persuaders*. Her co-starring role was possibly dubbed. She made her entrance in yet another skimpy bikini.

For the BBC Imogen played a glamorous but wicked Irish colleen in the cop show *Softly Softly—Task Force*.

As 1970 bowled along Imogen appeared in five movies in a row: *Carry On Loving*, *Incense for the Damned*, *The Virgin and the Gypsy*, *Tomorrow* and *El Condor*.

Incense for the Damned, a very '60s horror film (working title *Doctors Wear Scarlet* and also known as *Bloodsuckers*) was in fact shot the year before, but its release was delayed by a rash of internal squabbles—involving several lawsuits and the removal of the director's name from the credits.

This time Imogen was the Greek Chriseis.

Based on a novel by Simon Raven, the film concerns a strange vacation to Greece by a young and handsome (but impotent) Oxford don played by Patrick Mower. When he fails to return his friends and fiancée follow his tracks only to learn that he has fallen under the spell of the mysterious and beautiful Chriseis.

Chriseis is a vampire—but is her lust for blood real or a perversion that provides the only means by which the young academic can achieve sexual gratification?

For Imogen's cult admirers the film is an absolute must. She is first seen topless, entwining her victim in the surf—cut to Chriseis dancing, scantily clad to the delight of poolside revelers—cut to Imogen and Patrick getting steamy on a settee—cut to Imogen and Patrick in bed naked.

The first 15 to 20 minutes of the film are devoted largely to some dark orgiastic ritual; a nightmare vision of a hippie love-in, shot in an appropriately trippy style—sex and drugs and lots of bare boobs, all to the tune of psychedelic muzak—escalating into the satanic and gory sacrifice of a naked maiden.

The evil Chriseis presides over these debaucheries. Later, intoning weird incantations she mesmerizes another helpless victim and gloatingly incites her thuggish henchmen to rape and murder.

Looking not unlike one of those determined little girls in the Thelwell cartoons, bouncing along on their barrel-shaped, shaggy ponies, Imogen does a great deal of galloping up and down the sun-drenched hillsides mounted on a mule; showing off her shapely thighs in an odd, low-rent costume consisting of an ethnic waistcoat slung over a chic white modern mini-dress.

Chriseis lures Patrick Macnee, a dashing British diplomat, to his death over the edge of a cliff. But she gets her comeuppance when she is caught in the act of biting the captive don's neck by his friend, Johnny Sekka. She goes down fighting, hissing and scratching and baring her bloody fangs.

The film must have seemed like a good idea at the time—a venture into psychological horror, a new slant on the vampire myth. It had a worthy cast including cameo appearances by Peter Cushing and Edward Woodward.

Imogen is dark and gorgeous, a joy to behold. Her performance, however, is terrible. So is the role and so is the movie, submerged in heavy breathing, soft porn and gore. It has all the qualities of true awfulness guaranteed to enshrine it in the cult hall of fame. And it will ensure for Imogen another shred of dubious immortality.

Incense was shot partly in Cyprus where Paul Sproxton, a reporter for the British Forces Broadcasting Service, was able to interview Imogen on location somewhere on the sunny slopes.

Imogen was lovely to talk to, Paul recalls. She had a fairly major part in the film and seemed quite happy and thought her career was going well.

Imogen turns on her sunny side for an interview with Paul Sproxton.

Imogen plays a sullen and smoldering Gypsy girl in *The Virgin and the Gypsy*.

Paul Sproxton brought a photographer along. There are three photographs. In one Imo is relaxed, laughing; it is a sunny face that her friends recognize. In the next she obliges with a sultry pin-up pose, showing a leg, the mini-dress hitched up dangerously. One for her public.

In the third photo she sits quietly, gazing into the camera. Imogen is smiling, but if you look into her face, you might imagine many things: a child's shyness; a hesitation and uncertainty; and deep in her very dark eyes, a certain wariness. It is also a face that her friends recognize.

The Virgin and the Gypsy should have been something good; it is D.H. Lawrence, after all. But it is so sanitized, very pretty to look at and not much more with slow-motion performances and too many pregnant pauses.

Imogen, needless to say, plays a Gypsy girl, sullen and smoldering. As ever, she makes good use of her mobile features and expressive body language. It is not a bad performance; physically she is eloquent and there is detail in what she does with her face, hands and body, which indicates that she put some thought into the role. Her efforts, however, are diminished by what is surely the clumsy dubbing of her voice and by the way her character is rendered merely incidental and then simply vanishes from the plot—left, perhaps on the cutting room floor. Imogen, in fact, told the tabloids that her great love scene was trashed because of the lackluster performance of her leading man.

In one scene she is breast-feeding a baby. Later, she would claim that this episode kindled in her a powerful maternal urge. This longing consumed her; she was desperate to have children only to endure recurring tragedy.

Imogen as homely Jenny Grubb with Terry Scott in *Carry On Loving* (1970).

Tomorrow, directed by the legendary Don Kirshner, was a film about alien abduction and a pop group featuring Olivia Newton-John. "This could achieve cult status if rereleased on video," according to the International Only Olivia Fan Club website.

El Condor was one of those innumerable, throwaway Westerns with Spain standing in for Mexico. Lee Van Cleef and Jim Brown starred as two amiable rogues out to steal a fortune in gold from a local warlord.

Imogen's performance as Dolores earned her a special mention in the film review column of *Mayfair* magazine: "An unexpected bonus for western enthusiasts in *El Condor*, now on general release, was Imogen Hassall's revealing nude scene."

Imogen's Dolores is a humble village girl selected to entertain one of the warlord's officers. But she is no blushing maiden and when rescuers break down the door she is waiting, wearing nothing but a wry grin and coolly lifts up the sheets to reveal the officer cowering underneath.

Later, it transpires that Dolores is a single parent and Lee Van Cleef appears to be forming a bond with her young son. However, this avenue remains unexplored, her character undeveloped and like the Gypsy, she simply disappears.

This time, it might just really be Imogen doing the accent and capably. Again, she is eloquent to the tips of her fingers; she is not merely rehashing some caricature, Dolores and the Gypsy are two distinct creations.

One is reduced to attempting to assess Imogen's abilities in the context of sub-standard fare on the strength of an appearance that can be summed up as little more than a spit and a cough—her screen time in *El Condor* is measurable in seconds not even minutes.

This is the aspiring actress who had surprised everyone when she went from LAMDA to the RSC and then into the West End, who was "fascinatingly hard and brittle" in *The Vortex* and "quite haunting" in *The Italian Girl*.

Carry On Loving: the Grubb clan interviews Jenny's prospective suitor.

"I have two careers," Imogen once remarked. "Actress and glamour girl." The stage actress is lost in the ether. The glamour girl, the starlet, is preserved for posterity in onscreen cameos that serve only to pander to the public's continuing misconception of her.

Imogen's career, like the rest of her, is full of contradictions.

Carry On Loving marked an attempt to set aside the historical romps and return to the old-fashioned seaside postcard antics and real-world, everyday settings of the early films in the series.

It is somehow typical of Imogen's career that the performance cited to give her some credibility as an actress was in, of all things, a Carry On picture. And it would have to wait until her obituary in *Screen International*: "...She played cleverly against type, a dowdy miss who eventually flowers and proved categorically she could act."

Imogen plays Jenny Grubb, a shy wallflower, who is transformed into a gorgeous glamour girl. She submerges herself in the character of the dowdy miss to good comic effect. After the transformation, big hair flouncing everywhere, exhibiting her phenomenal cleavage in a low-cut mini-dress, she plays very nicely in a bit of old-style knockabout farce opposite Terry Scott as they struggle to get down to amorous business on a settee, only to be distracted by constant comings and goings.

Those who doubt Imogen's potential as a dramatic actress concede that she had a good comic touch. She is a lot of fun in *Carry On Loving*.

On November 6, 1970, the film was reviewed in *Today's Cinema*: "...Imogen Hassall proves that she has comic talent as well as other more noticeable attributes."

Peter Rogers, at the helm of the Carry On enterprise, says "She was wonderful to work with and everybody liked her."

Jacki Piper played Jenny Grubb's flatmate in *Carry On Loving*, so they spent a lot of time together on set. Imogen was very sweet, says Jacki. They would often sit off to the side of the set, chatting and Imogen would pour out her troubles. "We were the same age but I was more like her mum."

Imogen informs Terry Scott that those falsies do not belong to her. (*Carry On Loving*)

Imogen spoke a great deal about her father. She appeared to be so insecure and unhappy. It was illogical. Imogen was too beautiful and talented to be unhappy.

Jacki spent much of the time trying to bolster her up. She tried to be logical with Imogen, to persuade her that she had so much to offer, so much going for her. But logic could not penetrate Imogen's insecurity.

The problem, Jacki suggests, was not in Imogen's mind but a chemical imbalance. Today, her balance could be redressed with subtle and sophisticated treatment. Back then, the problem either went unrecognized or was aggravated with pills that tilted her even further off her axis and led eventually to a self-destructive addiction.

A famous still from *Carry On Loving* is another scrap of immortality for Imogen. Her cleavage straining to escape, she is shown laughing, informing a much relieved Terry Scott that a stray pair of falsies does not belong to her. This image appears occasionally in the lower order of modern men's magazines. Thus, is Imogen remembered.

In 1970 Imogen was, or so it must have seemed, riding on the crest of a wave.

On the pages of the tabloids, she came across bold as brass: "People say bosoms are out, but I say they're in, laughed Imogen Hassall with all the confidence of someone who knows she hasn't got much choice in the matter."

Imogen had made seven films over the past 12 months and was finishing a documentary for the BBC about her celebrated family. She was getting a lot of attention. "With a family like that, people say, what are you doing being all sexy? You ought to be in the Royal Shakespeare Company! Well, I have been and I've done my share of struggling."

The starlet was doing well. She had money to burn and could afford to buy a house in trendy Fulham: "I moved in with an old brass bed and nothing else. But I made so much money recently that I've now got carpets, central heating, furniture—and a super bathroom. It's marvelous to have achieved something instead of just wasting money on silly things." Imogen's house was in Betteridge Road. Michael Saunders lived nearbyand his home almost backed on to Imogen's. He remembers the area as something of an actor's colony. "She seemed a very pleasant person and I believe she was well-liked by her neighbors."

Mrs. Fox owned the Hurlingham Dog Shop. Imogen, an incurable dog person, was a regular visitor. She would pop in at all hours to buy treats for her two little Shitzu's, Cassidy and Ratso—and Sylvia, the Afghan Hound.

Mrs. Fox can still picture Imogen arriving at the shop with just a raincoat tossed casually over her nightdress. "She was terribly funny and couldn't care a sod what anyone thought."

Imogen, says Mrs. Fox, was "a very nice person, a very charming and beautiful girl."

Mrs. Fox also remembers that Imogen seemed to have a lot of boyfriends, but she liked to keep that side of her life quiet.

Imogen was exceptional, says Mrs. Fox, more than "just one of those glamour girls showing their boobs."

Imogen was very proud of her bright blue terraced house in Fulham and was only too pleased to give visiting reporters a guided tour: "...As soon as you get through the door she's up and showing you all over the place, in the kitchen, up the stairs, through the louver doors into the bathroom and then into the midnight blue and white bedroom, with the big brass bed that creaks when you sit on it. She's very proud of her house, since she planned all the interior herself and since she owns it herself."

Imogen defended her castle fiercely. Once, when car thieves were outside the house in the early hours of the morning, Imogen threw the front door open and, with her big eyes and wild hair flying in all directions, sent them scurrying away down the road.

Imo always made a great occasion of welcoming visitors to her very own house, especially if they were from the press, inevitably with a photographer in tow.

She would invariably be over-dressed: "Since it was the middle of the afternoon when I went to see her I was a bit surprised to see the caking of make-up she was wearing and her dress which was both extremely tight and extremely short and didn't really look like lounging-around-the-house wear. Still, it did show off her one great physical attribute to its greatest effect."

Imogen told Jim Danforth on the set of *When Dinosaurs Ruled the Earth* she didn't know if her breasts were a "blessing or a curse."

Imogen's bust was her greatest asset and her greatest curse. She exploited it and showed it off, but bemoaned the fact that no one could see her real self and the real actress.

The special visual effects director of *When Dinosaurs Ruled the Earth*, Jim Danforth, recalled an incident on set at Shepperton Studios. As she waited her turn to go in front of the cameras, Imogen was adjusting the top of her Stone Age bikini. Suddenly, she looked up and said, "You know, Jim, I don't know if these things are a blessing or a curse."

Imogen might well have had a very different and a much happier life had she been flat-chested. As she told the *News of the World*:

> I remember having wanted desperately, as a teenager, to be flat-chested like so many of the girls at ballet school.
> Pleading with my father to let me have an operation.
> He just laughed and said: "You'll be grateful for a nice bust later in life." In a way he was right — but it was responsible for plunging me into depths of despair more often than not.

As ever, she made a joke out of it:

> I had a competition with a girl at school called Olivia Breeze to see who could get the biggest bosoms by the end of term. Nivea Cream was my method. They used to call me Sabrina at ballet school.

Imogen's breasts were the center of attention, as her spectacular cleavage became a regular feature at movie premieres, gala openings and first nights.

"You could almost call me the Rent-a-Boob girl," she once said.

There is no doubt that all this recognition, however shallow, excited her.

Old friends remember Imogen scouring the newspapers, looking for her face or name. Some say that she was a publicity junkie.

The merging of the '60s into the 1970s sees her transfixed, smiling in a perpetual dazzle of flashbulbs, forever arriving and departing in style on red-carpets.

"She was in love with fame and being on the front page," says David Wigg. "She was in love with being a film star."

Those organizing such glitzy bashes could always rely on Imo to turn up and lend the proceedings some daring and glamour. There would always be a free ticket for her in the post. Visiting male celebrities, anxious to polish—or falsify—their image by being seen with a

Imogen's main attractions opened the doors at premieres, galas and first nights.

gorgeous babe on their arm, would give her a call. Imo, sheathed in eye-popping outfits, was decorative company for some very big star names. "I'm the girl in a hundred little black books..."

She would phone her girlfriends afterward and entertain them with detailed, very funny and often unflattering reports of her latest escort's performance.

For the premiere of *Butch Cassidy and the Sundance Kid* at the Shepherd's Bush Odeon, Imogen alighted from a Wells Fargo stagecoach in an extraordinary confection of sequins, beads, flounces and feathers. "Some package!" exclaimed *Today's Cinema*.

Later that same year she appeared again in *Today's Cinema* at another gala occasion, this time looking very cool and elegant in a white, backless and almost frontless evening gown, standing next to the Queen of Hammer Horror, Ingrid Pitt, equally splendid in furs.

Imogen appeared in a line-up of Hammer ladies including Linda Hayden and Veronica Carlson. Most people who recognize Imogen's name say "oh yeah, she was in all those Hammer horror films," but she was only in the one. One might think Imogen should have been obvious for those roles but she only made the one Hammer film.

Imogen with Linda Hayden, Richard Harris, Lulu, Maurice Gibb and Honor Blackman leaving Heathrow for the Limerick Film Festival in Ireland.

Imogen and Ingrid Pitt

Ingrid Pitt remembers the occasion. It was a grand opening of some kind and she and Imogen sat together at the dinner afterward. They were both hit on by Telly Savalas, but he seemed incapable of choosing between them. Thoroughly underwhelmed by this display of the male ego, both Ingrid and Imogen got up and left him.

Ingrid recalls Imogen as lovely, very nice. Her problem, states Ingrid, was that she never found the right man.

For a while, it appeared that no showbiz event was complete without Imogen. Most of the premieres and openings had no connection with any play or film in which she had actually performed. She was becoming famous simply for being famous.

The press built her up and then they tore her down. The tabloids dubbed Imogen eventually one of the "Top Ten Bores of the Year."

Sunday Mirror

IT'S MAN-ON-THE-MOON DAY AND THE PAPER WITH COLOUR POWER GIVES YOU ITS OWN HEAVENLY BODY, BELOW. SEE ALSO PAGES 7, 13 AND 36

8d.   July 20, 1969 No. 327 · · · · · · · · ·

As the astronauts rocket on their way to the Moon Imogen Hassall, actress, relaxes in the Bahamas sun.   Picture by LARRY ELLIS.

The warning bells were ringing:

> ...Imogen has courted her publicity—and she could have turned it down. And her balance, her sense of values, has been up-ended by it. She has mortgaged her future fame for a temporary notoriety. She has fallen into a trap that has engulfed many lesser talents—the trap of instant recognition that eventually destroys respect. I don't blame her for it. She is a girl of quicksilver wit, some learning, and a shrewdness that has led her to promote herself beyond her professional deserts.

Even her own mother said, "Her publicity runs ahead of her achievements."

In 1969 Imogen was on top of the world. By the close of 1970 it had all backfired badly, and she knew it. She declared her intention to abdicate as Queen of the Premieres and stated her determination to prove herself as an actress, turning down offers to appear in *Playboy* and *Oh Calcutta*; scrapping plans to record a pop single entitled "Will You Take Me To Bed?" "I have to prove that I can act—that there's something more to Imogen Hassall than just a short skirt and a low neckline." "She was panicking," says David Wigg. She used to talk to him a lot about it and cry. "Oh David, why am I not getting the big leading roles in movies, what's gone wrong?"

It was too late. Producers dismissed her as a clothespeg for see-throughs. She was fast becoming a bad joke and no one would take her seriously.

Christopher Long recalls a time when Imogen found herself on a yacht belonging to the great Sam Spiegel, moving in exalted circles among some of the most powerful figures in the business. "If only they had been able to see something in her..."

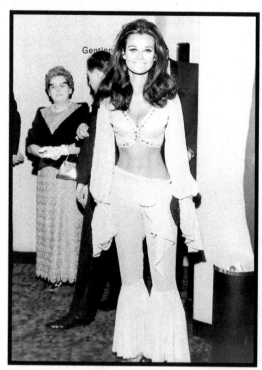

Producers dismissed Imogen as a clothespeg for see throughs.

And Imogen did not help herself by giving lurid accounts to the tabloids of her sexual encounters on board movie moguls' yachts.

She was always calling David Wigg—"What do you think, David, what do you think?"—should she do this, should she do that?

"You've got to make them believe you're more serious," he would tell her, over and over again. "You don't come over serious enough."

But you could never sort her out, because she would never listen. And she was so strong-willed in a self-defeating way, she would inevitably just go and do her own thing.

In Terry Johnson's play Imogen reappears in Sid's caravan on the set of *Carry On Camping* in 1969:

Imogen enters from behind the partition. She's drunk and not as vivacious as when we first met her. She finds her scattered clothes.

IMOGEN: I'm sorry.

SID: What for?

IMOGEN: Causing an argument. I'm always causing arguments. If there's men and me, there's usually an argument.

SID: Take no notice. He doesn't understand healthy desire.

IMOGEN: I'm surprised you even remembered me. I'm flattered, I mean, who was I then? I was nothing; a walk-on. This is such a strange business. You meet someone, you like them, you maybe sleep with them, the job ends, then you never see them again even though you always say you will, unless you've slept with them. I made some really good friends on *When Dinosaurs Ruled the Earth*, except Raquel [sic] of course, but she doesn't make friends, she just takes the odd hostage. Thing is I haven't seen anyone since. Everything's so...temporary. That's what's so nice about working with you lot; you're one big happy family. I'd love to work with you lot again.

SID: I'm gonna be needed soon.

Imogen carries on drinking.

IMOGEN: Oh that's all right. I only popped in to say hello. You know what I wish? I wish I had smaller breasts. Then I'd get to play some women with small breasts and they're always the best parts. I'd really like to play women with no breasts at all, you know, like in Ibsen. I should never have done the centerfold. I'm actually very versatile. "An impressive multi-faceted performance"; that's what they said about me as Jenny Grubb in *Loving*. And that wasn't just taking off the glasses and letting my hair down, that was acting actually. I was acting her repressed sexuality. What I'm saying is, I'm not just the

Countess of Cleavage; you know? People make presumptions. It's been hard trying to convince them I'm a serious actress, but I really think it's beginning to happen. I've got an audition for the Royal Shakespeare Company. And last month I did *The Persuaders*. Only the pilot but both Roger Moore and Tony Curtis were very complimentary and said there was a good chance my character could become a regular.

SID: I'm glad it's going well for you.

IMOGEN: Oh yes.

SID: I'm glad you popped in.

IMOGEN: I'm glad too.

SID: Thing is, um...

IMOGEN: Imogen.

SID: Imogen. What we just did...

IMOGEN: I know, I know. I don't know why we did that, I mean, I know you had a full house, but I mean why so suddenly, I mean, that's not why I came, I don't want you to think I'm a complete tart or anything, I always liked you.

SID: Well, these things happen.

IMOGEN: Yes they do; it's just a spontaneous thing and nothing to be ashamed of an expression of one's sexuality. I hope you don't think I do this a lot.

SID: I'm sure you don't.

IMOGEN: Because I don't. It's not why I came. I came because I wanted some advice.

SID: What's that then?

IMOGEN: Well you see, if I get the job with the Royal Shakespeare Company it's going to clash with *The Persuaders* if *The Persuaders* goes into a series, which it should, I mean it's got Roger Moore and Tony Curtis in it, but it's not definite and I'm not sure if I should do it. I'd rather be in the Royal Shakespeare Company but the problem is it's not a huge part. In fact I don't speak and I have to take my clothes off, but it is the RSC. Anyway; you've done a bit of everything so I thought you might advise me. What do you think I should do?

SID: *Persuaders*.

IMOGEN: But that's not definite.

SID: Shakespeare then, definitely.

IMOGEN: But I haven't actually been offered it.

SID: I'd take *The Persuaders* then. God, I'm knackered.

IMOGEN: But I don't want to act in rubbish, I want to act in really good stuff.

SID: Then if I were you, I'd hang out for the Shakespeare.

IMOGEN: The money's not very good.

SID: That's why I'd tend towards *The Persuaders*.

IMOGEN: Of course, I might not get offered either.

SID: In which case, take the other one.

IMOGEN: I need a job. A proper job. I don't mean to sound desperate but this is not working; it's driving me mad.

SID: I'll see what I can do.

IMOGEN: Oh, I didn't mean that you should...

SID: No trouble.

IMOGEN: That's not what I...would you? I mean I hope you don't think that's why I came.

SID: What are friends for?

IMOGEN: I thought if I did the centerfold at least they'll take notice. They did for a while, then just took advantage. Anyway, I mustn't be negative. Things might turn around,

Imogen in the gardens of Pinewood Studios

Tuesday's Child

tonight even. I'm meeting Michael Winner at L'Escargot. Just for a chat, but you never know, do you?

SID: That's right; you never know.

IMOGEN: So if it happened again, well...

SID: It mustn't happen again.

IMOGEN: Absolutely. That's what I...I mean if that's what you...that's fine.

SID: You see, I'm being strictly monogamous at the moment.

IMOGEN: Oh, I'd hate to harm your marriage.

SID: My marriage has nothing to do with it. I'm trying to prove to someone I can be faithful to her. She doesn't think I can do it.

IMOGEN: Oh well this was...we both know what this was, this was...

SID: A pleasant mistake.

IMOGEN: I feel a bit woozy.

SID: It's just if she walked in right now, I'd be in a right pickle.

Sally opens the door. She's wearing huge Wellingtons and carrying a suit and a selection of trilbys.

SID: Gawd blimey!

SALLY: Only me...Oh, I'm sorry.

SID: Come back in half an hour, will you?

SALLY: You haven't got half and hour, Sid; you've got 10 minutes.

IMOGEN: I think I'd better lie down. Do you mind?

SID: Um...

SALLY: They've rescheduled. They want you at three.

SID: I should be getting ready.

IMOGEN: That's all right; I'll just have a little snooze.

She collapses. Sid picks her up and lies her down behind the partition.

• • • • • • • • • • • • •

Imogen was trapped:

> The big hallo at first nights, the dress designed to reveal skin rather than personality, the photos that had her with jutting bosoms like castle parapets—all this composes the image that is Imogen Hassall.
>
> It is an image she has recently resented and tried to discard. For it is a great whopping lie, a betrayal of her true nature—and, I believe, in the end destructive of her real talent.

Imogen, realizing that things had gone horribly wrong, was floundering and, anxious to put things right, was only too available to a tabloid press ever ready to make the most of it:

> She wants now, she says, to be taken more seriously (go on, I bet you guessed, didn't you?). Her agent has told her to steer clear of premieres, and in fact she admits that she really hates them. The glamour was a fascination, but it also brought out a great deal of antagonism in people.
>
> "The next morning everybody would want to knock you down flat," she says.

"I don't want to be known as a zombie, but there are lots of girls who go to these shows, so is it my fault if the press takes my picture? I am what I am. If I show my navel off, then I show it off. They wouldn't photograph it if they didn't like it, would they?"

Other forces were at work, bringing about her sobering self-revelation. It was in July 1970 that Imogen and Christopher Long took out a special license to marry at Chelsea, only to part, unwed, four hours later:

I think he wanted a quiet wife not a boisterous one. My enormous public-ity has brought me more problems than success.

Imogen's professional and private troubles were always stumbling over each other, but now they were beginning to merge in a more serious way.

Her private ups and downs, as Timothy West had noted, had a tendency to distract her from her work. Even at the best of times, as Jackie Ingham says: "She was a good actress, but she larked about." Now it all seemed to be blurring into one great big mess.

Imogen was taking a long, hard look at herself. For once, the jokes had a certain bleak-ness about them:

"Well, it's been a helluva week," she said, moodily helping herself to a taste of my dessert. "Last Wednesday I was all set to be married and then four hours later it was all off. Finished. Then somebody in a newspaper voted me one of the Ten Biggest Bores of the Year."

"At least you were in the top 10," I said. "Think of the bores who never get a mention."

Miss Hassall said that she would have to analyze the compliment and continued. "Tomorrow I fly to Spain to see a producer about a part. Not to work, mark you, just to be looked at."

"What kind of part?"

"It will be my third prostitute," she said slowly. "Just look at the credits—eight film roles and they include one virgin, three whores and a stone-age woman who just had to stand there and grunt."

"Grunt me something from it."

"CRACKSTA!"

"Thank you."

"You're welcome"

This all makes Imo seem very sad, and she is a sad picture, painted by the press. Her friends say that it paints a false picture, that Imogen rarely meant what she said in the newspapers as seriously as it may have sounded or came across in print. The joke was always in there.

Taken at face value, Imogen does seem to be feeling rather sorry for herself:

Nobody recalls that when I played in *The Italian Girl* on the stage I re-ceived rave notices. Nobody mentions nowadays that I spent two years in *The Reluctant Peer*. It seems to be forgotten that I was once with the Royal Shakespeare Company—admittedly in bit parts—that I was in ballet and repertory.

Imogen and Ratso

Imogen with Roger Moore in _The Saint_

Imogen was in a no-win situation. She had already damaged herself professionally by exposing much of her anatomy for the popular press and the pin-up photographers. Now she was opening deeper wounds by baring her soul in public. She was becoming the object of thinly veiled ridicule. However she may have appeared to her close friends, her public persona came across as sad and foolish:

> Certainly she is the most sought-after female in London for any first night or launching party, to add a little icing sugar to the merchandise.
>
> Showing me her wardrobe in the tastefully arranged house in Fulham where she lives (with one au pair and two dogs) was like an actress displaying the costumes of her most famous roles.
>
> "I wore that for the premiere of _The Virgin and the Gypsy_. That one for the Simon Dee Show. This for the opening of _Butch Cassidy and the Sundance Kid_."
>
> It was the same sad, nostalgic tone war veterans use surveying the battalion colors "Ypres...Verdun...Vimy Ridge."
>
> But Miss Hassall's first-night campaigns are over (she says). She has fought on the beaches, in the foyers, on the stairs to the Royal Circle, and has neither faltered nor flinched.
>
> "But now I'm finished with all that," she declared. "I have to prove that I can act—that there's something more to Imogen Hassall than just a short skirt and a low neckline."
>
> And on that stirring note, she flew off to Southern Spain, to prove it.
>
> But those foyers will never be the same.

That was July 1970. On September 22:

Today, the clothes-peg lies in hospital, suffering from an overdose of drugs and the stress of trying, and failing, to be herself.

Imogens close friends and colleagues struggle with the complexities that were expressed in her ultimately, inevitably, fatal cries for help—and the result is so many contradictions. In 1970, the not unsympathetic press ventured its own theory:

It's easy to scoff at Imogen's moth-like attraction for the limelight. An unknown girl stands a million-to-one chance of a break. A girl who has at least registered as a shape in the public prints has something going for her. And showbiz is a harsh world, where thousands feel they ought to be chosen and a mere handful get to the starting-post of an interview.

And let's face it, Imogen Hassall has succeeded with her over-exposure. In the last eighteen months she's made six films, including box-office successes like *The Virgin and the Gypsy* and *El Condor*. But the big, above-the-title prizes have eluded her. And Imogen has an ambition · as vital as her statistics.

Most of us are impatient with the emotional turmoils of thespians. We see them, parading the fashions we covet, taking off at airports, escorted by male pin-ups. We envy their luck. We shrug off their stresses.

But the strains are real. They are especially puncturing for a girl of Imogen's temperament. For she is an intelligent girl who can rub monosyllables together without tripping over the sense. She has acted with the Royal Shakespeare Company and shone in an Iris Murdoch play, *The Italian Girl*.

"Why," I once asked her. "Do you run so hard?" "Because," she mused—and she has the ability to muse. "I want so much to be a star. Partly because my family has always been gifted, and I suppose I want to be in that tradition. But also because I do want to express myself. There's nothing I wouldn't do—except sleep with producers—to get the chance to be recognized."

Imogen is 25. She has renounced even permanent love for her professional drive. "I like being in love," she told me. "But every six months." She has been iffy-and-butty with her long-standing boyfriend Chris Long, for many a year.

...She is basically introverted—but showbiz is an extrovert world.

I know it's difficult to wring a tear for a girl who has bought her own home and furnished it on her earnings.

Imogen Hassall has done everything for her contours.

The lesson she must learn is that, sumptuous as they are, they're not sufficient to keep her permanently on the map.

Imogen took her need for attention and protection to its extreme; the most direct and dramatic means of letting the world know that she was in a mess and wanted someone to come and sort it all out for her.

She phoned David Wigg many times: "Oh David, I've done something silly...I can't go on, I can't go on, it's all a disaster, I'm never going to make it...!"

And David would call the ambulance or rush to her side. But he never thought that she really meant it or believed that she would ever actually succeed.

Christopher Long rode in an ambulance with her. Jackie Ingham was furious and terrified, because, one time, she really thought that Imogen had gone and done it; lying there—Imo, such a force of life—with tubes coming out of her, hooked up to machines.

No one who knew Imogen believes that she ever really meant to kill herself, not in 1970 and not even the last time—although they never knew what really happened on that November night in 1980.

CHAPTER SEVEN
DEMONS

> Sex is really like a game...a super sort of game...and you can play
> whenever you want—a game where nobody ever has to say no—just
> yes, yes, yes...

Those lines are spoken in the film *Take a Girl Like You*, and were indeed the rules of the game in the Swinging '60s and the hedonistic 1970s. Imogen appeared in the film, based on the book by Kingsley Amis, in 1971. She did not play the lead, a North Country lass struggling against all the odds to preserve her virginity; that went to Hayley Mills.

It would take a rare man, having bedded an incredible animal like Imogen, to admit that the sex was anything less than splendid. The male ego does not permit the slightest inference that the woman was left less than completely satisfied.

But would Imogen's girlfriends, in whom she confided, say different? Some say she was too highly strung to be able to relax sufficiently to enjoy sex.

With each affair, would Imogen despise all men a little bit more, and did her already damaged self-esteem sink even lower?

In July 1971 Imogen was telling the *News of the World* that she yearned for a pure love:

> Men these days seem to think that you've got to be either good or
> bad in bed and that's love.
> I don't think a man is clever just because he knows 69 different
> ways of doing it.

In the autumn of 1971 Imogen met her first husband. Some would see the failure of that marriage as a turning point, a breaking point.

That year Imogen was back onstage at the Duke of York's in *The Jockey Club Stakes*, a comedy by William Douglas Home, which revealed devious doings among the horse racing fraternity.

Taking over from Julia Lockwood, Imogen was cast as Lady Ursula Itchin, the spoiled, headstrong daughter of the Marquis of Candover, the Chief Steward, played first by Alaister Sim and then Wilfrid Hyde White.

Cast member Alan White says that Imogen was excellent in the part and describes her onstage as natural and free-flowing. Perhaps she was, at last, achieving that spontaneity which her teachers at LAMDA had labored so hard to instill in her.

The director had insisted that the actress for the part must be a lady. Alan White notes that Imogen had this quality naturally. She was cast as Lady Ursula because she was so lady-like despite the character having been conceived by the author as tall and blonde. Nicholas Hassall recalls, "Part of the reason why she had such a striking appearance was because of her exceptional deportment."

But, as so often with Imogen, here again there was an underlying darkness. The source of her extraordinary poise, such a vital element of her charisma and beauty, was the injury which had robbed her of the ballet—described by her brother as curvature of the spine. "And the reason that she had such deportment was because she was obliged to always sit up ramrod straight. She could not slouch, because if she did she immediately suffered acute back pains."

An unlikely couple: Imogen cuddles up to Wilfrid Hyde White.

The Queen of the Premieres was doing good work, and it may have seemed to the would-be serious actress that the signs were hopeful. In November 1971 at the conclusion of the run she gave an interview to the *Radio Times* under the title "New Image Imogen."

> There was a time, not so long ago, when you could hardly open a newspaper or a magazine without seeing the face and elegant figure of starlet Imogen Hassall. The gossip columnists chronicled her every outing and no first night was complete without her.

"Yes, I was queen of the premieres all right," she chuckles, "but I've played that part and now it's time to move on."

Moving on means getting rid of that old image and establishing a solid reputation as a stage actress. For most of the year she has been in William Douglas-Home's *The Jockey Club Stakes*, and she starts rehearsals for another play in January...

But Imogen doesn't regret any part of her career. In fact she says she's had a ball...

If Imogen was sincerely cherishing any hopes for her career they were false. She had many regrets and she was soon to accumulate some more.

For all her good intentions, Imogen let herself down again.

The Jockey Club Stakes inspired Imogen to take positive steps towards improving her public persona. She called upon David Wigg to help her find a PR who could be entrusted with the task of making her more serious. Such a person was identified, willing to take Imogen on.

The plan was that Imogen should give a Halloween party for the media on a boat on the Thames. The PR went to great lengths to instruct her charge as to how to dress in keeping with her new serious image—something attractive and glamorous but *not* revealing.

Imogen was a draw, says David, who was one of the guests at the party, and all the photographers were there promptly at one o'clock. Food and drink were lavished upon them—it cost a lot of money—and, glamorously but tastefully attired, the new Imogen posed for pictures.

By three o'clock the PR thought that it was safe to leave. All was well, Imogen had got it right, the new look, the new image.

But the next day the PR opened her morning paper to be confronted by photos of Imo in a witch's hat, topless, holding two candles up in front of her breasts.

The PR resigned.

Alan White's memories of working with Imogen are happy ones. "She got on wonderfully well with the rest of the cast...the description of Imogen's personality—'*joie de vivre*, energy, laughter and excitement'—is absolutely accurate."

Like everyone else, Alan was struck by Imogen's unusual beauty. "Like a young Vivien Leigh."

Sometime during the run of *The Jockey Club Stakes*, Imogen wandered into Pleasures of Past Times, one of the many little bookshops and galleries that cluster together in Cecil Court, a narrow lane between the West End theatres.

The proprietor, David Drummond, recalls her speaking about her famous grandfather. It was widely reported that her various homes were decorated with his valuable and collectable work. Alan White says that she was well off. She was working on stage, films and TV. And Eve was routinely sending her daughter money. Eve was very loyal, says Alan.

Imogen hung around the little shop to chat. She was always a naturally sociable sort and she seemed to want to talk.

As she talked Imo unwound and appeared to relax. He enjoyed their chat. "There was much more to her conversation than her glamour girl side."

Everyone who knew Imogen says that she was educated and well-read. Alan White calls her refined. Others recall her voice as very sophisticated, filled with an infectious laughter.

Alan says that Imogen was not a great thinker but a very lightweight character, happy and upbeat. Imo, he says, was always very direct and didn't put on an act, she was never obnoxious; she was charming and everyone adored her.

But he also recalls that she was on overdrive all the time, she did everything wholeheartedly. He could detect the tell-tale signs of her inner fragility.

Imogen, says Alan, was not a manic depressive. Her problems, he is convinced, were biological not psychiatric.

Tucked away in the program for *The Jockey Club Stakes*, there is in small print, a note: "Imogen Hassall's clothes kindly supplied by Imogen's Boutique, 274 Fulham Road, London SW 10, 01-352-0488."

Imogen regarded the establishment as little more than a novelty, and the novelty soon wore off. The business demanded interest and application and failed to enthuse her. She rarely put in an appearance.

When it was suggested to her that it might be a good idea if she showed a bit of interest, Imo would just look unenthusiastic and distracted. "Oh...Let's go have lunch...shall we...?"

Kenneth Ives replaced Terence Skelton in the cast of *The Jockey Club Stakes*. He is remembered by Imogen's friends as a theatre and television director, but he began his career as an actor. He read English Literature at Oxford and, like Christopher Hassall, was a member of OUDS. After Oxford came a commission in the Royal Navy and then a scholarship to RADA. His early credits include seasons at the Oxford and Nottingham Playhouses, and many television appearances; the best known was Hawkeye in the BBC's *The Last of the Mohicans*.

In the Autumn of 1971 *The Jockey Club Stakes* left London and went on tour.

As the company arrived at Aberdeen, the city's Pro Arte Singers were presenting *An Evening of Ivor Novello*. Reviews of the two productions appeared side by side in the *Aberdeen Press and Journal*. Imogen received only the briefest mention, while her father's contribution to the lasting appeal of Ivor Novello was ignored altogether.

The *Press and Journal* failed to make the connection, and one wonders whether the Pro Arte singers were aware that Christopher Hassall's daughter was in town. Imogen may have felt disappointed—surely she would have been invited to be the guest of honor.

At least there would be the royalties.

If Aberdeen failed to notice Imogen, Glasgow more than made up for it.

The *Daily Record* splashed her across four columns and over half a page. Looking very kittenish showing off a shapely thigh set off to perfection by knee-length trendy boots, she is perched on the lap of a somewhat surprising companion:

> A lithe, tanned girl with legs which seemed to go all the
> way to her chin sprang into the loving embrace of veteran
> actor Wilfrid Hyde White in the afternoon tea lounge of
> Glasgow's Central Hotel yesterday.

They made an odd, but affectionate couple, the 68-year-old actor—"the most darling man in the world," according to "Imogen Hassall, starlet, swinger and aspiring serious actress." It was all quite innocent and above board. From their home in Palm Springs, Wilfrid's wife had been quoted as saying that she was placing him in Imogen's care for the duration of the tour. And it was duly noted that Wilfrid had driven up on his own to Scotland, while Imogen, ever the jet-setter, had flown north from London.

"It's all a lovely fun thing," Wilfrid explained before Imogen arrived "so electrically" for their reunion at the hotel: "Imogen is really the most delightful little girl and she looks after me. I can think of safer people to be placed in care of. My God, this girl wants to keep going until 6 a.m."

An exhausting party animal, she was nevertheless wonderful company, insisted Wilfrid, although he was perpetually left in a spin by her whims and escapades.

They had been to Drury Lane to see Marlene Dietrich, and Imogen had entrusted him with her lipstick and the keys. "She is always being swept off by someone and at a party afterwards she disappeared. What she did without her keys I don't know."

It is not hard to imagine just how Imogen got by without her keys. But before any such speculation could be entered into "the pouting dolly bird of British films appeared in a flame red maxi dress split up the center and advanced upon us. After some cooing, hugging and hand-clasping, Wilfrid went off for a nap and we got down to a dissertation on what makes the latest sex bomb of the London scene really tick."

Imogen was still preoccupied by the gulf between the glamour girl and the actress. While dressing the part of the glamour girl, the actress was talking a good fight:

> "Ever since I played a wild nymphomaniac in a play called *The Italian Girl*, I have been stuck with the image of a sex bomb," she purred.
>
> "But I want to climb out of the mold I'm in, for God's sake.
>
> "Everyone wants me to bare my bosoms, swing until dawn and party it up like a mad thing. But unless I become known as an actress, I will be dead.
>
> "At the end of the day, the name of the game is talent. I'm trying like hell from here on to prove I have what it takes."

She sounds deadly serious and was no doubt utterly sincere. But simply wishing for something will not make it happen. All those who knew and/or worked with Imogen are united in their belief that—whatever their Imogen, an absolute delight or a nightmare walking—her mixed-up, distracted chemistry lacked the basic ingredients that might constitute the necessary dedication.

But, as her brother will remind you, the fact that she could sustain any kind of career at all in itself was an achievement.

For all her best efforts and good intentions, Newcastle's *The Journal* was unimpressed; Imogen failed to live up to expectations:

> That well-known lady, Imogen Hassall, has a surprisingly small part for her billing.
>
> Perhaps it's the fact that the character, Lady Ursula Itchin, is supposed to be a silly nonentity, and Miss Hassall's impression on the play is disappointing.

Her publicity ran ahead of her achievements, as her mother might say. Nevertheless, it was Imogen's picture that adorned *The Journal*'s review. Her image was a guaranteed attention-getter, even if the text then went on, as it so often did, to disparage her.

Imogen and Kenneth Ives pose on their wedding day.

Others, however, were singing Imogen's praises. According to the *Brighton Evening Argus*, Lady Ursula was "delightfully played by Imogen Hassall."

In any event, Imogen may have had little time for serious career planning. She was about to embark on another romance.

It was love at first sight but Kenneth Ives and Imogen did not tie the knot until 1974. Imogen looked blissful in the wedding photographs. But, although the marriage lasted, on paper at least, for four years, according to Imogen the smiling soon stopped. In June 1975 she would go to court, unsuccessfully, seeking a quickie divorce. She would tell the tabloids that it was all over after eight months.

As much as a part of her yearned for the security and shelter of a reliable Mr. Right, it appears that marriage and Imogen did not mix. Some of her friends claim that the failure of her marriage to Kenneth Ives—combined with the tragic loss of their child—was the breaking point that set Imogen on the downhill slide.

After that, the *joie de vivre* became heavy, depressing—things changed after the failure of her marriage. A sense of failure weighed heavy on Imogen as she grew older. In 1978 she would relate to a friend how her parents told her that she was someone who would never succeed, who would never see anything through.

She must have regarded herself as a failure. Her career did not satisfy her thirst for recognition and stardom; it did not live up to the famous Hassall name. Her relationships had all self-destructed; she had failed as a wife and the joys of motherhood had cruelly eluded her. She would seek them desperately for the remainder of her life.

Imogen saw the collapse of her marriage as further proof of her own failure, but in public she was dismissive of the whole affair. Contradictory, as ever, Imogen would also tell the tabloids that she longed for a reconciliation, while at the same time being photographed on the arm of another man. On January 27, 1978, *The Times* announced:

> Miss Imogen Hassall, aged 33, the film actress, is seeking divorce from
> her husband, Mr. Kenneth Ives, the actor-producer.

Imogen must have been deeply wounded by the failure of her first marriage. All the more so as her sense of inadequacy would have caused her to regard it as a self-inflicted wound.

Her desperate longing for stability and the guarantee of someone always being there to look after her—while denying this to herself by her impossible behavior—were among the many conflicting elements in her uncertain and contradictory chemistry. Her disappointment was a scar that never healed; its poison would erupt without warning in disturbing, lacerating outbursts, inflicted upon those close to her.

Imogen's brother met both of her husbands and came away with the impression of two charming people, behaving perfectly normally.

It was Kenneth Ives who had given Nicholas Hassall his one and only professional commission as a composer. Kenneth had directed a program for the BBC and was seeking incidental music for it. "Why don't you ring my brother?" suggested Imogen.

"She was always thinking of me," says Nicholas.

Nicholas recalls that both of Imogen's husbands were nonplused by her unpredictable, volatile nature. He saw both of them trying very hard to placate her.

Nicholas insists that Kenneth Ives can't be held responsible for Imogen's decline:

> ...If someone was as psychologically disturbed as she was, it would be
> very hard for anyone to live with her. She wound them up—it would
> have taken the patience of a saint. And anybody taking on my sister had
> a handful.

Nicholas suspects that Imogen's husbands may have imagined that they could take her in hand. "They couldn't do it. Even I gave that up when I was 12 or 13. I saw immediately that there was no point—she did exactly what she wanted."

Her husbands may have genuinely believed that they could help Imogen, that they would be good for her. But how can you help someone who will not help herself?

Imogen had begun 1971 much as she had finished 1970, all over the tabloids:

Imogen looks positively doting in this still from *The Virgin and the Gypsy*.

MUM'S THE WORD FOR MISS SEXPOT

If you imagine—and you may have had reason—that the important thing in Imogen Hassall's life is reaching stardom, then you've been misjudging the young lady.

Miss Hassall, who abdicated as Queen of the Premieres six months ago (haven't the West End foyers become deflated since?) has got herself a fresh set of values.

"I don't want stardom as much as I want to have a baby," she confided to me this week. "No, I'm serious—I mean it. I don't think any woman's life reaches fulfillment until she has given birth to a child."

Imogen's friends say that she longed to have children, a yearning that grew into desperation as she got older. The all-powerful need for motherhood consumed her, and each failure—and there were several—would fracture her already brittle nature more and more.

She told the *Daily Mirror* that she had been secretly hoping to become pregnant all through her relationship with Christopher Long. "I don't know why it hasn't happened. It's not for the sake of trying, although I haven't dared tell my boyfriend Christopher that."

Christopher says that "part of her would have been a wonderful mother." Others have their doubts as to whether Imogen, with her butterfly temperament, could have shouldered the responsibilities of motherhood; whether having a child would have been a cure for her troubled chemistry. The attendant hormonal excitements might well have destabilized her further.

If you believe what you read in the newspapers, Imogen's maternal instincts were first stirred while making *The Virgin and the Gypsy* in which, perched in a gaudy caravan, she had to simulate breast-feeding a baby. Imo does look positively doting, although the baby seems slightly bemused. The scene was fraught with difficulties:

> Four babies were brought to me on the set but because they had all been bottle-fed they just howled their heads off. Luckily, the fifth baby was a natural breast-feeder and he was kept content, even if the flavor was honey.

In January 1971 Imo appeared determined to seek the quiet life. But Christopher Long would fade from the scene:

> You know, he won't marry me. I don't suppose he would even if we were lucky enough to have a baby.
>
> Why won't he? I think he's ashamed of me. He doesn't like this sex symbol image.
>
> He probably thinks I'm not ready for marriage, but I'm twenty-six and I think it's time I was married and had children and settled down.
>
> Oh I could have the jet set life if I wanted to, but where would it take me? I think it is more important to have a home and a family.

Christopher knew all too well how Imo would one minute be talking about home and family and the next be off to have more pin-up shots taken.

Amanda Richardson and Maggie Guess, however, remember how frantic Imogen, as she approached 40 in 1980, was to have a child—how she was still trying and tragically failing.

Jenny had told a friend at LAMDA many years before that she would sleep with anyone to have a child, "I'll stand on my head all night so all the sperm goes down!"

In the Autumn of 1971 Kenneth Ives stepped into Imogen's life. In time she was expecting.

Jackie Ingham says that Imogen took herself off to a party in Paris in the middle of a very difficult pregnancy. With her fragile chemistry, she should have been kept wrapped in cotton wool. But it is not hard to imagine how she would have chaffed at such constraints.

The baby was born—a daughter—but was very premature and lived for only one week.

The birth of a child should be the greatest joy, a consummation of love, the fulfillment of hopes and dreams, the inspiration of new promise. The death of the baby was devastating.

There have been enormous changes in attitude and treatment over the past 20 years, and parents are now actively encouraged to acknowledge the loss of their child rather than attempt to deny what has happened.

Photo BEN JONES

Imogen Hassall

Representation :
A.L.S. MANAGEMENT Tel. 629-9121

1972 BRITISH FILM AND TELEVISION YEAR BOOK   173

Imogen's listing in the 1972 *British Film and Television Year Book*

At the time Imogen lost her baby, the theory was to encourage the mother to forget about it as soon as possible, leaving her with a grief and emptiness that she could not identify, having to come to terms with a bereavement that she was not allowed to mourn.

Mothers whose babies have died often suffer disturbing and distressing physical symptoms. They may experience the distress of having breasts engorged painfully with milk meant for a baby that is no longer there. In addition to the predictable loss of appetite and insomnia common to any bereavement, the mother may feel phantom fetal movements or even hear phantom crying.

A grieving mother would have to endure unhelpful contributions that, however well-intentioned, are often best left unsaid. She would be told to never mind, she could always have another baby. She would have to sit and listen to all that forced, cheerful, meaningless small talk, when all she wanted to do was talk about her loss or suffer the quick change of subject when she would suddenly start crying.

 So-and-so's situation must have been much harder, she might be assured, as if that was meant to make her feel better. It might be implied that, as the baby hardly lived at all, mourning it would be relatively quick and painless.

How terrible must Imogen's sense of failure have been in someone already afflicted with such low self-worth.

The awfulness of it is almost too much to comprehend, the intensity of sadness, loss and failure; a mother's breasts full of milk meant for her baby, her arms aching to hold her baby, missing her baby with her entire body.

It is a depth of grief that returns in waves of shocking force, over and over again, long after everyone else has moved on—when one least expects it; and with every anniversary of conception, birth and death, with every Christmas and Easter that might have been a family holiday; seeing pregnant women everywhere, women wheeling babies in prams—and grieving for the might-have-beens of a baby's life.

In the context of Imogen's several suicide attempts, her friends have described her initial reaction to hospitalization following a crisis as one of frustration and impatience. She would be anxious to leave her bed and her grim hospital surroundings as quickly as possible.

Only when she was safely home would the pain and remorse come to the surface.

Nicholas Hassall says that the baby was brought to term too soon and was put in an incubator but could not survive.

Imogen, according to Nicholas, had two abortions when she was younger. She was negligent when it came to contraception.

After the death of her child, Nicholas remembers, Imogen was incredibly depressed and was threatening to kill herself. "I would have looked after the child," she said.

Imogen's friends say that she never recovered from the loss of her baby and the disintegration of her marriage.

The pain and the sense of failure stayed with her, always close to the surface.

Although Alan Whitehead was 30 years old when he met Imogen, he says that she made him feel like a mere boy.

Alan says that Imogen was 34 when they met and had an affair that lasted for a year. It was 1975/76, halfway between her wedding and formal divorce, during her separation.

At the time Alan was the drummer in the successful pop group Marmalade, past their heyday, but still a hardworking, touring band. He was first introduced to Imo by a mutual friend. "You have to meet a very troubled friend of mine."

Perhaps it was thought that Alan might do Imo some good. He was certainly not the kind of man that she was usually associated with. Alan was a typical spindly, long-haired pop star and, being heavily into meditation, peace and love, was of an unruffled and placid nature. With his long wavy hair and occasional beard, he cut quite a Christ-like figure, or so he was often told.

Alan was overwhelmed by Imogen. Her intelligence and beauty, he says, mesmerized him. "She was well-read, educated with an agile, quick mind. You couldn't bullshit her, she would see through it immediately."

He had never met anyone quite like her. She was an engaging personality to sit and talk to, and he would love to listen to her talk about all the famous people she knew.

Their first date, Alan recalls, was at Trader Vic's. Halfway through dinner Imo put down her knife and fork and announced, "All right, you've seduced me with your eyes, let's go."

She took him to her terraced house in Fulham.

Alan bore witness to what he can only describe as Imogen's violent hatred of men. "Macho men were a prime target for her razor-sharp tongue."

Imogen, he says, "could be crude in her sexual poison."

When they went out together, Alan remembers, Imo would not cling to him. She would be off and circulating. Inevitably, she would gather a crowd of male admirers around her. Then she would parade Alan in front of them.

"You all thought you were going to fuck me," she would taunt her startled audience. "Well, I'm going to take him home and fuck his brains out!" "Take me away from these wankers!" she would command, before making a grand exit with Alan on her arm.

Imogen, says Alan, seemed to go out of her way to deflate men's egos and wound their pride. The bigger and huskier the men, the more she would lambaste them.

Alan can still see the expression on Imo's face: a look of utter disdain, her eyes full of poison, her mouth cruel. She could be bitingly unpleasant in a foul-mouthed way. Once, Imo told him, "All men's sexuality is their Achilles' heel."

She would pour her poison upon anything that a man might take pride in—from his driving to his endowment.

Sometimes, out of the blue, she would hurl her venom at him. They would have perfectly normal sex and then in what should have been the warm and tender afterglow, Imo

Alan and Imogen out on the town

would start without warning, "I think your prick's too small...haven't you ever been told that before...? Your real problem is you're gay...my gay friends all say you are..."

Alan did not take any of this personally. He sensed that it was not directed at him, but at all men. He would not try to dispute the matter. Rather, he would attempt to discuss it rationally, which only wound Imogen up into a fury, "You're not a man! What does it take to get you angry?"

Sitting up in bed, Alan would apply himself to the lessons he had learned in his meditation classes. Adopting a calm and light tone, he would turn the tirade into a bizarre seminar, "Really? Do you think so? So you think that size does matter...well, what is it exactly...is it the length, the width...? ...That's really interesting...some of my gay friends have told me 'you'll turn one day'...I wonder what they mean..."

This was not the response that Imo was used to, and certainly not the response that she wanted to provoke. She would look at him as though he were mad. Calmly and patiently Alan would carry on, exhausting each topic in turn. It could last for hours.

And then, suddenly, he would look and see that she was crying. "I don't know why I say these things. Why do I try and hurt you? Why do I want to make you angry? Why do I want to make you hit me?"

Alan recalls that Imogen would lash out when she was at her most vulnerable, at the moment which should have been the gentlest and most loving—the warm afterglow of lovemaking. It seemed to be a kind of defense mechanism.

Imogen gave Alan the impression that she drove many of her men to violence. Intelligent men would find themselves—frustrated, lacerated by Imogen's poison tongue—lashing out, behaving in a way that was alien and abhorrent to them.

What was happening to them? No wonder that they backed away, disturbed.

As to the source of Imogen's distrust of men, Alan has a single theory.

He was left in no doubt, by Imogen, that the damage was done years before by Christopher Hassall. As much as she admired him as a talent and a creative force, Alan says that Imogen spoke bitterly of her father and even claimed that at an early age he would make advances on her teenage boyfriends.

At 13 Imogen was already well-developed and was attracting the attention of older boys. Alan says that, according to Imogen, Christopher would take her to functions where her budding charms would draw young men to her, an opportunity, which her father with his charisma would take advantage of.

This is a startling revelation. Most would hold up their hands in horror and say that even if Christopher was gay, he was certainly not capable of such behavior.

Imogen told Derek Wright that it was troubling to her to be the daughter of someone thought to be homosexual. Beset by her demons, she might seek to emasculate a lover by accusing him of being really gay. And then there are these stories about her father, remembered by Alan Whitehead.

But Alan also recalls that Imogen felt comfortable in gay male society—unthreatened. It would not be the first time that a female sex object found refuge in such a milieu being the focal point of a gay male circle.

Alan says that Imo seemed to take a mischievous delight in introducing him to her gay admirers and then sitting back to enjoy the fun.

Imogen had other shocks in store. There was, it is alleged, a Sunday newspaper interview in which she claimed that she had shared an incestuous relationship with her father.

These are stories that sit uneasily with what others have said and observed of Imogen's relationship with her father; and what she herself said about him on countless occasions. Elsewhere, she spoke of him with great affection and admiration, even as the model for her ideal man, her Mr. Right.

"Nice, intelligent, aware—a sane and well-balanced individual," is how Bernard Palmer remembers Christopher Hassall—"a lovely man."

Bernard Palmer says that he must have known Christopher for over a decade. In all that time, while he was aware that Christopher was an object of desire for both sexes while at Oxford, it never occurred to him that he might be gay—not until after his death.

According to Bernard Palmer, Christopher doted on his daughter.

Malicious nonsense is how Norman Painting reacts to reports of Imogen's revelations about her relationship with her father.

Christopher Hassall "was not actively gay." The man that Norman Painting knew, as Joan's loving brother, was a quiet, pleasant person. He was easy, sociable, not selling anybody anything, just a pleasant, professional man.

Imogen would say anything to get a reaction, says Norman Painting. And if she was motivated by some sense of rejection, then this was groundless. Christopher not only doted on his daughter, but also did a great deal for her; he supported her and pulled many strings on her behalf.

"You wouldn't find anybody who knew Christopher Hassall who would give any credence at all" to the things that Imogen said, says Gillian Patterson. "He was rather conventional, rather shocked by that sort of thing and found it difficult to understand."

Gillian is sure that some of Christopher's friends made passes at young Jenny and that her father was horrified when he found out.

There is no doubt that both sexes were attracted to Christopher. He told Gillian how he once woke in the middle of the night to find that the son and heir of the house where he was a guest was climbing into bed with him. As Christopher told it, as the ardent young man climbed in one side of the bed, he was jumping out of the other.

Women were drawn to Christopher by his good looks and charm. Time and time again, at some party or function, he would be backed into a corner. "He was too nice to be rude to them—he was always having to be rescued, which I used to do."

Gillian says that Imogen came out with such stories about her father while he was still alive. Her mother was as appalled as he was.

"We were all aware that Jenny was very creative with her stories," says Nicholas Hassall. "Usually to Mother and myself it was just a matter of shrugging the shoulders and going on living. Occasionally even Mother's patience was strained to the limit."

"None of us could understand why she was doing it," Gillian recalls. "All we could think of was that she needed the money and was being a bit off-beam, saying what people wanted her to say and making things up."

The saddest part was that to those who really knew Imogen, it was so unlike her. "It was out of character—she was not an unkind person—something odd drove her."

And having said these things, says Gillian Patterson, Imogen would have put it right out of her mind. It would have all seemed quite superficial to her.

"It is absolutely unthinkable," says Nicholas Hassall, "that father would have attempted any form of seduction of anyone, male or female. He was a Victorian puritan to the depth of his soul. He confronted his own sexual drives by saying, quite categorically, that sexuality was a drive that had to be rigorously sublimated in the work ethic. I believe, therefore, despite statements made by Jenny and on occasion even by Mother, who had more reason to resent his attitude and physical neglect of her than anyone, that my Father lived 100% by his precepts. My own belief is that behind his attitude was a deep fear of his sexuality."

Christopher, says his son, was "incapable of resolving such homosexual tendencies that arose within his psyche in any form but mild hero worship."

"I'm very much concerned about your Income Tax," Eddie Marsh once wrote to Christopher, concerned also about Eve having to manage the household single-handed. "And it seems dreadful that Eve should have to go without service. We must discuss this when we meet, meanwhile please don't make any bones about using this check merely to make her comfortable."

Christopher's reply is resonant with the hero worship that his son alludes to:

...Eve shall know of it, and Nicholas Edward shall eat of your goodness transformed into mashed carrots. I have long ago given up trying to keep account of all I owe Providence for putting me in the way of your love. I await the day when, finding Nicko and Imogen of an age at last to understand, I take them as Prospero took Miranda, and tell them of Gonzalo who of his gentleness did furnish me with stuffs and necessaries...and volumes that I prize above my dukedom, until, like Miranda in the play, they exclaim, "Would I might but ever see that man!" But I trust they will already know him well.

There was, recalls Nicholas, suspicion that his father was having some sort of physical relationship with two of his female literary colleagues. "It was more likely that father's incredibly strong puritanical nature and iron will interceded to prevent that ever happening"

Peter Charlesworth remembers the stories. He heard them from Imogen herself.

Imogen told Peter that it was her father's fixation with the ballet that drove her to take it up. But then in the course of a single evening the story would vary from love to hate and back again. "She was hinting broadly at the depth of their relationship."

Peter says that Imogen appeared to be obsessed with her father. "I'm of the impression that she was in love with him—her obsession was so great."

And the obsession grew as time went by. Imogen's father was still one of her favorite topics—"rarely a conversation would go by without her talking about him and his work and his relationship with her. Her obsession was enormous."

Peter wonders whether in Imogen's tales of incest there was an element of wishful thinking. "My impression was quite definitely that she was in love with her father. I think that the stories were what she would have liked to have happened."

Young girls often develop a crush on some senior male authority figure, a father, brother, uncle or teacher. It is an acknowledged part of growing up and they usually grow out of it. Peter Charlesworth's Imogen, it seems, was still somehow afflicted.

The child was always close to the surface with Imogen, unpredictability and the flights of fancy can be disturbing in a grown woman.

Peter Charlesworth only met Christopher Hassall briefly once or twice, but he is certain that the stories are untrue. He regarded them as fantasies that were the product of Imogen's illness. He felt she was a very disturbed human being.

The scale of her obsession, as he saw it, convinced him. "This led me to believe that there was a deviation between the truth and what she was saying."

And like so many who knew Imogen, Peter insists that her tale-telling went against her true nature. "She was actually a very nice person."

It is easy to speculate, to construct the train of logic, a runaway train; propelled by Imogen's child-like eagerness to please—to give them what they want, to get a reaction, an ever bigger and more gratifying reaction; and warped by the distorted perspective of her unbalanced chemistry.

Imagine Imogen, escalating from Aunt Joan the so very plain; to Aunt Joan, jealous of Imogen who is beautiful and has so many boyfriends; plain Aunt Joan who never had any boyfriends; come to think of it, she was probably a lesbian; and actually when I was a child she tried to seduce me...Imogen watching the way a child watches when she wants to make an impression, watching as her listener's eyes grow wider or a reporter's pencil scribbles faster and faster.

Or Imogen, out of the blue, venting her sense of rejection upon her father's memory; her jealousy of the attention that he received and gave to others. His charm always drew a crowd of admirers, male and female; he was always the center of attraction. Was this jealousy elevated and distorted into advances made upon her boyfriends, upon the boys who should have been paying attention to her? And he gave so much of his attention to others—were Imogen's alleged claims that they had shared an incestuous relationship wishful thinking, a manifestation of her extreme obsession; or revenge for the denial, as she saw it, of the love that she craved so desperately and the love that she had to give?

Many say that Christopher doted on his daughter. His son sees it a different way.

"It is true that Jenny loved him dearly," says Nicholas Hassall. "And for that she received zilch in the form of any emotional return from him. He hardly noticed her apart from being flattered that such an exotic being as my sister could feel so deeply for him. I maintain one of the causes of my sister's later instability was due to the complete indifference of my father. Jenny would not have been able to consciously accept that the object of her deepest affections was so completely and utterly indifferent to her. She therefore covered up from her conscious self this appalling deficiency, making up what stories that were needed to maintain the fiction of his interest in her."

For a child who is so outgoing and giving, who has a great volume of love to give, the worst of it is not in failing to receive love. The worst of it is when such a loving child feels that the love she longs to give has been ignored or rejected.

Nicholas Hassall confirms that his sister liked to embroider a tale—"the little fibber."

He says that she never mentioned these things to him—"I have no inkling of that."

She did, however, tell him all kinds of stories. "I remember myself hearing things from my sister—I said 'Look, Jenny, I don't know about this, I can't really believe this, but if you say so'—and I'd leave it like that because I didn't want a row."

The consensus is that Imogen adored her father. Was she, as Alan Whitehead says, simply lashing out blindly in pain? "Her pain made her attack anything she loved."

Imogen explained it quite clearly and convincingly to the *News of the World* in the interview that was published in three parts on July 18 and 25 and August 1, 1971.

Many recall a single interview that Imogen gave selling her life story to one of the tabloids. They remember it as the interview that did all the damage, that severed her ties with her family and many important and influential family friends because of what she said about her father.

They cannot recollect which newspaper it was or which year it was. What they do remember is that Imogen said that she had an incestuous relationship with her father.

But that is not what Imogen said. Not exactly.

The notorious interview must be the "Exclusive" that Imogen gave to the *News of the World*, serialized in three consecutive editions, "A Little Girl In London's Orgy Set... IMOGEN HASSALL TELLS ALL—the story they said was too hot to handle!"

Imogen spilled the beans on her love life and the orgies and the love-ins and the jet set, dropping some very big star names along the way.

She also spoke at length about her father: "...The first man with whom I fell in love was my own father. It would be fair to describe our love for each other as incestuous. No, we never actually slept together. But that apart, we were as close, physically and psychologically, as father and daughter could get..."

According to Imogen, their bond was strengthened by the failure of Christopher's marriage. "I never really missed my mother. I transferred all my love and affection to my father...Daddy seemed bent on deliberately fashioning me into the image of a wife. He needed somebody to be beside him; someone he could show off to the lords and ladies, actors and actresses who attended our house parties. He adored me as much as he could any woman. I am certain that he never had an affair after my mother left. His love for me was tremendous and complete...to many of his friends I became known as Mrs. Hassall..."

Harking back to the night that she learned of her father's death and her plans to break the news to her father of the loss of her maidenhood, Imogen expanded upon the nature of their relationship: "My father and I had an incredible, almost incestuous love for each other. He still thought of me as his virginal daughter. He had been the greatest influence on my life and had taught me always to be totally honest about everything. And so I was determined not to deceive him over the intimate side of my life. I realized he would be deeply hurt and it would, in effect, be like breaking up a marriage."

Both father and daughter gave of their love greatly and desired love greatly. It was in their nature. As brother and sister, Joan and Christopher were unusually close and intense. It is no surprise that father and daughter were the same.

It is not unusual for a daughter to assume the role of lady of the house and her father's escort after the mother has died or a marriage has dissolved.

Adored is the word most often used to describe the bond between Christopher and his daughter. And it is not unheard of for a young girl to fall in love with her father, or for a father to be utterly captivated by his beautiful daughter and to be jealous of any other object of her affections.

All that Imogen is doing is acknowledging the unusual intensity of the bond that she shared with her father. Unusual, but not un-natural.

But where there is an unusual intensity of love, there is also an extraordinary capacity for pain. Imogen was hurt by her father. The pain lasted a lifetime and the scars never healed.

There are many stories that people tell, stories, they say, that Imogen told them. But the story that Imogen told the *News of the World* has a certain ring of truth about it.

When Imogen was about nine, she had a little playmate—"he was the most beautiful creature I had ever seen." Smitten, Jenny asked her young chum to marry her; he laughed and "sent me up something rotten," and they went back to their children's games.

The little boy's father was a very distinguished man and a great friend of Christopher Hassall. Years later when Imogen was about 15, the father came to stay at the Hassalls' country home for the weekend. He offered to take Jenny to Battersea Fun Fair and show her the sights of London; and suggested that she should come and stay for a few days at his home.

Christopher readily agreed:

> It was lovely at the fair. But when we got back to his flat he made a grab at my dress and tried to fondle me...
>
> ...He kept on telling me he had talked to my father about me, and that Daddy had expressed the wish that he should be the first man in my life.
>
> It was utterly ridiculous. Father was a very religious man and would never have countenanced such a conversation, let alone such an outrageous suggestion...
>
> I rushed across the room, wrenched the front door open and ran helter-skelter into the street. I phoned Daddy from a coin box...

Confused and distressed, expecting words of comfort from her father, Jenny received instead a terrible blow, "To my horror and disbelief this usually kind man said he thought I was an evil little girl and had made it all up. In other words, a schoolgirl fantasy!"

Imogen (right) with Ratso and friends at Alan's pool

It must have seemed to Jenny that her whole world had fallen apart:

> This had a profound effect on me. I felt bitterly upset that my father,
> whom I loved and admired so much, thought me both a liar and, worse,
> a sexual day-dreamer.
>
> And shocked that his friend, who had seemed so cultured and re-
> fined, should turn out to be a frustrated middle-aged man fumbling up
> a child's skirts.
>
> I suddenly got it into perspective that this was probably men in a
> nutshell. And believe me, I can speak from experience...

Imogen's lifelong mistrust of all men and the source of her unhealed pain—was from
the awful shock of her father's rejection.

For a year Alan Whitehead had to live with Imogen's pain, the darkness that would
rise up without warning. Her pain was amplified by the pills that she took because she had
trouble sleeping and the booze. Imogen, he says, was a whiskey drinker and it made her
aggressive, "It was difficult to sit through a day when you knew she was going to be drunk

all day."

Alan can recall Imo looking at him with a face full of pain, through a blur of pills and booze. Confused, she would see his face, with his long hair and beard and seem to lose all reason. "Heal me, Jesus, touch me, take this pain away."

Alan cannot define Imogen's pain. "A shadow would pull at her soul."

He remembers how her face would change—"her knitted brow, eyes like lightning striking; her mouth would become cruel."

Although disturbed by her entreaties and her vision of him as her Savior, Alan was willing to do as she wished if it would help.

He would touch her forehead, "The lines of hate and tension would fade away and she would be a baby again."

When he touched her, she would relax at once and drift off quietly to sleep.

Alan tried to suggest that Imogen seek some form of therapy, but she

Imogen in sunny and happier times

reacted to the suggestion badly, "Why, do you think I'm mad!"

Alan was well aware of how self-destructive she was. He knew all about the suicide attempts. Imo would describe them in lurid detail, reserving particular relish for the time that she tried to slash her wrists, "...the blood hit the ceiling..."

Schooled in meditation and contemplation and a particular, passive view of the world, Alan came to regard Imogen almost as something sent to test him. She was a severe test.

He never took her tirades as being directed specifically against him. He never rose to the bait—which, of course, would drive Imogen on and on until, all of a sudden, there would be a sobbing, helpless baby.

What spared him for so long was that, as much as he cared about her, he never fell in love with her. He saw the mayhem and the pain that surrounded her and was not going to be sucked into that.

Imogen's whole personality, says Alan Whitehead, "was a complete conflict of different people. She just wanted love, but her reasoning, her judgment, was flawed. She was too disturbed to know what love was."

Inevitably came the explosion that was so severe there could be no going back. There was nothing left, no pieces to pick up.

It was all quite trivial. Alan was away on tour with the band. He phoned Imo to assure her of his prompt return, but circumstances intervened and he was very late, arriving at Imogen's new home in Putney at 5:30 a.m.

By this time, Imo was seriously drunk and abusive, having consumed at least three-quarters of a bottle of whiskey. Among other things, she accused him of dallying with groupies. As hard as he tried, Alan could not reassure her; and the harder he tried, the worse she became.

As the flood of invective grew ever more toxic, Imo suddenly decided to have a bath. Alan lay on the bed and listened to the continuing tirade coming unbroken from the bathroom, echoing off the surface of the bath water.

Finally the futility of it all was just too much. Alan got quietly out of bed. With Imo still in the bath and still shouting, he tiptoed out of the house.

She was on the phone as soon as he stepped through his own front door. He says that she must have called at least 10 times during the rest of the day.

"You're not a man," she was shouting. "What does it take to get you angry?"

Imogen was shouting that she was going to commit suicide. Well, said Alan, you certainly know all about that.

By the time that Imo had called for the 10th time, even Alan was starting to crack. His voice had a new tone, "You're just a waste of my time. I don't want you to call me any more!"

He swears that there was a note of triumph in her reply, "So you have got some fire in you after all. I can make you angry!"

She had won at last, but she had lost.

Alan paints a dark picture of Imogen's demons unleashed. But he states that the darkness only represented a small part of the year that they spent together, "She was 90 percent kind, loving and caring, 10 percent difficult."

Imogen, he says, could also be "compassionate, protective, almost motherly."

She would come along to some of the Marmalade's gigs and joke about being the oldest groupie in the business. At home she was an enthusiastic cook and many an evening was spent simply relaxing and playing backgammon.

Alan says that he hardly met any of Imo's friends. She liked to keep him to herself. Some of her friends were disparaging and would comment on his unsuitability, "He looks a bit frail for you, Imo."

Imogen would defend him in his absence. She could be very protective and mothering. She "was very loving most of the time."

"Imo is one of the few ladies left in London," Alan once said of her. "She's a real lady, if you know what I mean."

He never judged Imogen and made no demands on her. He was happy just to be with her.

When it was too late, Imo told a friend, "Perhaps I shouldn't have let that one slip through the net."

When Alan thinks of Imogen, it is with fond memories. He remembers her sparkling sense of humor.

He recalls the essentially domestic person—"happy just to sit around and chat. It was a really nice relationship in a funny sort of way. She was quite happy flopping about in the garden or going for walks."

Alan has some lovely snapshots of Imo poolside wearing a bikini and a silly hat with her little dog. In one, she is standing in the pool as it is being drained, the water level barely reaching her knees. Judging by the big grin that lights up her face, it was a day when the pool was half full for her, not half empty.

Alan Whitehead's Imogen was "a unique individual. My life was enriched by knowing her."

CHAPTER EIGHT
OUT OF THE FRYING PAN
AND INTO THE FIRE

Despite all her troubles Imogen was still a working actress. Even her closest friends are surprised when they look at her credits and see how much work she did.

Between 1962 when she left LAMDA and 1980, her last tour, 1977 was the only year Imogen spent entirely resting. Considering the nature of the business Imogen might even be deemed successful — in anyone's terms but her own; she was neither the serious actress nor the star she so very badly wanted to be.But she was working and living comfortably. As Alan Whitehead noted, she could afford not to have to work all the time.

In 1971 Imogen was touring in *The Jockey Club Stakes*, seen on TV in the comedy s *On the House* and on the big screen in *Take a Girl Like You*. The next year she appeared in "Stones of Venice," an episode of *Jason King*.

She also appeared in *Images*, a series of sketches spoofing TV advertising. She wrote one of the sketches herself. Imogen sometimes said that she wanted to write but could not bring herself to compete with the ghost of her father. At one time it was announced that she was going to write a book about her talented family. In her biographies in various theatre programs notice was given of its impending publication but no trace of such a book exists. Just another of her occasional pipe dreams.

"Countess Is Taking The Road to Laughs," said the *Sun* on August 3, 1972:

> Having lunch with Imogen Hassall is rather like buying a restaurant.
>
> Suddenly waiters who were off-hand when you came in materialize out of the carpet like genies.
>
> Your meal arrives quickly and quietly. And while every other man in the place is waving energetically for service, you have two waiters who would put the salt on for you, if you let them...

Despite the declared abdication of the Queen of the Premieres, Imogen the actress still had to work. Publicity may have been an addiction, but it was also a tool of the trade.

August 14-26, 1972, Imogen was in rep at the Marlowe Theatre, Canterbury in *The Little Hut.* According to The Stage: "Miss Hassall displayed more than obvious sultry beauty as she played her lovers off against each other." Rehearsals had been blighted by illness but Imogen and her co-stars "worked like demons to tighten and trim the production into a well-timed and homogeneous whole...a living expression of the show-must-go-on-manship."

If she wanted to be taken seriously, however, she was talking to the wrong people and saying the wrong things:

> Imogen, who appears in *Images* tonight...did not appear to notice the fuss.
>
> She sat back happily, drinking Greek wine and picking at a kebab, while she admitted disarmingly to being a nutcase.

Imogen meets Archbishop Makarios, President of the Republic of Cyprus

> There was the time, she said, when she went around
> Greece with a party of travel experts who never spent a
> sober moment from Monday to Saturday.
>
> On Sunday, she dropped out of the tour and promised
> to meet them on the way back. But in the meantime she
> had already convinced the Greek hoteliers that English
> women were out of their heads.
>
> "Perhaps," she mused over the coffee. "It was because
> I was dancing on the tables."

The Queen was still making public appearances throughout the 1970s. Imogen was finding it hard to relinquish her crown.

In July 1971 she attended the London premiere of *The Last Valley* and was photographed poised on the cinema forecourt showing a leg and her perilous cleavage.

In March 1975 she was still frozen in the glare of the flashbulbs on a red carpet, between cordoned ranks of fans, at the premiere of *At Long Last Love*, hoping to see Burt Reynolds and wondering who Imogen was.

But it wasn't all a shallow show. Imogen was also busy doing good works. She would willingly put her shoulder to the wheel for charity, especially for handicapped children.

Motives are often mixed when celebs turn out for good causes, the cynical among us mutter darkly about tax deductions and publicity-seeking. Imogen's motives could be very mixed, but she had a good heart. She had a lot of love to give and she appreciated the uncomplicated affection of those in need, particularly children.

In Imogen's resume in the program for the 1978 tour of *Say Who You Are* there was this postscript, "If Imogen has any time at all to spare in her busy life she is always gladly available for charity work."

David Jacobs says that Imogen was absolutely sincere. She was very much involved with the Stars

Imogen and the bicycle

Organization for Spastics and was tremendously helpful, turning out whenever asked without hesitation.

For David Jacobs one image sums up the fun and enthusiasm that she always brought with her. He remembers driving a tractor around the track at Thruxton with Imo perched cheerfully behind him, leaning over him with her ample bosom.

Imogen was a great sport—and, says David Jacobs, with a smile in his voice, a great flirt—fun company.

She always had a big grin for the cameras. Peter Fenton can still see Imogen scouring the newspapers for any mention of herself. Good publicity or bad, it hardly seemed to matter. He says that she treated even her disasters and worst embarrassments as just another bit of publicity, even when on June 24, 1975, *The Times* announced:

> Imogen Hassall, the actress of Hurlingham Road, Fulham, was fined £10 at West London Magistrates' Court yesterday for riding a bicycle while unfit through drink or drugs early on Sunday morning in Fulham. She pleaded guilty.

Imogen laughed it off as a big joke. Needless to say the tabloids soon got wind of it and came running. There are the predictable poses—Imo straddling a bicycle with a big grin on her face.

She had other things on her mind at the time—the breakdown of her first marriage. "Miss Hassall In A Hustle," said the *Sun* on June 24, 1975:

> Actress Imogen Hassall arrived by bicycle for a special command performance—in a court.
>
> She was saddled with a £10 fine at West London after she admitted riding a bike when drunk.
>
> Then the lady-in-a-hurry dashed off by car to the High Court, hoping for a divorce. But she was out of luck there too, when the judge refused to speed up the wheels of justice.
>
> He told her she must wait for three years before seeking a divorce from her husband, actor Kenneth Ives.
>
> She married Ives—who played Hawkeye in the TV serial *Last of the Mohicans*—just 13 months ago.
>
> Later Imogen relaxed and spoke about her fast-moving action before the courts.
>
> The 31-year-old starlet said: "It was amusing being charged with being drunk in charge of a bike, but divorce is no laughing matter."

Thirty-something and still a pin-up

"The 31-year-old starlet..." she was almost 33 and still only a starlet.

As far as the tabloids were concerned it was "The Day Imogen Wobbled On Her Bicycle." And even in *The Guardian* it was "The Actress And The Bicycle." It was reported that Imo had borrowed a bicycle and was on her way home from a party, thus marking the occasion of National Bicycle Week.

Imogen had been observed by police Constable Cove at 1:10 on a Sunday morning pedaling along Daisy Lane, Putney, in a somewhat erratic manner, weaving from one side of the road to the other.

She was on the wrong side of the road as she turned into Hurlingham Road and P.C. Cove noted that her bicycle had no lights.

"It was noticed that her eyes were glazed," the constable told the court. "Her speech was slurred and her breath smelt strongly of drink."

It was reported that Imogen said: "Is it dark? I don't think it is."

Brought up before the magistrate Imogen said that she was sorry and was fined £10 and ordered to pay £11 doctor's fees. The magistrate asked her whether her behavior was indicative of some problem or merely the result of excessive celebration.

"I don't believe I was drunk," Imogen replied. "I won't ride a bike ever again."

Outside the court Imo obliged the photographers, looking lovely and elegant in a cream, embroidered two-piece and a broad-brimmed hat fit for Ascot. She was still protesting her innocence. "The policeman said my breath smelled. I thought it was the garlic I had eaten and not drink. Anyway, it's no more bikes and no more garlic for me."

The 1970s began where the '60s left off—Imogen was busy.

1973 was a particularly active year. She went on tour in the comedy *The Mating Game* in which she played one of the leads opposite Ian Lavender of *Dad's Army* fame.

by arrangement with JOHN GALE & RAY COONEY present

ian
lavender
(from 'dad's army')

imogen
hassall

david
stoll

joanna
henderson

and

carol
hawkins
(from 'the fenn street gang')

in
london's latest smash hit
comedy from the apollo theatre

the
mating
game
by robin hawdon

directed by maurice stewart   designed by hutchinson scott

Darlington
Civic

Theatre Director: PETER TOD.   Telephone: 65774
Tuesday 13th November until Saturday 24th November, 1973

"How to play 'The Mating Game'" advertised the *Wimbledon News*:

> The rules are as follows: All you require is a lavish London apartment with only one bed in it. Take Draycott Harris, a smooth, suave bachelor who is a TV star and his brother lovable, cuddly James. Then add two delectable girls, Honey Tooks and Julia Carrington. The referee is Mrs. Finney, a dragon of a charlady. Then sit back and enjoy the fun.

Imogen was not the glamorous Honey Tooks, but Julia Carrington, described as "the short-sighted and censorious secretary."

"It was not one of the more pleasant of my experiences" is all that Ian Lavender is prepared to say.

David Stoll, a fellow member of the touring company, says that the tour did not seem to be a happy experience for Imogen. He remembers her as "a lovely lady, but a very sad one. I don't think she enjoyed the tour very much, as she seemed to have so many private problems, that they appeared to interfere with her professional work at times. I'm sure, if her home life had been on an even keel she would have attained the star status she so badly wanted."

Sad she may have been, but as always with Imogen, comedy was never far away.

The Life and Death of Imogen Hassall   **147**

In October 1973 *The Mating Game* was playing at the New Theatre in Hull. On the last night of the run, Imogen was told that she had an admirer who was anxious to meet her. Straight from the stage and still in costume, resplendent in "a beautiful white lace ballgown with my hair piled up in ringlets," she went to the stage door to be met by a man bearing an unusual token of his admiration:

> He was a very sweet, charming man, who said he was representing the R.A.F. base. He had a present in his hand. It looked like a bottle of champagne. When I realized that it was two pounds of frozen haddock, my face must have been a picture. I was lost for words.

Nevertheless, Imogen accepted her gift with her customary graciousness and asked her dresser to wrap the haddock carefully in plastic bags. She was planning to drive all the way back to London that night and wanted to take the fish with her.

Unfortunately, the heat inside Imogen's Mini began to defrost the haddock as the long drive south dragged on. Then, to make matters worse, the car broke down at four o'clock in the morning just as she reached Cricklewood.

By some miracle a taxi happened along and the driver agreed to take Imogen and her luggage home.

Leaning into the Mini to extract Imogen's bags, the driver was assaulted by the smell of the thawing haddock:

> He refused to take me and the haddock. So I had to leave it in the gutter in Cricklewood. I just hope the local cats enjoyed their breakfast that morning.

Imogen's stage career would now consist largely of touring, the stresses and strains of which could only aggravate her increasing mental and physical fragility. She would play in some prestigious local theatres as well as the far-flung provinces in demoralizing theatrical backwaters. She would never appear on the West End stage again.

She was cast, more often than not, because she was a face familiar from TV and her name would put provincial fans in seats. She played leading roles but out there in the sticks who would ever get to hear about it?

Derek Wright toured with Imogen in *Barefoot in the Park* in 1973. "I found Imogen delightful to work with. Very pretty, very professional and eager to do her best. My scenes with her were always a delight to play."

Imogen had a huge part in the play—she "never stopped talking." It was obviously a daunting prospect for her: "On the first night I went to wish her good luck before the curtain went up and found her standing at the side of the stage waiting to make her first entrance, understandably very nervous with such a long part. 'I'm all right as long as I don't have to say anything.'"

Derek Wright became something of a father figure for Imogen. She confided to him "how difficult it was to be the daughter of someone thought to be bisexual/homosexual."

Barefoot in the Park was produced by Barrie Stacey, who recalls Imogen vividly in his book *A Ticket to the Carnival*, published in 1987. He "fancied Imogen Hassall to play the lead for many reasons."

It was duly arranged that they meet in town for tea to discuss the proposed tour: "Imogen came to tea in a large picture hat, the thinnest chiffon dress, and looked absolutely beautiful. She was fluffy, sexy and infuriating, therefore utterly feminine. We got on like a house on fire."

Barrie did not have great expectations of Imogen as an actress—"she was obviously not going to give Dorothy Tutin a hard time"—but he was plainly inspired by her charisma: "Nevertheless, she looked ravishing and full of promise, Her outfit was straight out of *A Yank at Oxford* [a Vivien Leigh picture]. After two cups of tea we were inseparable, and swore an oath to do the play—or die."

According to Barrie Stacey, the tour opened at Richmond to a packed and most appreciative house—"although Imogen was not going to worry Jane Fonda either in the acting department."

Like Derek Wright, Barrie Stacey remembers Imogen having trouble with her lines. Other members of the cast, however, were able to cover for her, "...and with her sex appeal the audience were not following the same line of thought anyway."

The play completed its short run at the King's Theatre in Southsea and, as Barrie Stacey recounts, Imogen did not merely stop traffic, she brought the defense of the realm to an abrupt halt: "When the Navy got wind of Imogen, no boats were put to sea. So when we had a press reception for the play, the Navy turned up in such force to meet Imogen that if invasion had taken place that morning, we would all have been gonners."

Imogen had always been "a favorite pin-up with the Fleet in Portsmouth," reported the local *Hampshire Telegraph*—keenly anticipating her arrival in Southsea with a large photo of a smiling Imo in a bikini and the bold headline "Pin-up Imogen to go barefoot at the Kings next week."

Imogen must have lapped it up, being the center of attention, surrounded by eager admirers, showing her happy face, tossing her head back with a broad smile, that silent laughter—ever the Gracious Lady, giving autographs and accepting compliments—a Star.

The owners of the King's Theatre loaned their flat to Imogen while the tour resided at Southsea—"we had quite a week," wrote Barrie Stacey. He was evidently inspired by Imogen. In the publicity for the tour, she was billed above the title:

Grapefruit Productions present
Imogen Hassall
In Neil Simon's brilliant comedy...

There is a generously proportioned and very sexy portrait of her, and Imogen's bio dwarfs those of her co-stars, blowing her trumpet loudly:

> Imogen Hassall is an actress of many talents, and appears frequently on the stage, in films and on television. She started her professional career after studying at the Academy of Dramatic Art, with the Royal Shakespeare Company in *Troilus and Cressida*, and she appeared with them at the Edinburgh Festival. She then went on to the West End, appearing with Dame Sybil Thorndike in William Douglas-Home's *The Reluctant Peer* and in *The Italian Girl*. And now to films. Here she has worked with some of the leading names in the profession—Yul Brynner, Jonathan Miller, Hayley Mills, Peter Cushing, Franco Nero, Lee Van Cleef—in successes like *Carry On Loving* and *The Virgin and the Gypsy*. She has appeared on

television with Michael Redgrave in Anouilh's "Monsieur Barnet" in the Evelyn Waugh trilogy *Sword of Honour* and in many other programs.

It comes across as a venture intended to elevate Imogen to star status. They "swore on oath to do the play or die," in a scene vaguely reminiscent of John Counsell's meeting with Eve Lynett—although the daughter lacked the mother's modesty and good sense.

Or was it simply a case of a face that could guarantee a full house?

It certainly is an abrupt leap to the top. To date in the billing Imogen had more often than not hovered in the relegation zone, or at best languished mid-table. Putting her name above the title and giving her the lion's share of the limelight must have raised a few eyebrows.

It certainly came as a surprise to the theatre critic of *The Whitehaven News*, who pronounced it to be "*Not just a one-woman show.*"

> Sadly, Neil Simon's *Barefoot in the Park*...was billed as though it was Imogen Hassall's "one-woman" show, as though Miss Hassall was the leading light and everything else was to move in her glow like so many moths.
>
> Miss Hassall was bright in a bouncy sort of way but was hardly what one had anticipated...

The reviewer appears to have been provoked by the somewhat blatant tone of Imogen's publicity and gave special praise to the fine all-round team effort of her co-stars—Lawrence Trimble, Mavis Rogerson, Derek Wright and Glynn Sweet—"showing that the leading light was not going to dazzle anyone, at least not in this context":

> All those enticing posters about the town with Miss Hassall seductively slipping the zip on her dress while pursing her smoldering lips can now be seen to have been rather like an advertisement of a nude clutching a bar of soap in order to sell the commodity. Fortunately, the soap proved to be of good quality, so much so that the nude was to some extent forgotten.

Imogen's publicity for *Barefoot in the Park* mirrors the fatal contradictions in her career—her glossed-up resume juxtaposed with a pin-up picture. The pin-up always drew a crowd, but the actress did herself no favors.

After all the preceding excitement, Imogen's actual performance won no praise at Southsea, "Imogen Hassall seems determined to play capering Corrie at the fastest possible tempo."

And the *Northern Echo* said merely that "Imogen Hassall gives a very decorative performance," at the Georgian Theatre in Richmond, Yorkshire.

In 1973/74, Imogen was also busy making a movie—a homegrown, low-budget affair, marking the screen debut of David Jason.

White Cargo, like so many of Imogen's films, has been banished to the early morning showings in the twilight zone of TV scheduling. It is a sort of spy spoof, a saucy seaside postcard comedy about a Walter Mitty character prone to 007 fantasies, who foils a gang of white slavers operating out of a Soho strip club.

Imogen plays Stella, an undercover policewoman disguised as a stripper. She makes her entrance in a shabby blonde wig and blue sequin bikini. At 32 she looks impossibly slim and unusually pale, even unhealthy.

Her forte was light comedy and she plays it efficiently, albeit mechanically. The dancer is still in there in her tendency to strike poses instead of moving naturally; and in her exaggerated expressions. Her acting on screen at least, tends towards a series of set expressions rather than any genuine spontaneity—her friends recognize some of these as classic Imogen faces. As Stella she assumes a cockney accent, which slips occasionally. When her true identity is revealed, Imogen reverts to her normal posh tones, enriched when she takes command of the situation—Imo just playing herself again?

Imogen does not appear to be attacking this role with her usual enthusiasm, which is hardly surprising. She seems out of sorts, listless, even sullen. As a piece of work the role and the vehicle could have given her scant satisfaction. Or, is there a hint of her private troubles escaping onto the screen?

In the film, Stella has a little black-and-white Shitzu. At one time Imogen had as pets Cassidy and Ratso. Could this be the faith-

Imogen portrays a policewoman in the spy spoof *White Cargo* **(1974).**

ful Ratso, co-starring with his mistress? It is not hard to imagine Imo so needing her little friend for comfort that she took him not only on set but onscreen with her. She was probably just having a lark, making her doggie into a movie star.

Imogen's screen career had fizzled out. She would not be seen on the big screen again until 1979. And that was in *Licence To Love and Kill*, a B-movie secret agent caper starring Gareth Hunt, of *The New Avengers*. In the USA it was called *The Man From S.E.X.*, which says it all.

Musician Donald Clisby had known Nicholas Hassall since 1965 when Nicholas was playing French horn for the Festival Ballet. Nicholas wanted to be a composer and would in time withdraw to focus all his energies on that. He "has a remarkable brain," says

Donald Clisby. "Into all kinds of esoterics; the occult, mysticism," science, physics and chemistry."

In 1973 Nicholas, then living in Crouch End, called Donald and said: "come round and meet my sister, she wants to meet you."

Donald had established a reputation among his friends and colleagues as a palm reader. He says that he did it mostly for laughs and even describes himself as a fake but adds that he did have a knack for hitting things on the head.

Imogen duly arrived in Crouch End clad in a splendid white trouser suit. "It looked very good on her," recalls Donald. Nicholas introduced him as an expert in reading hands. His sister, interested, offered her palm for inspection.

Hers was not a good hand Donald remembers; the lines in it lacked strength.

Although Donald Clisby knew Imogen only briefly, she left a lasting impression. On one occasion, when Donald happened to be visiting Nicholas at Crouch End, Imogen telephoned her brother and proceeded to engage him in conversation while she was quite clearly in the middle of having sex.

There was an abrupt interruption, as Imo rounded on her unknown lover, "You're soft! You've gone down!"

In 1974, the one-time Royal Shakespeare Company player and West End actress was appearing in pantomime. There is nothing wrong with panto and the panto season has, traditionally, always been welcomed by actors as a seasonal improvement in their employment prospects.

Caroline Lange appeared with Imogen in *Puss in Boots* at Whitehaven. Imo, she recalls, was playing the Princess, the daughter of the Dame and was having trouble remembering her lines.

The silence would stretch until it was screaming. Then one would see Imo thinking to herself, *Oh my God, it's me*!

Whenever she dried, Imogen would fall back on the one line she could remember, "Oh Mummy, I'm so fwightened!"

The panto at Whitehaven was another of Barrie Stacey's productions. This Imogen of 1975 came across to Barrie Stacey as a much more troubled personality than the leading lady of *Barefoot in the Park*. "She was very nervous, a little temperamental and prone to several horrendous outbursts."

One evening, Imo took exception to the show's choreographer and threw a bottle of whiskey at her. As Barrie Stacey relates it, the choreographer was more than capable of giving as good as she got. She caught the flying bottle and threw it straight back. "Imogen went on with a whiskey rinse hairdo."

Barrie Stacey supports accounts of Imogen's problems with her lines. He recounts how the Dame had a stock phrase to cover Imogen's lapses—"Oh, daughter, you haven't got lost in the woods again? You must stop picking the daisies!"

Once again, Barrie Stacey had put a star on Imogen's dressing room door. The show was advertised as:

Puss In Boots
Starring Film, Television and Stage Star
IMOGEN HASSALL

And the billboards were dominated by Imogen's seductive, sultry poses.

The Whitehaven News sent a reporter to the rehearsals. Since it was only rehearsal, Imo was working in a "most un-princess like outfit of black sweater and jeans and had her flowing black hair tied in a tail at the back."

As if sensing the journalist's disappointment, Imogen was only too happy to oblige the inevitable photographer by changing quickly into one of her glamorous costumes. "She told me that this is her first ever pantomime and that Whitehaven audiences are to be treated to her first public performance as a singer!"

No doubt prompted by Imo, *The Whitehaven News* stated that her theatrical career had begun at the age of 16 as the youngest member of the Royal Ballet Company, "...and if she isn't too confident about the singing part of the role, at least she doesn't anticipate any trouble with the dancing — the pantomime role calls for her to dance the Charleston and do a bit of ballet as well."

For all the build-up, Imogen

was barely mentioned in the review of the show, although it was noted that she proved popular with the young audience.

The production was a troublesome one for her. She must have been a continual source of stress for producer Barrie Stacey, as she all too often was, but it is plain that Barrie remembers her with great fondness and regret: "I wish I had spent more time with Imogen. She needed love and attention, and had much more potential than she was credited for. She needed to re-think her image, as it is always later than one thinks. The train of life never slows, not even for a passenger as beautiful as Imogen Hassall. Her early death was a sad blow and ended what could have been an interesting career. She used to ring me at four a.m. just to chat and invite me over. After an hour, even the mightiest weaken. She used to threaten that she was going to commit suicide, and I would often jest to friends, 'I think I'll send the razor blades over.' How very sad that she really meant it."

Bill Homewood, another member of the *Puss in Boots* company, remembers Imogen with tremendous affection. He depicts a more confident performer than others might recall, but hints at the low self-worth that hid behind the public show. "My short relationship with Imogen is a rosy memory. She was very special — self-deprecating privately though capable of impetuous and barmy publicity stunts, she was fearless and relaxed on stage and wonderful company in private: hilarious, passionate and quixotic."

Briefly, Bill and Imogen were lovers. Bill was a few years younger than Imogen and was married at the time — "I was not looking after my marriage very well." Imogen, meanwhile, was on the rebound from the breakdown of her first marriage.

They liked each other immediately and fell into each other's arms. The bond was a shared sense of humor. "Hilarity drew us together."

Imogen and the cast of *Puss in Boots*

For a few short months, they had a really grand time—"we mainly stayed in bed and never went anywhere or did anything much"—living together during the panto's run, or secluded in Imogen's pad in Fulham. "We made a desert island out of wherever we were."

Bill was impressed by Imogen the professional and saw much more in her than the shallow image that decorated the tabloids. "She was a personality who also had a craft. She was good at her job."

Imogen, he says, was "a tremendously authoritative actress." He is convinced that she had it in her to tackle the great roles.

And she could still dance. In the panto, there was a choreographed fantasy scene. At 32, Imogen arrived at rehearsals with her ancient point shoes. She tottered about tentatively for a few moments, holding on for support, then suddenly took wing and began to improvise, accompanied by the pianist. She did the entire piece on point to the astonishment of the watching chorus girls.

Onstage she would appear to lose herself in the mood of the dance, then suddenly mutter something funny as she glided past the wings.

Did Imogen's memory wander all the way back to the summer of 1952 and the sunny lawns of Elmhurst when she danced?

Imogen's old school remembered her. In 1973 Elmhurst had launched a Development Fund appeal for £250,000 to build new premises for staff and pupils. In the brochure for the Fund the name of Imogen Hassall appeared as one of the "talented performers produced by Elmhurst."

Imogen had other talents. She was a skilled designer, says Bill Homewood, recalling the enormous efforts that she put into decorating her house. She lavished special attention on the garden with statues and water, amplifying its confined spaces with a clever use of mirrors.

Socially Imogen always made a tremendous impact. Bill remembers her as the life and soul of a Christmas party hosted by Lord Sieff. At charades Imogen was truly inspired.

Conversationally Imogen was "an intellectual force to be reckoned with." She could hold her own on any topic and always drew people to her.

Her beauty, says Bill, stopped traffic. Of her many lovers, he observes, "She had a huge affection and was capable of tremendous giving. She was emotionally ample."

Above all, Imogen was one of the funniest people he had ever met.

But Imo was not popular with her family. The things that she had said had caused a great deal of distress. Although she may have appeared to shrug these things off at the time that she said them, it was something that worried her. "She was terribly upset to have lost the faith of her family. She had burnt her boats and didn't know how to get back." A newspaper had dubbed her the Britvic heiress. Imogen hinted that she had forfeited any inheritance.

Bill and Imogen shared happy times on their desert island. Just once, Bill caught a glimmer of Hell and saw "what was behind the door that she kept shut."

It came out of the blue.

Bill was surprised to hear Imogen crying in the upstairs bedroom. Entering to investigate, he was confronted by a hysterical, harrowing scene.

Imogen was on her hands and knees crawling about on the bedroom floor groping, searching, sobbing frantically—"my baby, my baby, where's my baby? She was in such a trance of grief that she really believed that her baby was somewhere to be found."

Bill did what he could to console her. His impression was that her child "had lived long enough for her to know it." The death of her baby had a massively profound effect on her. It was the core of the pain that would never leave her.

During the short time that Bill knew Imogen she admitted herself into a hospital for psychiatric treatment. Others report her resistance to such a course of action, an indication, perhaps, of just how very low and desperate she felt now.

Typically Imogen was very funny about it.

Not long after the run of *Puss in Boots* Bill was working in America. Imogen moved on to other relationships. Amicably, they drifted apart.

"She was a very moving woman," says Bill Homewood. "I really adored her."

Those were drab times in the career of Imogen Hassall. The heady days of the Swinging '60s, when the world was beating a path to her door; when she was everywhere—on the West End stage, on TV, on the silver screen—all seemed like a very long time ago. She had peaked, or so it appeared, and was now on a downhill slide.

To hear her tell it, Imogen's life was one long hard luck story.

"The Countess of Cleavage Is Out In The Cold," declared the *News of the World* on June 29, 1975:

> Imogen Hassall—the girl dubbed the Countess of Cleav-
> age—last night told me how her glamorous showbiz life
> has turned into a nightmare of despair and loneliness.

Imogen was still smarting and feeling hard done by after having been busted for riding her bicycle; an affront aggravated by her failure to get a quickie divorce from Kenneth Ives:

> At her West London flat, Imogen, dressed in a purple
> low-cut dress, told me: "This week is the culmination
> of the worst six months of my life. Drunk in charge of a
> bike, I ask you!
>
> I pleaded guilty so I can't complain. But honestly,
> since I had jaundice I hardly drink, and I'd had three
> glasses of Portuguese rose wine that night.

I don't get drunk, I get zany, and I thought I was being
friendly waving at the policeman.

With my luck now if I get a part I'd fall down and
break my leg."

Imogen told the *News of the World* that for her "stardom is just a dirty word":

"I had some good years, and I made a bit of cash," she
said.

"Luckily I put it in bricks and mortar. But at the
moment I'm in the red and my bank manager isn't too
happy.

"I've been offered skin-flicks soft porn to do, but
no way.

"I haven't earned a penny since Christmas, and I don't
even qualify for the dole since I'm still married."

Imogen's catalogue of misfortunes was infused with a touch of bizarre comedy. "I was
driving to see someone I thought could help get me a script—and my car blew up. I'm now
looking for a second-hand Mini."

She had turned down cript only to have a young man from the film company appear
on her doorstep—who started taking off his clothes, "He just stood there and said 'I'm a bit
warm' and took every stitch off."Imogen told him she had to water her lawn. At this point
she got her finger caught in the sliding door and cut it, "It was absurd, me holding a cut
finger and this nude stranger standing there. I said to him 'I don't know about you but I'm
off to hospital for some stitches.' When I got back he was gone."

Imogen had another more sinister admirer—"an ardent and persistent admirer who
regularly stands in her front garden gazing at the house." She called the police several times
but there was little they could do. "He also sends me Premium Bonds, often about a fiver
a week with 'From me, with love to you' written on them. In my financial state I suppose
I should encourage him."

Imogen then turned to the subject of her faltering career—"I haven't been offered a
part in six months and no one seems to want to know."

She claimed she was a victim of British inhibitions:

The British are so bloody puritanical. They can take foreign birds with good looks and a big figure, but not when
it's the home-grown variety...

It's ridiculous. I'm a good actress, I really am, and
I've got a good body.

In France or Italy I'd be a star. But not here, oh no.
We don't mind ogling Scandinavians and Continentals
but not our own.

On the subject of stardom Imogen reflected with grim irony on the gulf between the
public image and the private reality—with imagery that was positively Dickensian:

At Christmas I was in Whitehaven in a room in digs, alone.
I was opening in *Puss in Boots* on Boxing Day.

On Christmas Day I could hear the family having a
right old time, and I sat in bed with three woolly cardigans
and a half-bottle of whiskey for company.

I thought to myself, "You're a star all right, Imogen,
look at all the glamour the public think you're surrounded
with. You're having a right old time, living it up."

Imogen's proclaimed loneliness led her on to the subject of her failed marriage. Despite
the fact that she had recently been to court seeking a divorce and was seen conspicuously with
other men, she claimed that all she really wanted was a reconciliation and a settled life:

I didn't even know where my husband was. I've never
been as lonely in my life.

At that moment I would have given anything—films,
stardom, premieres, even acting—for a husband, a couple
of kids...

I still love my husband Kenneth," Imogen declared.
"And if he came to my front door there's nothing I'd like
better.

All I really want to be is a married lady with a couple
of kids. I hate being alone.

But he never calls, he never rings, and I never hear
from him.

His career is booming—and mine as an actress is
non-existent.

It was recalled that a previous broken love affair had prompted one of Imogen's cries
for help. "I'm not suicidal, I'm almost happy in a depressed, pessimistic, cynical sort of
way. I can't see how things can get worse."

Just as all seemed hopeless offers of work came out of the blue, a tour with Brian Rix to
be followed by another pantomime. Imogen stated,. "I thought I was forgotten and finished
as an actress. I have been through a year of worry, illness and depression. My agent said
that my publicity had gone against me."

"I think I am a good actress," said Imogen, her confidence somewhat restored, add-
ing that "one of my first parts was with Lord Olivier," just as she had once been quoted as
claiming that she had understudied Diana Rigg at the RSC.

While her stated purpose was to re-establish her credibility as an actress, Imo was not
quite ready to shed the glamour. "But I still enjoy going to premieres. I am a very zany
person and like enjoying myself. Some people don't understand that."

"Imogen Back In The Limelight," was the headline in September 1975 as Imogen attended another gala. She was still talking about a reconciliation of her marriage:

I still love him and he has said he still loves me, but he
won't see me or talk to me.

I tried to get a divorce so that the marriage could
be cleared up one way or the other, but I didn't get one
because my husband said he didn't want one.

Imogen was offered a tour with Brian Rix in *A Bit Between the Teeth*.

> It's crazy. I don't know where I am. I would like a
> reconciliation but it doesn't seem likely.

Imogen was declaring her hopes for a reconciliation with Kenneth Ives on September 6, 1975. The day before she had been photographed at the premiere of *Rollerball*, cheek to cheek with Alan Whitehead with whom, it was reported, she was spending summer weekends.

Confusing times but Imogen was optimistic. "Still, with so much work to look forward to, I can forget about depressing matters for a while. I hope this will be the end of one of the worst times of my life."

1975 saw Imogen back in panto as Maid Marian in *Babes in the Wood*, a very successful production in Bournemouth with Dora Bryan.

Dora Bryan remembers Imogen fondly as a good friend. During the run in Bournemouth, they stayed in neighboring flats, Imogen on her own and Dora with her 15-year-old daughter, with whom Imogen was very close.

Dora's Imogen was a lovely girl and she remembers lots of giggles. Imogen was also very professional and while Dora was aware of her troubles with the drink and the pills, they did not intrude upon her work in *Babes in the Wood*—the pills were not in evidence.

Imogen's appearance in Bournemouth afforded the *Evening Echo* the opportunity to reflect upon a Hassall family connection:

> While giving the memory a test, there's the name Hassall
> to recall for some a great time in our orchestra's history
> and the tribute paid in verse by Christopher Hassall.

And here's attractive daughter Imogen in Bournemouth again, displaying her charms as, who else, Maid Marion.

Before rounding off the year in panto, Imogen had been touring again in the Brian Rix farce *A Bit Between the Teeth*.

Terence Alexander's Imogen was a far cry from that of Peter Bowles or Derek Wright. "I think Imogen had a very difficult and probably very sad life but she was also a nightmare walking. She was not easy to work with and stirred up trouble off-stage."

Terence Alexander refutes any suggestion that Imogen was in any way malicious. "She let her personal life get in the way of her professional life—and this could be very irritating to other members of the cast. She usually did over dramatic things and that's what I meant by stirring up trouble. I don't think she was malicious—just very obsessed with herself and her rather wretched private life." "I had met her when she was about 18 years old in a TV play—I think her first—and she was very beautiful and seemed very charming... In later years she identified very strongly with Vivien Leigh—that was after Vivien's death—and was similarly unbalanced in my opinion. She was a menace but I feel very sorry for her."

If Imogen appeared to be somewhat distracted by events in her personal life, perhaps she had good reason. Bradford's *Telegraph and Argus* proclaimed. "Actress Imogen Hassall today pleaded with the man who is threatening her life, 'Get help—you are a sick man.'"

Imogen's sinister admirer was still making his presence felt. The full story emerged, across two columns, beneath a publicity still of Brian Rix and a scantily-clad Imo, threatening to burst out of her skimpy bra.

Imogen revealed how she had been plagued by an obviously deranged stalker from the moment her life story had appeared in a Sunday newspaper. "I believe this man needs help—I want to see him in a mental home rather than behind bars. He has written some terrible letters and made horrible telephone calls threatening suicide and my own life. It is making my life a misery."

According to Imogen, her "maniac follower" had even journeyed from Liverpool to camp out on her doorstep—"I had to sell up and move away. When I saw him in London he said he would do anything I told him. I'm telling him now—go to a doctor."

The *News of the World* had reported what may have been the incident that prompted Imogen to sell up and move out:

Actress Imogen Hassall is in the heart unit of a London hospital today recovering from what she described as a night of terror.

The glamorous 31-year-old brunette says she was forced to flee from her Fulham home in a flimsy nightie...

Imogen was asleep in the bedroom when there was a lot of shouting and banging at the front door. It was 2 a.m. and she was really frightened.

She just sat in bed until she realized someone was trying to open her bedroom window.

Then she lost her nerve and ran into the garden, jumped over a fence and collapsed.

The next thing she remembers is waking up in hospital...

The Life and Death of Imogen Hassall

The hospital said that Imogen was being kept in with a respiratory infection. A police spokesman commented: "Miss Hassall hasn't made any statement to us about this and we aren't investigating."

Alan Whitehead's memories of the event are more in keeping with the bizarre slapstick that dogged incident-prone Imo.

His account has Imogen's rare sleep being disturbed when she thought she could hear noises. Befuddled by her pills and believing in her distracted, doped state that burglars were breaking into the front of the house, she ran out of the patio doors at the rear and into the garden. Still in her night-clothes she clambered over the garden fence only to collapse in the neighbors' fishpond. There the neighbors found her, semi-conscious and lying in the water. With the best of intentions they forced a double-brandy into her. This prompted a cardiac arrest and Imogen had to be rushed to the hospital.

Imogen had received several dud telephone calls that very weekend as *A Bit Between the Teeth* arrived in Bradford to play a week at the Alhambra. Judging by the postmarks on his most recent correspondence, her warped admirer was back in Liverpool. In two weeks' time the tour would be moving on to Merseyside. Imogen was dreading it. "...He may be in the audience. The police are doing all they can to help but it is still a terrible feeling he could be out there."

There being no business like show business, it might be observed that you could not buy publicity like that, adorned as it was by a picture of Imogen stripped down to her underwear.

There are other sources for incidents involving a stalker around this time. These accounts do not mention Liverpool. It is claimed that this sad individual was duly identified and turned out to be a civic dignitary from a popular seaside town.

It was the performance given by Imogen's underwear that caught the eye of the *Cardiff Western Mail*. Imogen's bra won praise for "...playing a pretty crucial supporting role."

The *Peterborough Standard*, however, looked beyond Imogen's obvious charms and made note of her comedic gifts. She was "not only voluptuous but clever with it."

Good farce is technically demanding and Imogen, the *Standard* declared, relied not only on her good looks but on her "great skill" too.

The *Norwich Evening News* was equally complimentary. "Imogen Hassall, exposed in one sense but hidden in another (behind doors, curtains and under an eiderdown) timed all her antics to a nicety."

Although temperamental and unreliable—Imogen knew her craft.

Before touring with her in *A Bit Between the Teeth* Stuart Sherwin had been on nodding terms with Imogen at the Buckstone Club, an actor's club in Suffolk Street behind the Haymarket Theatre.

Stuart has enjoyable memories of his Imogen. Life with Imogen was always full of surprises: "She was good fun to be with and I remember one occasion when we were in Norwich...and I took her to the Mustard Shop. When she saw the various posters, etc., she remarked that her grandfather was an RA and had painted them. This was mentioned just as an afterthought, but when the manager heard that, he asked us to wait a moment. He, unbeknown to us, phoned Colman's factory and a few minutes later we were whisked in a large motor car to the factory for a guided tour and a chat with the directors!"

Life with Imogen was always exciting. Stuart Sherwin can testify to the thrills and spills of her driving: "It was terrifying, she drove at great speed and seemed to be unaware of other traffic and most of the time talked to me without looking at the road. I arrived in Norwich a nervous wreck and refused to make the return journey with her. However, came the Saturday last performance and I was persuaded, much against my will, to make the return journey with her. It was a repeat of the first trip, only in the dark! At one point we were stopped by the police and it took all of my powers of persuasion to convince them that Imogen was sober. The rest of the journey it was all I could do to persuade her to go above 10 miles an hour!"

Amanda Richardson recalls how she would sometimes resist Imo's attempts to climb into the driving seat of the sporty Datsun she owned in 1980, and took the wheel herself.

Stuart Sherwin watched Imo pursue one of her many pipe dreams and experienced her child-like resistance to the voice of reason: "Near the end of the tour she spoke to me about doing cabaret. It was, I think, just another of Imogen's fantasies and I spent one very late night trying to bring her down to earth and tell her of the problems and pitfalls, but she honestly thought she could just get on a stage and that was it. Some weeks later I read in a paper of Imogen being given a very bad reception in some club, something which the press would seize on and take every delight in. It was all very sad and even if I had seen Imogen that time and said I told you so she wouldn't have listened."

Imogen had turned to Dora Bryan for help in putting her cabaret act together. Dora did what she could, suggesting a few songs. She says that Imogen went so far as to organize a press call to herald the event and even performed a few excerpts from the show. Imogen was a capable singer, says Dora, at least for the purposes of panto. She was certainly not lacking in confidence, however misplaced.

Stuart Sherwin suggests as an actress Imogen was good in the type of play that they were doing, light comedy, but she expected too much from her chosen profession: "She certainly wanted to be a star, quite how she thought she could achieve that I don't know. She certainly had talent but I think along the way she didn't listen to the right people. Maybe she only listened to those who told her what she wanted to hear. There have never been enough good parts in plays, films, what have you, for attractive young actresses and, in any case, there are always dozens, even hundreds, of these lovely ladies like Imogen waiting for the opportunity. To make your mark in that jungle you have to have something which, maybe, Imogen didn't have."

"No Rix farce would be complete, of course, without delectable young ladies running about in bras and briefs," said the *Scarborough Evening News*; and Imogen, the reviewer affirmed, suited the requirements of her role admirably.

Imogen did not always merit a mention in the eyes of the provincial critics. If she did, it was often a mere passing nod in the direction of her good looks and spectacular attributes: "lovely Imogen Hassall"; "luscious Imogen Hassall."

Newcastle's *Evening Chronicle* took a limited view of Imogen's contribution to the night's entertainment. "...Imogen Hassall, does not have much of a part—although she does have a lot of everything else, all of which is made to waggle."

Week after week, year after year, she scanned the columns making do with such crumbs. It must have been galling, wearying, but she persevered.

Stuart Sherwin could see that Imogen could be her own worst enemy. "One of Imogen's worst faults was, I suppose, her habit of talking unguardedly to the press. She seemed to attract the worst of the press people because I'm sure they expected her to say something outrageous."

The company would hold a press call at every place it played. The journalists would take every opportunity to get Imo to say something they could use.

Touring with her in 1980, Maggie Guess and Amanda Richardson would see the same thing—Imo opening her mouth and putting her foot in it, again and again, the hacks hardly needing to prompt her then lapping it up. Her friends would attempt to advise and restrain her but it was no use, Imo went her own merry way.

BILL KENWRIGHT & ROD. H. COTON
(for David Gordon Productions)
present

"STEPTOE"
WILFRID BRAMBELL

GEOFFREY DAVIES
"DOCTOR ON THE GO"

IMOGEN HASSALL
in

KILLER

A NEW PLAY by BURTON GRAHAM

Directed by JOHN FORGEHAM

Stuart Sherwin sums up his Imogen very simply—"she was fun." But he was well aware of her complex and contradictory nature. "She was irrational, could be infuriating and I am sure that she had many fears both real and imagined; she was generous and had a great sense of humor, she was certainly never boring. Her death and its manner were very sad and although I only knew her for a little while I'm grateful for that."

In 1976 Imogen was on the road again this time in *Killer*—a mystery that was standard provincial fare.

Killer was a three-person play unless one counts the assistant stage manager who appeared nightly as a corpse. The sinister plot concerned a successful public relations man, played by Geoffrey Davies, who clawed his way to the top, only to have a stranger (Wilfrid Brambell) emerge from his murky past and destroy him. Imogen had the role of the PR man's glamorous and efficient secretary with whom he may have been having an affair.

Geoffrey Davies recalls the Imogen of 1976 as still very much the vivacious young actress—"still very bright and buzzing. I liked her tremendously, she was a very, very nice, warm person, always great fun."

The tour with *Killer* took Imogen back to Bradford but this time she was stalked only onstage. The critic sent by the *Telegraph and Argus* regarded her as welcome compensation for an otherwise lackluster drama. "...Happily, Imogen Hassall brought an elegant beauty to the unrewarding part of the secretary."

"Imogen Hassall prowls elegantly," said the Bath *Evening Chronicle*.

1977 appears to have been the odd year out. Imogen was unemployed. It is possible that she may have appeared on one or another of those TV panel game shows that are a refuge for resting actors; an opportunity to show one's face and say, I'm still here.

The work was dwindling; Imogen had acquired a bad reputation and agents and producers were starting to shy away from her.

Peter Charlesworth says that Imogen approached him several times during the 1970s and asked him to represent her. "I declined because I knew her very well and I knew it was a massive headache."

Peter recalls that the last seven to nine years of Imogen's life were impossible. Imogen was not particularly talented but she was a very competent actress—"she could walk on the stage, she could do it, She was very competent—she was very decorative."

The problem was her unreliability. She was, by this time, "a very disturbed human being," her problems accelerated by an addiction to barbiturates. "It was obvious that the rot had set in."

Peter adored Imogen as a person—"she was great fun and very nice"—but professionally she was not worth the risk—"particularly with the drugs."

Her moods were unpredictable—disturbingly so. She could vacillate violently from one personality to another. "One day she would be sweetness and light and the next day it would be all madness."

With Imogen you were on edge all the time. That she still had any kind of career at all, she owed to the kindness of those who cared about her. "The other actors were terribly good to her. They carried her because they liked her."

Peter was enormously fond of Imogen because he knew that the real Imogen was a warm and caring person—but he had to avoid her professionally.

Peter felt that Imogen should not be in the business. Hers had always been a modest talent. Her best days, the dizzy days of the Swinging Sixties, were now far behind her; her era had gone. She was really no more than one of those glamour girls of the time, who had been over-hyped.

DARLINGTON CIVIC THEATRE
Theatre Director; PETER TOD. BOX OFFICE, DARLINGTON 59411
Monday 18th. September until Saturday 23rd. September

cts
ARTISTES AND THEATRICAL SERVICES
(MANAGEMENT) LTD.
In association with
CROSSKEYS PRODUCTIONS
LTD.
present a
HARROGATE THEATRE
PRODUCTION

ANDREW KNOX DOCTOR ON THE GO
ROSALIND BAILEY
IMOGEN HASSALL
RODNEY DIAK

In the Smash Hit Comedy Success by
**Keith Waterhouse
and Willis Hall,**

SAY WHO YOU ARE

Designed by Peter Fairchild
Lighting by Charles Whitworth

Nightly at 7.30pm. Friday 8.00pm. Saturday 5.00 and 8.00pm.

And she was so terribly troubled; it was all too much for her. "The poor girl was ill—it was unfair."

1977 was the lull before the storm.

In January 1978 Imogen was at last able to file her petition for divorce from Kenneth Ives. The hearing was undefended.

"I have a number of boyfriends," Imogen said. "But no plans to remarry. I now have a new agent and plan to re-start my career in real earnest."

It was not to be. Fresh from her divorce from Kenneth Ives, Imo ran full-tilt into the arms of a grand and ill-fated passion.

Say Who You Are was a comedy by Keith Waterhouse and Willis Hall and, according to *The Stage*, was "an exposé of feminine stratagem...presenting the modern image of the single girl on the sexual merry-go-round," sowing the seeds of marital discord. When the play went on tour, Imogen took over the role of "the bachelor girl, Valerie, who is forlornly in love, but not for keeps."

Set designer Peter Fairchild remembers Imogen as "a lovely lady and an intriguing actress."

Peter recalls the Harrogate Theatre failed to meet Imogen's requirements. The shabby state of her dressing room reduced her to tears and she refused to enter it. Despite a limited budget, it was promptly re-painted and decorated for her.

Imogen Hassall

Management:
RICHARD EASTHAM

1978 INTERNATIONAL FILM AND TV YEAR BOOK   187

Imogen struts her stuff but hardly in the manner of a serious actress.

The sight of that drab and Spartan dressing room must have been thoroughly dispiriting for someone with a star inside her. It must have seemed as though the Royal Ballet School, the RSC, Wyndham's and the Duke of York's had all happened to someone else.

Imogen made headlines in the local papers during the tour. Once again it was for the wrong reasons.

Sylvia, her Afghan hound, devoured a farmer's goose, beak and all. There was something of a fuss and according to Peter Fairchild Imo was very upset about it.

She was upset enough to seek a manly shoulder to cry on. That shoulder belonged to fellow cast member Andrew Knox. Peter Fairchild observed that soon "they were very much involved with each other."

The son of actor Alexan-der Knox, Andrew was born in Hollywood and educated at the City of London School and Clare College, Cambridge, graduating with a degree in English.

He first appeared with the Marlowe Society at Cambridge in classical roles. This he followed with a year treading the boards in Nairobi and a year spent on both coasts of the United States in experimental theatre.

On his return to England Andrew continued to work in the theatre then moved into television. He will be best remembered as Gascoigne in the popular *Doctor on the Go* comedy series.

Imogen Hassall and Andrew Knox—a marriage made in tabloid heaven.

Gina Batt was A.S.M. and in charge of wardrobe on the tour of *Say Who You Are*. The director asked her to look after Imogen. He knew that she would need a keeper.

The production people also knew Imogen well and knew what it took to keep her happy. They gave her a blank check to choose her own outfits; Gina recalls trips to Harrod's to pick out patterns. These tended to be red, backless with a low cleavage and fit like a second skin.

As for Imogen's performance Gina says that she could be awful or brilliant depending on her mood. When she set her mind to it Imogen had a unique electricity onstage, a charisma—she was mesmeric.

Nicholas Hassall thought that his sister was not a good actress, but "she kept at it—she plugged away at it."

Nicholas watched Imogen onstage and as time went by his opinion altered. "Now," he said to himself "she is beginning to act. She wasn't a dedicated actress because her interests were dead. She was a ballet dancer." But she had no choice. As his sister told him: "It's all I can do...there's nothing else I can do anyway."

She tried to do it the right way. She went to LAMDA and from there to the RSC and into the West End. Her screen career is disposable but she did some good work onstage.

Nicholas Hassall does not blame Imogen's publicity-seeking for the erosion of her career. "She had tremendously good contacts. She would have gone on despite the popular press. The serious professionals didn't take all that much notice of the *News of the World*."

The problem, says Nicholas, was that she was unreliable and had a bad reputation. She was trouble, "under terrible emotional stress—and was taking too many barbiturates. You mustn't underestimate the psychological pressures she was under, which were always militating against her being a good professional...feeling psychologically overwrought, to the immense extent that she was and trying to keep up a professional job..."

Nicholas gives his sister credit for the strength and courage that she showed, just to keep at it. The fact that she had a career, despite it all was a considerable achievement. "She would have been a good actress—she was improving—she got better and better."

Touring with Imo was about lots of bags and dogs. Imogen took all her fluffy stuff with her on tour. No simple kimono for her—everything, even her slippers, had to have fluff.

When the tour started, there was both Sylvia the Afghan hound and Ratso the Shitzu. The former was always in trouble, while the latter was a bad tempered, grizzly creature. Gina Batt, having been a Shitzu owner herself was familiar with the breed—it gave her and Imogen something in common and they hit it off right from the start.

Gina tried to do the driving as often as she could, especially at night, when Imogen had been drinking. She usually got her way except when Imo was being belligerent. Being driven by Imogen, says Gina, was "a nightmare from hell," especially with the Afghan's head hanging out of the car window all of the way. She was thankful when Sylvia was sent home eventually and Imo was left only with Ratso the grizzly Shitzu.

Gina was Imogen's constant companion on the tour of *Say Who You Are*. She ensured that Imogen was never alone because Imogen would often say how much she dreaded loneliness. She told Gina that she did not want to die alone.

As the tour progressed around the country Gina would do the cooking and the cleaning and had the job of washing the hairpieces that now substituted for the gorgeous mane of Imogen's youth. She recalls that Imogen was drinking but pills were never a problem. Gina says that she was "a minder 24 hours a day" and made herself the custodian of Imogen's pills.

As they traveled from town to town, the two of them enjoyed themselves, finding ways of keeping themselves occupied. Imogen liked going places; she liked to be out and about, being seen. Whenever they took to the streets Imogen always dressed her best—on went the hairpiece and the make-up. Imogen always turned heads wherever she went; she loved being looked at—"it was a tonic," says Gina.

Nicholas Hassall says that Imogen's narcissism was her only safety valve: "She was born into a background where she was inevitably going to be successful as long as she didn't blot her copybook too fast. That milieu encourages narcissism and if there's a fatal psychological flaw...Her only real drug was the appreciation she felt she got from other people looking at her—a very sad state of affairs really."

As soon as they arrived at a new town, Imo would be keen to go exploring—"let's go for a wander...let's find a nice antique shop." Although she had extravagant tastes she would seek out the local Woolworth's; she loved browsing in Woolie's. And there were handbags and shoe shops, lots of shoe shops. Imogen, of course, always chose the most expensive pair.

Often Gina would accompany Imogen on long walks along the seafront or across the moors. This was a more relaxed and natural Imogen, restrained and casual with a simple turban on her head. Sometimes in such moments, Gina would catch Imogen staring silently into the distance, somewhere very far away. Then she would return and Gina would wonder whether her friend had been in a happy or a sad place.

Imogen would talk about certain parts of her life but leave so many questions unanswered. She was so soft, so caring, says Gina. She cared desperately about other people but had a problem accepting that others cared about her, crying out for help and then pushing it away. Gina sensed that Imogen wanted to give to others all the things that she had been denied.

When Imogen did talk about herself the recurring theme was her childhood and her relationship with her parents. She spoke of these things in a disconnected way, giving Gina glimpses seen through a glass darkly, impressions of darkness, fear and loneliness.

Imogen adored her father but had obviously been deeply wounded by him. She could not understand why her adoration had not been returned. "Why did he push me away, why did he reject me?"

Imogen's account of her family life left Gina with an impression of four people living entirely separate lives in a house that was very big and very dark; of a child's fear of the creaking in the shadows. Gina's impression was one of an environment lacking communication and affection; there was no hugging or kissing.

As a child, Imogen said, she was always being dragged to things for Daddy. Her father was always surrounded by a group of distinguished men. Little Jenny, like a pretty doll, would be passed around this thrilling, wonderful circle of men and bounced on their knees, only to be banished when it was time to get down to business. This abrupt switch from being the center of attention to seeming rejection left scars which, 30 years later, were still raw and bleeding.

In her adulthood Imogen's brother Nicholas was a vague, peripheral figure. It appeared to Gina that brother and sister were very close as children. Gina says that when Imogen spoke of her childhood, everything was we—but, at some point, for some reason, Nicholas distanced himself from his family and the we became I.

Imogen's accounts portrayed young Nicholas as a blond cherub, but also as skinny, sickly and weak. Brother and sister, said Imogen, were not allowed to play together because of Nick's frailty. And Imogen also claimed that her mother would not let her have any other friends in the house. She said she was frightened of her mother. It seemed to Gina there was no love there.

Her parents instilled in her the idea that she was someone who would never get anything right, who would never finish anything that she started. As they walked and talked, Imogen gave Gina the impression that fear was a constant factor in her childhood. She said some odd and disturbing things. She said that she liked to sit on her father's knee but Nicholas did not because he said it hurt. Nicholas, Imogen suggested, was always afraid.

Nicholas Hassall says. "I don't believe my parents systematically undermined my sister—more the opposite. My mother encouraged my sister in whatever direction she wanted to go. My father really couldn't adapt to a family life, but even he tried and he certainly didn't undermine her."

At the time, says Gina Batt, she did not really understand what Imogen was talking about. She was just left with impressions, a feeling that something was not right, a sense of fear that was somehow associated with Imogen's parents—"and fear is associated with pain and hurt."

Before long Imogen had new distractions and new pain to pre-occupy her in the shape of Andrew Knox.

Gina Batt says Andrew was not the kind of man that Imogen needed. Gina describes him as emotional and volatile, living in the shadow of a cold, arrogant and unemotional father. He was just the sort of man who would fuel Imogen's insecurity. It was as if she willed such men upon herself, men who could be provoked into an extreme reaction and give her the response that she wanted; as if she was seeking constantly to prove a point.

Imogen could not bear to be on her own. She always needed input from a male. That she would seek out male company from among her touring companions was inevitable.

For the first few weeks there was a lot of flirtation and laughter between Imogen and Andrew. Imogen did the full come-on, turning on the glamour, batting her eyelids. Imogen could make marvelous use of her exotic eyes.

When it came to attracting men, Imogen never gave herself credit for the intelligence that she had and never considered that she did not need to rely on her body alone. It was a symptom of her zero self-esteem. Imo was so often her own judge, jury and hangman.

Geoffrey Davies co-starred with Andrew Knox in the popular *Doctor* series. He describes Andrew as "charming, very eccentric, very amusing." Andrew was unusually eccentric for a young man and it manifested itself most conspicuously in his dress sense, "...Rather Bertie Wooster—a lovely character—rather a Bertie Wooster type of character..."

Andrew sported an assortment of bow ties and colorful waistcoats and cut a decidedly old-fashioned figure in the star-spangled, wide-lapeled, kipper-tied, voluminously flared, stack-heeled, disco-maniac 1970s. "An extraordinary character, a lovely fellow."

Others recall that Andrew was equally at home in jeans and a T-shirt, although he could go to exotic lengths and turn up in baggy Indian shirts and trousers.

John and Allison Kane knew Andrew Knox before, during and after his relationship with Imogen. John had also worked with Andrew in *Doctor*. He remembers him as a very sweet individual.

Andrew liked the company of women, although Allison claims that he was too much of a romantic to be a womanizer; he enjoyed flirting.

He did drink "and one gathers he let drink run away with him"—and smoke pot—"he always had a fair supply of that"; but Andrew saw no harm in his indulgences and meant no harm to anyone.

To Allison Kane, Andrew was "a very sunny personality," who was constantly entertaining and amusing. He could be "wonderfully silly. He had an immense energy and naiveté to him," says John. "Very sweet-natured and generous, a little feckless perhaps. There was an old-fashioned quality about him, a naiveté, immensely likable."

Andrew had "a very pukka sort of accent." As an actor, he would have been perfect for all of those naval films that were so popular in an earlier time.

The impression of Andrew that one gets from John and Allison Kane is of a certain innocence, a boyish charm and great enthusiasm,

Above all he was a gentleman, "...a parfait and genteel knight—there was that quality about him..."

It took about six weeks for the relationship to get up and running. Inevitably, the rows began.

Imogen and Andrew's marriage was made in tabloid heaven.

They did not really know each other. Gina Batt says Andrew thought that he could tame Imogen and realized too late that it was impossible.

The rows were loud and sometimes violent. They argued everywhere. On one occasion there were complaints from the audience to management that their enjoyment of the play was being spoiled by the sound of raised voices offstage.

Late one night, Imogen was driving Andrew and Gina back to their digs across a dark and lonely common. The row began in the car and continued out on the common until Imogen stormed back to rejoin Gina waiting in the car, and drove off leaving Andrew stranded in the vast and empty darkness.

"He can walk back!" huffed Imo.

It was only on condition that Gina did the driving that Imogen was persuaded to turn around and retrieve Andrew. The lovers did not speak to each other all the way back and then proceeded to row all night.

Events took a turn for the melodramatic in Malvern. In the play Andrew's character was involved romantically not with Imogen's character but with another. This purely fictional relationship posed in Imogen's mind a potential threat. When Imo was in a bad mood she could go for anybody; she developed a hatred for that other actress, who had done absolutely nothing to offend her.

Backstage Gina saw Imo pick up a pair of scissors and stalk up behind her imagined rival, aiming at a spot between her shoulder blades. Gina quickly and quietly stepped forward and plucked the scissors from Imo's hand.

Gina was convinced that the whole scene was staged by Imogen and that she had made sure, by her conspicuous and exaggerated actions that she would not go unobserved and unhindered. It was done for effect, just as she would often say things for effect and then elaborate if she felt that she was not getting enough of a reaction. It was all part of the child in her; she was in so many ways "a little girl that never grew up."

At the end of the tour, Imogen and Andrew were no longer on speaking terms.

"We're finished," Imogen told Gina. "I'm never going to see him again."

Not long after Gina received a telephone call, "We're getting married! It's so exciting!"

John and Allison Kane were not optimistic. "We thought it was a bad idea—we knew Imogen was not entirely stable...and the combination of the pair of them...!"

John expressed his doubts to Andrew, who seemed convinced that he could help Imogen. "I can give her stability, I can help. I understand her demons and I can help her cope with them."

Andrew, says John, was not entirely stable himself; and he doubted whether Andrew knew what he was getting himself into. "He didn't really know what marriage entailed, certainly not marriage to someone like Imogen. He would have gone into it because it was a new experience—he was always keen for new experiences."

John describes Andrew as a kind man, not a saint by any means, but "there was a niceness about him, a decency about him. He genuinely thought that this would be a good thing for her, that he could take this thing on."

"Wedding Bells For Imogen," chimed the *Sun* on January 15, 1979. "Sexy actress Imogen Hassall takes on a star role today...as the bride at her wedding...Imogen, ex-wife of TV director Kenneth Ives, said last night: 'We have never been out of each other's pockets for months—and it has been wonderful'."

It was, by all accounts, a case of two large personalities meeting head on.

By May 1979 it had all gone horribly wrong and Imo was giving her account of the courtship to the *News of the World*:

In fact, when we originally met it was a case of hate at first sight.

It was on the opening day of rehearsals for the play *Say Who You Are...*

He made a dramatic entrance wearing only swimming trunks.

It turned out he liked to go swimming before work and had come straight from the pool.

I thought he was a bit peculiar.

I didn't like him at all. I actually found him quite nauseating and rather childish.

And I discovered later that his first impression of me was just as bad. He wrote in his diary that I was "dim, dull and raddled."

But during the weeks that we were on tour with the play we gradually became jokey friends.

You can't help it when you're on the road—especially when you're playing lovers on stage.

It's a tough life being on tour with a small company and you have to share and share alike. You're thrown together all the time and finally you end up in the same bed.

It was actually quite a time before Andrew and I became lovers.

What clinched it was when my Afghan hound Sylvia ate a goose!

Andrew and I, two other members of the cast and the stage manager were sharing a beautiful farm cottage while we were appearing in the North, because it was the cheapest way to live.

One day we came back to find that Sylvia had eaten one of the farmer's geese. She demolished the whole thing, beak and all. It caused a terrible fuss.

The story made the local television news and hordes of pressmen descended on the village pub. In the end we had to leave the cottage.

I was very upset about it all. Andrew had to console me and one thing led to another...

By the time we got back to London the gossip columns had got us engaged, despite the fact that I had no intention of getting married again.

My divorce from Kenneth had only just come through and, anyway, Andrew hadn't asked me.

But the idea began to grow on him until, for reasons best known to himself, he became determined to marry me.

As for me, it was fear of loneliness more than anything which led me into marrying him—against my better judgment.

The wedding took place at the register office in Berwick-upon-Tweed, Northumberland, where Andrew's parents lived in baronial splendor. Imogen depicted the ceremony as a complete farce:

The night before the wedding I was sobbing on my future father-in-law's shoulder, telling him that I didn't want to get married.

But being an old Hollywood star used to actresses getting melodramatic, he just didn't bat an eyelid.

He just told me not to worry and said everything would be all right.

I decided there was no way I could call it off, so the next morning I drank several stiff Scotches and got on with it.

It was all a last-minute thing. Andrew had to borrow the money to get a special license and I had to borrow a fur coat.

I had no proper clothes for the occasion. I wore a turquoise lamé suit and arrived at the register office looking as if I was going to a nightclub rather than a wedding.

When it came to repeating the marriage vows I couldn't understand what the registrar said because he had such a strong Scottish accent.

I had to say: "I beg your pardon."

He said: "It's very important that we get this right."

So I told him: "In that case you'd better write it down so I can read it."

Meanwhile, my father-in-law was falling about in hysterics saying: "I knew we should have had a rehearsal."

I didn't know a soul at the reception—my family refused to come.

And what with the drinking, excitement and general craziness I was in such a state by the end of it all that they had to call a doctor who gave me an injection to put me to sleep.

She said to Andrew in a strong Scottish accent: "I hope ye'll no be troubling your wife, tonight, Mr. Knox'."

Imogen dismissed her second marriage as one "that never had a hope." She said that after only three days she knew that it could not work:

Two weeks later I came home to my house in Putney to find that Andrew had taken all his belongings and moved out. In that time we'd only spent about six nights together.

The wedding was all a big joke that I didn't quite see.

In retrospect I think Andrew probably saw the whole thing as a big publicity stunt.

But I actually persuaded myself that at last someone wanted me for myself.

I was in love with the idea of marrying, settling down and having a family.

I managed to kid myself that it might actually turn out that way.

Andrew, I think, was in love with the idea of marrying a glamorous sex symbol amid a blaze of publicity.

He fell for the phony image of me that had been built up over the years.

I was certainly never really in love with him and I'm pretty sure he was never in love with me.

As she told her side of the story to *News of the World*, Imogen's agenda appeared to be to diminish her sex symbol image by playing down her love life and by criticizing her lovers:

In the 1960s everybody wanted to know me. I had a glamorous image as a successful, sexy, beautiful starlet...

I had plenty of work and plenty of money. Life was fun.

But in the '70s everything started to change.

All the publicity I'd been getting started to backfire.

Suddenly I found I'd got a bad reputation as somebody who was flip about life, an easy lover and who would do anything to get her picture in the paper.

Gradually I found that nobody wanted to know me any more.

In the last few years it's become more and more difficult to get work. A few weeks ago my agent actually dropped me because he said nobody in the business would touch me with a barge pole.

At the moment I'm working in a shop for £30 a week just to make ends meet.

The sick joke is that my image as a sex symbol couldn't be more false.

If only people knew the truth. The fact is that my sex life is non-existent...

Andrew and I didn't have a very exciting sex life...

Right from the start he had his own separate bedroom. We'd never lived as man and wife in the normal sense.

This monologue echoed Imo's tirades, a drop of her sexual poison. Equally suspicious are her pleas of poverty, although the houses kept getting smaller ending with the semi-detached cottage in Wimbledon Village.

Work was getting rarer. Once there were movies, TV and the stage, all at the same time. Now there might be a single short tour, like a tiny island in a vast, empty year.

Her life was shrinking. Once there was Sam Spiegel's yacht. Now, Jackie Ingham recalls, Imo would save and hang up last year's Christmas cards, as her mail dwindled.

Scarcely pausing for breath Imogen described her sexy image as a myth and a curse:

The trouble is that, because of that image, the right men won't come forward...

They don't have the courage to approach someone they assume is a femme fatale.

The boyfriends I've attracted are often homosexuals who think my sex symbol image will do something for their reputations or they're guys who just want to be seen with me.

It's true that I'm seen with a lot of different men and, to the outside world, it might seem that I'm having a right old time.

But almost invariably they are arranged dates who ring up out of the blue and say they would like to meet me.

Like the peer of the realm who invited me out to lunch at the House of Lords the other week.

Nothing ever comes of those meetings.

People don't realize that I go to bed alone every night with a glass of milk and a couple of sleeping pills. Imogen Hassall the sex queen? I should be so lucky,

Andrew Knox rose up to defend his manhood—in the same edition of the *News of the World*:

It's bull that we had a poor sex life...

I think it's a bit naughty of Imogen to suggest it. Our sex life was splendid. It was rip-roaring. We were fornicating rotten all the time we were together, which wasn't just two weeks. It was two months...

We spent an awful lot of time in bed and she told me I was the best lover she ever had.

Few men ever admit to giving anything less than complete satisfaction. But how many of Imogen's lovers were embarrassed when her demons spoke—"I think your prick's too small...your problem is that you're really gay"—or were belittled in the detailed reports that would amuse her girlfriends? Having attended to the dents in his ego, Andrew then presented his version of the wedding:

The idea that I married her for a publicity stunt is totally untrue.

If it were true, I'd have married her in town in a blaze of publicity.

But instead of that we went to the country because we wanted a quiet wedding.

Also, when I first met her I didn't know who she was.

And when it comes to publicity she is the expert.

It's a shame really because all the publicity makes people forget she's a good actress.

It's true that she was a bit upset the night before the wedding.

She burst into tears. But then she was always doing that.

I said to her then, "Look we don't have to get married. We can go back to town and carry on being friends and lovers."

In fact, when I went to bed I switched the alarm off.

I had it set because I had to have the papers that we need to get married by 9 a.m.

But Imogen woke me up and told me I had to get the papers in. I said, "I thought it was off." She said, "You must get the papers in."

Imogen was taken ill at the reception.

She spent our first night throwing up. The next day we had to call a doctor to give her an injection.

I married Imogen because she is a great lady.

Our life was fiery and passionate, but we just couldn't live together"

Kenneth Ives declines to speak about his private life. In 1987 Andrew Knox also took his own life. He boarded the Jersey ferry for the mainland and was not on it when it docked. He claimed that he was going to stay with an old friend in London but she said later that she had no notice of his coming. His parents held fast to the conviction that it was an accident.

Any account of Imogen's marriages thus relies on the fragmented memories of those who watched from the sidelines—who had the inside story told to them by Imogen or read it in the newspapers.

The truth—the contradictory, confused and embellished truth—is thrown to the tender mercies of the tabloids.

Aunt Joan read all about it in the newspapers. "Poor Imogen has been in the tabloid papers again first for getting married and then for coming unstuck in eight weeks. It is no use wishing that her life could have some settled happiness in it because she might find it dreadfully boring."

For as long as Imogen and Andrew did live together, be it Imogen's two weeks or Andrew's two months, they lived in Schubert Road, Putney.

The least of their worries was a parked car, persistently blocking their driveway, but in defense of their homestead, they summoned the cavalry.

George Pegler, then serving at Wandsworth police station, answered the call and over the course of a weekend was able to resolve the matter:

> As soon as I arrived I was invited in and introduced to them both. Having taken details of the problem, Imogen and her husband invited me to have a drink (which I refused as I was on duty!), and took me on a guided tour of their house. I spent quite a long time with them and was made to feel almost a friend in a very short time. We then got another call on the Sunday afternoon regarding the same problem and I attended again. This time I was met very warmly and, having got to grips with the problem, Imogen not only invited me to have a drink, but asked me if I could stay to Sunday dinner which was nearly ready and she was sure she could find enough for me. Unfortunately, I had already had mine and had to decline her kind offer...
>
> I do remember her as a very kind and likable person, and she was very happy having only recently got married...

Imogen, it appeared, was thrilled by her newlywed status and eager to show off her married home and her cozy, Sunday dinner domesticity.

All for a marriage that was doomed from the start.

Or was it all a hollow sham, a performance staged for the benefit of this lone representative of her public?

Gina Batt recalls the violence in the relationship. On tour in *Say Who You Are* Imogen more than once went onstage with make-up disguising a black eye.

Gina remembers visits to their home in Putney after the tour had finished. There were bruises on her face and arms and Imogen would strip off to display the marks on her body. "Look at my bruises!"

It was almost as if she was proud of them. Imogen felt some compulsion to drive her men to such extremes, as if she had a point to make. Gina believes that the roots of this compulsion are to be found in the hurt and bewilderment that Imogen expressed in her childhood reminiscences. Not knowing why she was hurting, she created a source of pain, physical proof of her pain.

Imogen bruised with remarkable ease, says Nicholas Hassall. She had only to bump into something and it seemed to him that she had abnormally soft skin.

Imogen told Gina that she had suffered a miscarriage after Andrew pushed her downstairs.

"That surprises me," says Geoffrey Davies. "I would never have put Andrew down as a violent person, especially towards women."

Geoffrey says that Andrew was brought up as a gentleman and was always very gentlemanly towards women,

However, the *Doctor* series was finished before Andrew married Imogen and Geoffrey never got to see the two of them together. He had worked with Imogen before the marriage and was to work with her again after it collapsed. Geoffrey can remember Imogen telling him that Andrew was useless and that the marriage was never consummated.

Geoffrey did get to hear things about the marriage. Everyone was surprised when Imogen got hitched to Andrew—"he wasn't her type, they didn't seem like a pair." He says, "I do remember stories about their violent relationship."

For as long as Andrew and Imogen lived together in Putney, John and Allison Kane were practically neighbors. They remember visiting the house in Schubert Road when it was still a work-in-progress with Imogen busy doing it up—"she was very industrious." One peculiarity that they recall was a fully functioning toilet bowl as part of the bedroom furniture.

"She came to some of our parties and she was very pleasant," says John Kane. "One had heard stories about her but we never saw any sign of that wild side, she was just good company."

But there was also "an excitement about her, something scary too, something that made you a little nervous to be around her."

It was a surprise when Andrew started coming round, sometimes in tears, sometimes just to escape.

"He hated rows," adds Allison. "And yet the rows that he and Imogen had were monumental—he'd come round absolutely sobbing and sobbing and sobbing: I think she used to beat him up—I remember him coming round one night in a state of real shock."

Andrew kept regular and detailed journals. He must have written something which Imogen did not like. There was an explosion; Imogen took the journal away from him and Andrew sought refuge with the Kanes.

While Allison ministered to Andrew, John volunteered to brave Imogen's wrath and get the confiscated journal back. To his surprise, Imogen was perfectly calm and composed. She said that she was quite prepared to return the journal—"all he has to do is come round and I'll give it to him."

John stayed for a while and Imogen, who "couldn't have been more rational," told him of her disappointment with Andrew. He dithered; could not make up his mind; was not decisive; would say one thing and then do another. "He doesn't know what he wants, he's very immature."John says that he could not argue with that.

Some might say that this was a bit rich coming from Imogen; a case of the pot calling the kettle black.

For all the trauma, says Allison Kane, "Andrew was quite happy to let us know that it was the best sex that he'd ever had in his life."

Allison believes that some of the hurt could well have been sexual—"it was a very sexually charged relationship."

Andrew really did want the marriage to work and the fact that it was falling apart clearly devastated him. "The scenario that he'd mapped out in his head—he'd marry her and give her stability—he'd save her, they'd have great sex and a wonderful marriage—it was obvious that it wasn't going to happen—it wasn't that he didn't keep trying, it was going from bad to worse—I think he got out to save his own skin and I can't blame him."

Like Geoffrey Davies, John and Allison Kane are surprised by accounts of Andrew's violence. There was no hint of violence in his nature, they say—"he was a very gentle person. He got a bit crazy when he was drunk, but not in a violent way, he was never aggressive. He would have had to have been provoked very much," says John. And only under the influence of drink or drugs, adds Allison. "Andrew in his normal persona you wouldn't equate with hitting anyone."

The Kanes did not witness any of the rows but remembered, "It was a destructive relationship. They were both lovely people, positive people in a way."

David Daly, Imogen's agent, says that she was "madly in love," but Andrew "couldn't take her neurosis." Others suggested Andrew was hurt by Imogen's unfaithfulness. They were separated, but the name Knox was on Imogen's death certificate—and while there were other men, there is ample evidence that, at the same time, Imogen was still hoping for a reconciliation. Amanda Richardson shared lodgings on tour with Imogen in 1980, and witnessed the desperate lengths that she would sink to trying to preserve her second marriage.

Clive Graham would encounter Imogen as the years went by.

He recalls sometime during the late 1960s an Annual Star Gala Open Day staged by the Variety Club in the Festival Gardens, Battersea Park. It was a great event featuring parades with floats and a galaxy of stars mingling with their public, enjoying the rides and signing autographs.

Imogen was there to do her bit, lending glamour to the proceedings. At the time Clive had eyes for another. Imogen did not appear to mind; it was all very jolly.

Ten years went by before Clive crossed paths with Imogen again.

He cannot remember the exact year but it was the late 1970s and Imogen was living in Putney.

It was all to do with a Chelsea Nomads Cricket Club weekend mini-tour to leafy Oxfordshire. Imogen had accepted Clive's invitation to tag along.

She was delightful, Clive says, and looked stunning.

The team was hugely charmed by Imogen and being a friendly, sociable sort, she joined in and was welcomed into the fold. She knew some of the players from earlier social encounters, a few from many years back, LAMDA days.

Clive recalls the occasion as a welcome escape for her. "Although a few actors were members of the team, the Chelsea Nomads Cricket Club was essentially not a showbiz side. So, perhaps, being away from showbiz characters and chat, Jenny was able to relax, be her warm, fun, beautiful self and enjoy herself in ordinary circumstances with no pressure on her to perform or to impress."

She enjoyed all the rituals and did what the other women did: she watched the game from a deck chair and chatted and applauded; mucking in to assist with the refreshments.

For Clive, the day illustrated the atmosphere of normality and fun in which Imogen felt happy and relaxed; where there was no expectation that she should either be treated as, or behave as, the star.

It had been arranged in advance that the Chelsea Nomads would stay overnight in rural Oxfordshire, so as to be rested for the match. Before they set out Clive suggested to Imogen, tentatively, that they might share a room in the Churchill Arms at Ascott-under-Wychwood.

"Fine by me," she laughed. "I do know you rather well."

That night they were lovers again, just like old times. It was beautiful.

When they woke in the morning, happy and just a little hung-over, Imogen was bursting, "I have got to have a pee!"

The pub was ancient and did not boast en suite bathrooms. The facilities were far away down a winding corridor. When Imogen tried to leave their room, she found that the old door had warped and was jammed. As hard as he tried, Clive could not budge it.

By now, they were both bursting, bursting and laughing. Fortunately, knowing that boozers wake up thirsty, Clive had obtained two pint jugs of water, one for each of them.

Amidst much hilarity, Imogen somehow improvised and the jugs were then emptied into the flowerbed below.

Laughing they fell into each other's arms and back into bed.

It was like it used to be, all those years ago at LAMDA. "It was that kind of loving fun."

After the cricket match, they set off in Imogen's car with Clive at the wheel, conveying Imogen back to Putney.

During that long drive without any warning Imogen exploded. "An extraordinary, sudden outburst of vitriol and bitterness — sudden and extreme — based on the use that men make of women."

Imogen spat pure poison for 20 minutes — it came out of nowhere, springing from no argument or disagreement between them. Clive was stunned. It was shocking, frightening; she was someone he did not know. "It was as if the lovely weekend hadn't happened."

And just as abruptly, the torrent ceased and Imogen "reverted back to being a lovely person."

Looking back and seeking to explain Imogen's outburst, Clive says that he had no way of telling if she had been taking any pills.

She was not goading him, he says, she was not looking for a fight. It was almost ritualistic, something she had to get off her chest.

Perhaps she even chose that particular moment — the two of them en route in the car with him at the wheel — in order to spare him a more direct and prolonged confrontation. It was in a way, a protective thing.

By the time they reached Imogen's house in Putney it was getting dark.

"You don't have to go, do you?" said Imogen.

She did not want to be alone.

Nervously, Clive remained. They chatted for a while. Clive cannot recall the exact year, but he had no inkling of her second marriage. Clive had no idea that Andrew Knox even existed.

Imogen took Clive on a guided tour of the garden and parts of the house. She was very proud of her house and made a special point of showing off the fountain in the garden, a lit statue framed by beaded strands of water, like a glass birdcage; a bit of kitsch, a bit of fun.

As the tour progressed, Imogen began to interject with references to her marriage to Kenneth Ives. "She spoke about it as if it was a really deep hurt."

The references to Kenneth Ives came out of the blue. It was the first that Clive had heard of the loss of their baby.

Imogen was quite calm and relaxed, talking about it in a very matter-of-fact way. It was a very mixed conversation; one minute she would be speaking about a flowerbed or the statue and the next minute about the marriage. And so to bed...

But this was not going to be a repeat of the loving fun of that perfect, vintage night in leafy Oxfordshire.

Imogen lay down on the bed like a piece of meat. "Now you can do what you want with me," she said in a strange, dead voice.

Clive's heart sank. This was not something that his Jen would have said.

They did make love. But this time Imogen was someone Clive did not know. Unlike their night at the Churchill Arms she was extremely passive. She did not seem to want enjoyment.

Perhaps she felt that she ought to. It seemed to Clive that "she wanted the company more than the sex. It was the difference," says Clive, "between making love with and making love to a person."

The loving fun had died.

CHAPTER NINE
CURTAIN

1980 saw Imogen embark upon a marathon tour in Bill Kenwright's production of Richard Harris's successful comedy about a local cricket club, *Outside Edge*, that extended from February through to August.

"I owe my career," says Bill Kenwright. "to people like Imogen Hassall, who went off in the sticks and toured and toured, week in, week out."

The production was a case of keeping up with the cast changes. There seemed to be fresh faces at every venue.

Jennifer Wilson does not appear on every playbill, but she was there long enough to get to know Imo. "She was a delightful personality to be with when not depressed...she always seemed to be very generous and warm. I certainly liked her a lot...she was, we said, sometimes, as mad as a hatter, but I think everyone loved her...she had a very big heart."

Geoffrey Davies was another who did not stay for the entire run. He was there at the beginning and remembers that Imogen was having great difficulties in rehearsal. "The director came up to me and said 'I'm very worried about Imogen, I don't think she's going to be up to learning the lines.' " Geoffrey promised to have a word with Imogen about it; she was clearly very upset. "Oh," she said. "I'm not going to be able to learn it."

Imogen's character, Ginnie, spent a great deal of her time bikini-clad, reclining on a sun-lounger in her garden reading magazines. To Geoffrey the solution seemed obvious. "Have all your dialogue down in the magazines. If you do it now, we have two weeks of rehearsals left, you'll know it..."

Imogen was delighted. She and Geoffrey used to drive in together to rehearsals and, when he came to collect her on the following Monday, she was very pleased with herself. "I've done it, I've done all my lines in the magazines, I spent all weekend doing it."

From that moment on the rehearsals were a different ballgame altogether. "This is wonderful!" said the director.

By opening night Imogen was not even glancing at the lines concealed in her magazines; she knew them.

Norman Rossington recalls Imogen with great fondness, "She didn't do things by halves." He speaks of her "wicked sense of humor—she made me laugh a lot."

Bill Kenwright appreciated Imogen's loyalty to him and the people she was working with. On a previous occasion, his offer to Imogen of a relatively humble tour was competing with the more glamorous and lucrative prospect of a West End show. When that show's producer phoned Imogen, her response was, "I'd love to do it, but I do love Bill, he fucks me so beautifully."

Bill Kenwright received a call from his stunned rival—"no actress has ever spoken to me like that!"

As to whether he had ever bedded Imogen—"I'm not sure that I did," says Bill Kenwright. "I don't think I did. I think Imogen had it in her mind that I did."

Bill Kenwright does not remember the bad times. Imogen was not just another actress working for him—"she was very much a close friend. She wasn't like an employee, not at all. She was like one of the family, always coming into the office for a cup of tea."

Rod Coton, Executive Producer at Bill Kenwright Ltd, echoes Bill's warm sentiments with regard to Imogen. His most vivid recollections, however, are reserved for Imogen's mother.

Outside Edge: **Amanda in the white hat, Maggie in fur, Jimmy seated second from left with Norman on his left, Imogen is back row left**

Eve Hassall as she advanced in years remained a force to be reckoned with. She was living in a flat in Kensington, a stone's throw from Harrod's; and there are tales of a colorful lifestyle, of men and alcohol. In 1980, due perhaps to dwindling fortunes and capacity, Imogen would be obliged to uproot her mother and move her into a home—an experience which Imogen found so stressful and dispiriting that it incited yet another cry for help.

Returning from some social event, Rod Coton and his party were giving Hassall mother and daughter a lift to their respective homes. Having stopped en route to deposit Imogen on her doorstep, Rod was startled to see Eve, somewhat the worse for wear for drink, advance toward him with a predatory gleam in her eyes. "How would you like to make an old woman very happy?"

Eve had clearly been a beauty in her youth but she was well past her prime. Alarmed, Rod retreated, but not quickly enough. Eve was upon him, thrusting her tongue into his mouth.

Rod Coton tells this story with immense relish; and it is with such relish and much affection that, by and large, all the Hassalls are remembered, from grandfather John to Imogen.

Jimmy Ellis became established in the role of the cricket club skipper in *Outside Edge*. He is also remembered with great affection by his colleagues as the leader of the gang.

He met Imogen for the first time on the tour of *Outside Edge*. "She had a film star aura that was never fulfilled. It needed somebody to say 'this girl has got to be turned into a star.' She had an extraordinary, particularly feline kind of sex appeal. She should have been a star but nobody had the foresight, which they might have had in a Continental country."

Imogen herself may have lacked the necessary will to grasp at stardom, but much of it was due to that peculiarly British Carry On attitude to a pretty girl. The French, of course, would also have had Imogen's clothes off, but it would have been "in something with some purpose, with a script by Jean-Paul Sartre, " suggests Jimmy Ellis.

Imogen, says Jimmy, was "a great flirt, wonderful fun—it was like being at school almost. I could never work out what age she was. She seemed to me to be a perpetual little child.

"My fondest memory of her is that she was a great trouper and a great communicator. She went on smiling every night and gave it her best. It's not a job for a spoiled little film star, the spoiled little film stars don't hang around much for that kind of thing."

Imogen, Jimmy insists, did the business. She had her problems, that was obvious; but on the tour of *Outside Edge* she was a thorough professional. "I couldn't have faulted her, none of it seemed to affect her work. She managed to hang on in there till the curtain came down. We all had to do the same and then it's playtime after that."

Imogen and Jimmy formed a special bond as the tour progressed. They flirted like crazy, but it was just for fun. Jimmy was recently and very happily married and Imogen was very happy for him and would often tell the newlyweds how lucky they were and how much she envied them. Jimmy's wife liked Imogen very much and was always concerned that she was being looked after; and Jimmy trusted his wife's instincts. "There were no games—Imogen played no games with me. She never played any games either on or offstage, except for fun; larking about, fooling around in the wings. That's how you keep sane on tour. She never overdid it. She got herself on there and did the job."

And Jimmy knew that there was much more to Imogen than just fun. She was far from superficial. Like so many who knew her, he appreciated her intelligence and enjoyed her company and their conversations. "I found her complex and interestingly complex."

She was also dangerous. She was someone that he would have been wary of becoming involved with, even if he had been footloose and fancy free. "You might think you were just fooling around and find yourself in very deep water."

No doubt many men had floundered in that deep, dark water. Whether she saw him as a kind of father or elder brother figure, he cannot say. He was a rare man, a man whom Imogen trusted. Those rare men have very special memories of Imogen.

Amanda Richardson shared digs with Imo during the tour and, although Amanda was a younger and a junior actress, the two of them became very close within a short space of time. "She was great fun and spoke her mind when other people would be afraid to do so. She was very kind to me and we looked after one another on tour."

Amanda also remembers that Imogen was disillusioned. "Most of her problems at the time I knew her were because she was addicted to the prescribed drug Tuinal, which is now banned. She was apparently put on it at the age of about 18 with her mother's consent."

According to Amanda, Imogen was quite open about the tranquilizers and carried them about with her in her handbag. She was bitter that her mother had put her on this drug and was desperate to come off it.

At one point, they went to a doctor, who cut down her dose and gave her Valium instead.

Being Imogen, her own efforts to combat her addiction were extreme, distressing and comic. She would simply stop taking the pills for a day with peculiar side effects.

On stage in the middle of a scene with Amanda, Imogen suffered a sudden attack of lockjaw and could barely mumble her lines. Fortunately, the script placed her in the sun lounger with a book, which she was able to use to mask her face, while Amanda somehow contrived to speak for the both of them.

Just as suddenly, the attack passed and Imo sent the whole episode up afterwards with great hilarity.

That was Imogen—tragedy and comedy.

Sharing digs with her, Amanda was able to witness Imogen's midnight miseries at close quarters.

At night, Imogen would take her last scheduled dose of Tuinal. Only then did she appear able to relax enough to eat something. She would get up at 2 a.m. and gobble honey sandwiches.

Imogen had only recently split up with Andrew Knox and Amanda saw that she was still very upset.

Imogen, clutching at straws, was desperate to cling to her failed second marriage.

She dragged Amanda with her for moral support on an ill-conceived, impulsive visit to her aged in-laws in Berwick-upon-Tweed where the grand old Hollywood actor Alexander Knox lived in his castle.

Predictably, the visit was a disaster. Alexander and his wife gave Imogen a frosty welcome. Imogen's dog was dying and she herself had a terrible bout of flu.

Imogen slept in a bed she had once shared with Andrew and was very upset.

Her in-laws thought that her illness was only an excuse to stay and made it plain that she had outstayed what cold welcome she had received. Still very ill, Imogen was sent home to London while Amanda went back to the tour.

On this occasion Imogen's illness was genuine but there were times when her ailments were self-induced, imaginary; when she could not face the day, could not steel herself for the evening's performance—like a child that does not want to get out of bed and go to school.

In April 1980 *Outside Edge* was residing for a week at Lincoln. Bill Kenwright's diary noted three successive entries:

April 15—Imogen off.

April 16—Imogen—she was worried that I had got upset with her because
    she was off.

April 17—Imogen

It was so like her, not childish but childlike. To call someone childish, to tell them that they are being childish, is to belittle them. They are shallow, annoying. Childlike is something very different, more complex, fascinating, often captivating, sometimes disturbing. It was Imogen's innocence—"one can be falling into bed but still be innocent"—her eagerness to please; to make an impression; her need for reassurance and for protection; her desire to give love and to be loved. "There would always be that kind of phone message—Imogen off—Imogen the next day—is she still loved?"

Amanda Richardson recalls when she was on the Tuinal Imogen "did not really know what she was doing"—and she was drinking.

She was dreading the approach of 40. Although she was still only 38, Imogen would tell people that she was 40 and then burst into tears afterward if they failed to say that she did not look it.

As she got older Imogen's features changed in a way that was characteristically Hassall. Her face, like her father's before her, became broader. Apparently, it was something that troubled her.

Imogen's friend Suzanna Leigh remembers an incident at a party. A guest greeting Imogen called out "Hi, pugface!" She was not pleased.

She would always do her own thing, says Amanda, and hang the consequences.

"Oh, don't do it!" went up the constant cry. But Imo would go right ahead. At the regular press calls her colleagues would brace themselves. "She wouldn't ignore a crass remark."

And the press was always happy to see her.

"The drugs kept her unstable," says Amanda. "She could just turn on people."

There was a night at a restaurant in Aberdeen. Imo took offense at something unseen and unheard by anyone else and suddenly got up and flounced out into the pouring rain. She must have found a hotel, for she was not seen again that night. "Imogen did a lot of flouncing. She had a very good exit."

The costume budget for *Outside Edge* was very modest and the outfits provided did not match up to Imo's high standards.

"Bugger that!" she said, and took herself off to Harrod's. She outfitted herself as she thought appropriate and sent the bill to the theatre.

"Imogen always wore fabulous outfits," says Amanda. "But not always right for the occasion."

Once, Imo and Amanda found themselves in Imo's sporty brown Datsun—"too fast for her"—at a lonely petrol station in Handsworth. This was 1980 and Handsworth was a notorious urban jungle, a wasteland with the reputation of a war zone.

While Amanda made herself as small as possible, huddled inside the car, Imo, resplendent in a fur coat, high heels and pearls, strode about in the rain, declaiming, affecting to be thrown entirely by the simply outrageous notion of a self-service petrol pump.

"Do you actually mean that one has to put in the petrol oneself!" she exclaimed in her most ladylike and commanding tones.

Every inch the Lady, Imo simply stood there in the rain in her fur coat, holding out the nozzle disdainfully by her fingertips until a little man in overalls came running and put the petrol in for her. "Oh, how very kind. You're a sweetie!"

The tour of *Outside Edge* was an endurance race, lasting some 24 weeks. It must have taken its toll on Imogen, physically and mentally, but wherever she went, her charm left a lasting impression on those she met, however fleetingly.

"You're fantastic!" she wrote in the visitor's book belonging to stage door keeper Tony Burns. "It would be very cliché of me to say I thought Imogen Hassall was a lovely, vibrant, engaging, charming young lady, but that is the truth in her case. She was very kind."

For Maggie Guess touring with Imo was always an adventure.

The tour took in embattled Northern Ireland. At the airport, Imo was nervous and bored—"she had a very low boredom threshold," says Maggie. "I hate flying. I can't cope with this, let's go to the bar..." One drink led to another and by the time their plane touched down Imo was exuberant.

Imogen's autograph in a stage door keeper's guestbook

The company clambered into a waiting mini-van and set off for its lodgings. The sight of the British Army out on armed patrol was not something that they were accustomed to.

"Oh look!" shrieked Imo. "A soldier!"

The bemused squaddies did their best to look professional as Imo had her head out of the window of the mini-van shouting and waving at them. "We're terrorists in here, you can come and shoot us! We're IRA!"

Normally, says Maggie, if you just said, "Shut up, Imo, you're over the top!" she would calm down and behave herself. This time it took the combined weight of all of her companions nervously eyeing those guns to pin her down and gag her.

Hillary Crane remembers the trip across the Irish Sea vividly. It was the one and only time that she was thrown out of digs. It was a case of guilt by association and the culprit was Imogen Hassall. "She turned up at the airport wearing a very amazing all-in-one silver trouser suit and silver boots. She looked like a spaceman."

According to plan, the traveling players arrived eventually at Coleraine, a small, unpretentious and unsophisticated town not far from Belfast.

Accommodation had been pre-arranged in a local guest house. The landlady, Hillary recalls, was quite literally staggered by the sight of Imo, dazzling in her silver space suit. Imo, meanwhile, was singularly unimpressed by the facilities. "I'm not staying in this fucking dump!"

The landlady was outraged. She was not going to stand for that kind of foul language in her house. "Be off with you!"

In the wrong place at the wrong time, Hillary was also evicted. Homeless, they wandered the streets of Coleraine knocking on doors until they were accepted at another equally modest boarding house run by a husband and wife.

According to Hillary the husband "nearly died from lust," when he saw Imo standing on his doorstep.

It was an austere bread and breakfast. Breakfast did not mean breakfast in bed, but Imo—who had been given the best room in the house—had hers brought up on a tray by the salivating husband.

The Life and Death of Imogen Hassall   **183**

Imogen was a night bird, her internal clock unbalanced by the pills—the poppers, as Hillary describes them.

Imo would often be restless in the small hours because she was, says Hillary, "incredibly lonely" and because of the pills, which seemed to make her very hungry.

Hillary says that for all her loneliness Imogen had two boyfriends at the time, but one of them was married and the other, Imo said, was giving her a lot of trouble. She used to talk about how much she wanted to settle down and have children, but Hillary was never sure if she really meant it.

During their stay in Coleraine Imo took a shine to "two soldier boys" and went out with them in the evening. Exactly what transpired remained shrouded in mystery, but she came back to the digs very late and starving.

In the wee small hours, unable to bear her hunger any longer, Imo crept downstairs to the kitchen. Searching desperately for something to eat, she pulled open a cupboard door only to have an avalanche of pots and pans come crashing down.

Fearing invaders, the proprietors of the guest house burst into the kitchen.

The husband's eyes bulged out. Imo was stark naked.

The lady of the house was furious. Imo was packed off upstairs, still hungry with only a tea towel to preserve her modesty.

As far as the local *Chronicle* was concerned, Imogen was a star. Keen anticipation of the arrival of *Outside Edge* featured largely on its arts page; an award-winning West End comedy, coming to Coleraine. Bill Kenwright, it said, had "gathered together probably the strongest cast currently on tour"—and "the beautiful Imogen Hassall" in the opinion of the *Chronicle* was one of the headliners.

Imogen, said the *Chronicle*, was "out to prove that she has a lot more talent than the gossip columns give her credit for."

However, while Imogen features largely in the advance publicity, she is not mentioned at all in the actual review of the play. It is as if she does not exist. Interestingly, it is noted that other members of the cast "coped well with some last minute personnel changes." Could this, therefore, have been one of Imogen's spontaneous off days? Several of her colleagues on odd occasions throughout the long tour, found themselves re-shuffled so that one or another of them could at very short notice, play the absent Imogen's part.

And it would be just Imogen's luck that she would be off on the very night that someone came to review the play.

Maggie Guess saw Imogen over-the-top. She also saw the other side of her, her lack of confidence—when Imo came in search of moral support.

By this time Eve Hassall was residing in what Maggie describes as "an awful Council-run Home." Imogen obviously found it an ordeal to visit her there and asked Maggie to come along.

Imo was decked out in her full film star regalia—the high heels and fur cape. "My mother will expect me to arrive as a film star. I've got to do the bit for Mummy."

When they arrived at what Maggie remembers as a dreary and depressing place, Imogen dragged her in too. "I don't want to go in on my own."

Eve, while aged, appeared to be in full command of her faculties and made a big thing out of showing her daughter the star off to her fellow residents. Imogen behaved accordingly, putting on a show. "Hullo, Mummy darling, kiss, kiss!"

Like Amanda Richardson, Maggie recalls that Imogen's family seemed very far in the background. Amanda says that Imogen hardly saw her brother Nicholas.

Imogen struck Maggie as a rather lonely figure. She appeared to have "no bosom pals, no life-long friends." Unlike other members of the cast, Imogen never seemed to be going off with friends who had come to see her in the show. She hardly took part in any of the daytime things that the company got up to, unless it was to do with publicity, a press and/or photo call.

This may have been the impression that Imogen gave, and she would often describe herself as a lonely person, but others remember her as very much one of the gang. And surely she would have had some friends who came to see her: Jackie Ing-ham, for one, and Clive Graham.

Maggie remembers she so desperately hated to be alone. Day and night, she needed to have someone with her. And if there was no one, she would pick up the phone or be up and off to the King's Road, where she was almost bound to bump into somebody.

Imogen's craving for company was all the more desperate because her irrational impulses,

Happy New Year—Imogen is ready to party

extreme mood swings and spicy inventions plus the demands that she made upon friends' time and patience would drive people away.

She was always on the phone to them; they saw her almost every day. She might even ask them to sit up at her bedside with her into the early hours until she drifted off to her precious sleep.

How often did she allow a man into her bed simply because she did not want to be alone?

Her prop, or so it appeared to Maggie, was her pills. On a night train to Scotland, Imogen explained to Maggie about the pill that she took at night to knock her out and the pill in the morning to wake her up—and this on top of the booze.

"She was screwed up by unscrupulous, silly, trendy '60s and '70s doctors," says Jimmy Ellis, "who dispensed any old bloody thing to unhappy ladies, actresses; uppers, downers—they have a lot to answer for."

It was in the evenings, Jimmy recalls, that Imogen could get into trouble, although "she was adorable when she'd had a few glasses of wine. Always at night it was look after Imogen time."

She was very much an essential member of a happy family, a happy company, loyal to each other. There was a great team spirit.

They never went anywhere without her; it was always "Where's Imo?" and if necessary there was always someone to take her home. On at least one occasion Jimmy had to put Imogen to bed. He felt duty bound to call his wife and tell her where he was; she insisted that he stay and make sure that Imogen was all right.

Imogen was still pining desperately for motherhood and hoping for Mr. Right, although now, she said, she was looking for a normal man. "All I want to do is be settled down with children and not with somebody like an actor."

Jimmy Ellis says that Imogen "had an obsession—she desperately wanted to be a mother." She had "a burning desire" that was almost out of all proportion. And she feared that it was getting too late.

There were men, mostly anonymous. Imogen was still trying to become pregnant with near fatal consequences.

It was a Friday evening performance in Watford—Jimmy Ellis says that it was something of a VIP night attended by such luminaries as the Head of Drama at the BBC. "Oh my God," said Imo, "I've got a terrible stomach ache!"

She had been telling people that she was pregnant—the most likely candidate was a nameless sales rep—but not everyone believed her.

Maggie believed her and told her to be careful, advising her to see a doctor—"you're no spring chicken, you know"—but Imo just shrugged and said, "I will when the tour finishes."

There was always something wrong with Imo; she was always complaining of something. "You never knew with Imogen," says Jimmy Ellis. "Because she was up and down."
"Oh, take an aspirin," someone suggested.

Imogen was clearly in agony but there was no proper understudy. So Imogen, the trouper, went on.

While playing the scene, Maggie saw that Imogen was deathly gray and was sweating buckets. Jimmy Ellis' wife Robina happened to be in the audience, seated very close to the front. Imogen in her bikini was reclining downstage right in the sun lounger. "She was all goosepimply and looked kind of gray. She looked dreadful—in pain."

Imogen was able to play the scene until she had to stand up. Then, according to Jimmy Ellis, she "jack-knifed and just dropped, collapsed." The others all came and gathered around her. Norman Rossington scooped her up in his arms.

Norman recalls that "the audience thought it was a gag." So as not to alarm or disillusion them, he made a grimace and carried Imogen offstage.

Jimmy Ellis remembers a hasty combination of ad-libbing, covering up like crazy. Meanwhile, in the wings Norman Rossington was kneeling by Imogen's side speaking to her, comforting her. From the stage, Jimmy saw Imogen rise and force herself back on again. She got into position and tried to come out with a line only to collapse in agony once more.

This time the curtain came down. Jimmy Ellis told the audience—who were still half convinced what they were seeing was part of the play—that, for once, the show was not going to go on.

The theatre manager sent for a doctor. When the doctor arrived, his diagnosis was immediate and dramatic, "I've got minutes to save this girl's life, she's bleeding to death."

Imogen had dragged herself onstage enduring the agonies of an ectopic pregnancy. The fertilized egg had developed outside the uterus within a fallopian tube, which, the doctor said, had now burst.

Imogen was rushed to hospital.

That evening, Maggie was having dinner with some casting people. "Oh, was Imo drunk again?" someone said. The next day, another actress had materialized out of nowhere and was to be seen rehearsing with the company manager. She performed the Saturday matinee from the book.

No news of Imogen's condition was given to the cast, so Maggie and Amanda went to see her at the hospital. They found Imogen weak and very distressed. "I've had the production

Tuesday's Child

office on the phone. They want to know if I can be back at work on Monday. Please get them off my back!"When it sank in that Imogen was not going to be back at work on Monday, she was advised to go on holiday; so she went on a short cruise to rest and recuperate.Her colleagues awaited her return with eager anticipation. They missed her laughter..

There must have been a warm welcome for her upon her return; and the excitement was not long in coming—the Big Fight—the Battle of the Green Room. It all began with a kindness.

Miss X was yet another newcomer to the cast. She was very nice to Imogen after she came out of hospital. Imogen stayed with her for a couple of weeks and Miss X even insisted that she borrow some of her cruise clothes when it was proposed that the invalid take a holiday.

Unfortunately, Imo left items of Miss X's clothing lying on the seat of her car and some of them were stolen while Imo was busy indoors showing Amanda a new fur coat.

What had been a case of bad chemistry flared into a feud when Miss X demanded the return of the rest of her clothes, after Imo had hung on to them interminably—having neglected mentioning the theft.

Miss X had the surviving garments flung back at her in a crumpled ball in the middle of a theatre car park. A screaming match escalated into fisticuffs and the two of them had to be separated by other members of the cast.

An uneasy truce did not last for long. Battle was resumed in the Green Room at the Cambridge Theatre.

The cubicle-like dressing rooms at the Cambridge were arranged in a square around the Green Room, which was furnished with comfy chairs and settees. Members of the cast, including Miss X, were in their respective dressing rooms beginning their preparations for the performance.

It was Imo's custom to relax before the show by taking a short nap.

"We've got hours, darling," she announced, stretching out on a settee. "I'll have a little sleep."

Miss X's relaxation was her portable television. It was loud and the walls were very thin.

"Can we have the TV down," shouted Imo in her most commanding tone. "I want to sleep now!"

Miss X refused to comply.

"Why are you always so difficult?" demanded Imo.

"Talk about difficult!" Miss X retorted.

Instantly they were "yelling and screaming and swearing." Imo struck Miss X and scratched her face. The company manager had to pry them apart, and the combatants went onstage that evening with their battle scars thinly disguised with make-up.

Nick Hirst, then in his mid-20s, joined the *Outside Edge* tour as deputy stage manager during Imogen's absence. She was due back soon and the entire company was anticipating her return; it was a major event.

When Imo reappeared, somewhat restored and deeply tanned, she spoke of her recent misfortunes with typical relish. "I nearly died—onstage, darling—I nearly died!"

While she was away, Nick Hirst and Amanda Richardson had become very close. Imogen trusted Amanda as a friend and so Nick became a friend too. They made a comfortable three-some with Imo keeping a caring eye on her younger colleagues' progress in their relationship. There was a nice balance between them—by day, Imogen was like a mother or an older sister to Nick and Amanda; by night, they were her keepers. Imogen, Nick recalls, was still a bit frail; he suspected that she might be occasionally in pain but she tried to hide it.

Nick remembers the *Outside Edge* tour as both a good-natured time and a drunken binge across the nation. Touring is an intimate exercise and the members of a company get to know each other well, warts and all. But this, by and large, was a company that gelled and Nick's memories are happy ones.

There was a social core—with occasional variations—of Jimmy Ellis, Amanda, Nick, Imo and Norman Rossington. Those were the bad old days of restrictive licensing laws, which did not suit actors, whose average working day lasted from 6 p.m. to 10:30 p.m. But they had an uncanny knack, wherever they found themselves, for sniffing out a suitable venue for out-of-hours drinking. Regularly they were to be found entrenched behind locked pub doors, boozing into the early hours.

Actors have long been legendary drinkers but this band of happy troupers met its match in the form of the Britain's elite special forces, the Special Air Service.

As Jimmy Ellis recalls, the encounter took place in Hereford, home of the SAS. The company had, as planned, played a week in that town and were surprised when they were asked to stay on and make it two. A two-week run seemed a lot to expect of Hereford and there was a suspicion that the tour management had not got its act together.

Thus, the troupe found itself with a Sunday off that was not preoccupied by traveling. Sunday in Hereford with time on their hands; a bleak prospect.

There was, of course, the pub for a liquid lunch but when the pub closed, the long afternoon stretched before them. "The boys tried to break away, but the girls were in a giggly mood and wouldn't let us out of their sight."

Eventually, they lit upon what advertised itself as the Hereford Farmers' or Young Farmers' Club. Seeking manly pursuits the boys gained entry on the pretext of wanting a game of snooker. Not to be put off, the girls piled in behind them and refused to be deflected by the unpromising prospect of "a badly run down, dowdy old hall with two snooker tables."

Chalk and decent cues were in short supply and "as the girls still insisted on hanging around," Jimmy Ellis approached the proprietor and inquired as to whether something such as lemonade might be provided for his female companions.

"Oh, it's a drink you want," replied their host. "Why didn't you say so?"

The troupe were ushered into another private room which was full of men who were busy consuming daunting volumes of alcohol. "They were quite spaced out but terribly polite; polite and gentlemanly in spite of the drink."

These men were obviously not young farmers. Upon inquiry, the proprietor told the astonished actors that this was the Special Air Service and these were the very heroes of the recent Iranian Embassy Siege, freshly debriefed and under orders to go and unwind and get drunk for two or three days.

Actors are as persistent as any journalist when they get a whiff of a good story. Boldly, they approached the SAS men and said tell us all about it.

The SAS were charmed by their unexpected and glamorous guests and were surprisingly relaxed and forthcoming. "It was a perfectly ordinary, sociable day; the girls were open-mouthed."

The SAS told the traveling players that, as actors, they would be able to appreciate the necessary and detailed preparation that had gone into the storming of the Iranian Embassy. Like a stage set, as exact a mock-up as could be achieved had been constructed, down to the last light switch and door handle. It had taken many full-scale dress rehearsals before they were ready to go in—while, unknowing, the world chaffed at the delay.

Jimmy Ellis remembers one SAS man in particular, who was Irish and smaller than the rest. His mates joked that he was always the one who went in first as look-out, shinning up the drainpipes.

Jimmy noticed that the small SAS man was gazing enraptured into Imogen's eyes. Identifying Jimmy as the leader of the gang, he approached him with all due deference, "Excuse me, Mister, would it be out of order if I bought Miss Hassall a big bunch of roses?"

It was a Sunday afternoon and Hereford was shut. "She'd love it, but where are you going to get them?"

Despite the influence of the alcohol, the SAS man bent down and retrieved a roll of banknotes from his sock.

"Leave it to me."

The small man exited and duly reappeared some time later, bearing "the biggest bunch of roses you'd ever seen."

Imo was glowing. She accepted this token of admiration graciously and with great ceremony. Her admirer, having made his grand and gallant gesture, was satisfied and withdrew happy and contented—mission accomplished.

There is another version of this story—substitute Amanda Richardson for Imogen.

According to Nick Hirst, Amanda was the object of the SAS man's infatuation and the flowers were presented to her. For once, Imo was not the center of attention.

Besides, says Nick, Imogen might not even have been there. He recalls that Imogen could hardly drink because she was still on medication after her collapse. She might, therefore, have felt out of place at such heavy drinking sessions.

But it is a good story and it is true, as Jimmy Ellis says, that "Imogen inspired that sort of thing...men fell at her feet."

Imogen could be the Gracious Lady in the presence of her admirers. Nick Hirst observed she could also be a bit of an exhibitionist.

During the company's time at Hereford, while the rest of the cast had to make do with assorted digs, the company manager was staying at a local country house. The garden had a swimming pool and the company manager invited the troupe to make use of it.

It was a lazy, hazy, slightly drunken Summer's day and Imo, as she often did, decided to take things as far as they could go and sunbathe in the nude. This was much to the consternation of the company manager, who was anxious to spare the blushes of the owners of the house. Imo would not have given a hoot what anyone thought.

"...And where did she get that tan?" wrote one envious provincial critic, seeing Imo, bikini-clad, stage right, reclining decoratively on her sun lounger, still sensational at 38.

Imogen's all over tan was striking. Those were the days of fanatical sun worship, before ozone depletion and cancer scares. And she had a head start when it came to bronzing her head-turning body; her exotic genes. It does not come across in all the films, TV shows and photographs, but everyone remembers how naturally dark she was, how beautiful she was.

"She enjoyed being naked," says Bill Kenwright. "Whenever one knocked at the door, where most actresses covered up, I think she'd get it off before you walked in the door."

Nick Hirst's fondest memories of the tour, however, are of the daily domesticity of touring, of the domestic Imogen looking after everyone and a comfortable threesome, sharing digs.

In particular, Nick remembers a humble terraced house in Liverpool 8. Their bubble of cozy domesticity was an oasis of calm in a volatile, notorious neighborhood, where the simmering menace of gangs loitering on street corners would, in time, boil over into full-scale rioting.

Undaunted, Imo would set forth in the mornings to the corner shop. The arrangement was that Imogen and Amanda shared a room, while Nick had a room to himself. However, Nick and Amanda had become involved. One morning, Imo set forth to plunder the corner shop for milk and cigarettes. When she returned, her young colleagues were sharing Amanda's bed. Imo climbed quietly back into her own bed on the other side of the room. Too shy to get up and exit, naked in front of Imogen, Nick stayed where he was and so the three of them slept on.

Nick's image of Imo on the tour of *Outside Edge* is of her in the kitchen in a dressing gown, her hair wrapped in a towel, frying pan in hand, happily cooking breakfast.

Imogen's reviews for *Outside Edge* tended to concentrate on her bikini. "Raven-haired beauty Imogen Hassall is certainly bowling the fellows over in her latest role. For the sultry actress has the men in a spin when she appears in a skimpy bikini during Richard Harris's hilarious new play..."

38 and still a pin-up. She was always there for the photo calls, ready, able and willing with a daring neckline, showing a leg.

Her performance, as well as her bikini, drew favorable notices. She was "both decorative and delightfully dismissive," using "an elegant figure and throaty voice to delineate Ginnie, 'the scourge of Sainsbury's'."

Norman Rossington says that Imogen was "very good. She knew what she was about; she knew the job. She wasn't just a figure and a face."

"...one other of the cast of nine deserves special mention: Imogen Hassall," noted the *Stevenage Comet*, "as the poisonously jealous, neurotic wife of Bob...spitting venom from her sun lounger..."

"She wasn't a bad actress," agrees Bill Kenwright. "When you put her onstage you knew you were going to get a good performance."

The problem was that she was notoriously unreliable. Imogen was habitually late, very late; and sometimes she was off. But there was no question that she was capable. "She could have worked forever. She had style, confidence. She had confidence onstage, great aplomb. Certain actors, like footballers, once they have the ball you feel safe. Imogen, when she walked on stage, she had the audience in the palm of her hand."

During rehearsals Imogen told Geoffrey Davies, "I think I've got it together, I think I'm ready to get into the character parts."

Geoffrey believes that had Imogen lived, she might have developed into a very interesting character actress. It was her underlying vulnerability that gave her depth. "Even when she was playing quite brittle parts her vulnerability came over, which made it very interesting."

Geoffrey was surprised and pleased to hear Imogen speak with such mature reflection. What she told him made him hopeful for her: "I'm quite looking forward now to moving into the character parts. I've resigned myself to the fact that I can't play the glamorous parts anymore. I'm quite resigned to the fact that I'm going to move into the character parts and I'm looking forward to it."

Geoffrey soon realized that it was just a phase, "when she was in a logical mood. When she was in another mood and became illogical, that was all forgotten."

For the benefit of the press, Imo was striking a positive note. "I keep fairly busy, but although I do film and TV work, theatre is my first love because of the close communication with the audience."

According to Imogen, there was "an American TV series with Tony Curtis, in the pipeline" when the tour finished in September.

"She just wanted to work," says Bill Kenwright. "The idea of a career that went somewhere was lost in the ether. It was just I want to work and anyone that will give me a job means they love me and they want me and that's what I want to do."

The breaking up of a happy company, says Jimmy Ellis, is a small bereavement, and Imogen was to miss her *Outside Edge* family dreadfully in the remaining weeks of her life.

The veterans speak of that tour and of Imogen with a special fondness. "An old-fashioned romp," says Jimmy Ellis. "Everybody was delightfully mad."

On Maggie Guess's shelf is a little gift that Imo gave her when the tour closed. It is a large, decorative glass test tube with a cork stopper—a joke, a novelty, meant to be a kind of pocket flask—just the sort of thing that would have tickled Imo's fancy.

They got to know Imogen well on her final tour—heart and soul. Says Jimmy Ellis, "Her whole past, her whole career, seemed to go past our eyes like she was a drowning girl; that last tour summed up everything."

Nick Hirst had the impression that there was nothing in the offing after *Outside Edge*. Practically a neighbor, Nick remained in close touch with Imogen after the tour closed. They saw each other two or three times a week and spoke on the phone almost every day.

Peter Charlesworth last saw Imogen around the time of *Outside Edge*. He was having dinner with Norman Rossington and Imogen joined them at a restaurant in Hampstead. As so often with Imogen, her dinner companions were on edge all evening. This was a far cry from the bright young thing that Peter had first met in the early 1960s. "I got the impression that everything had finally beaten her—she was no longer in control of herself."

Inevitably, Imogen launched into a tirade about her father. The flow was irrational—"she was shooting off in 10 different tangents. As she took a few more glasses of wine the story changed—one minute from hate to the next minute what a great artiste he was, how talented he was and how she's kept all his work..."

In the course of a single evening, Peter saw the many Imogens flash by. "The personalities appeared like a pack of cards—one black, then a red one, then another black one, then two more red ones...there was the kind Imogen, warm—Imogen the gay—Imogen the impossible—Imogen the demented..."

Peter says that Imogen telephoned him not long after and said that she wanted to see him. "I edged round it as I'd done before—there was nothing you could do for her."

In 1980, Imogen had another new home. She left Putney and moved to a compact, semi-detached, ancient cottage in Crooked Billet, Wimbledon Village; on the edge of Wimbledon Common right next door to the Crooked Billet pub. "It saves a hell of a lot on replenishing the drinks cabinet—and if I'm hungry I can always pop in for a snack."

And company on tap, a crowd—better to be lonely in a crowd than lonely all alone—people she could take home with her when she did not want to be alone.

Nick Hirst recalls that Imo was "so proud of her little cottage," but he says that she was living beyond her means. There was vague talk of money coming from somewhere, but it never seemed to amount to anything. As Nick describes it, "she saved on the pennies but was extravagant with the pounds."

Imogen always overpsent with her constant generosity. Nick and Amanda were always having to talk her out of paying for everything. And there were her expensive impulses.

During the tour, Nick remembers, Imo was getting about at one time in a "clapped out" Lotus Elan. When a fellow female cast member acquired a brand new car, Imo promptly determined that she must have one too. She repeated this, almost like a mantra, while Nick toiled to talk her out of it.

Imogen was away on tour in *Outside Edge* for eight months and had hardly any opportunity to settle into her new home. But now, as she told the *Wimbledon News*, she was looking forward to some rest and relaxation.

She spoke at length about her family:

> Just recently, I've had the sad task of arranging for my mother to be taken
> into a home to be cared for and giving up her London flat.

The Life and Death of Imogen Hassall

Sorting through my mother's things was very nostalgic and brought back memories of a happy childhood...

The increased stress caused by the admission of her mother into a home had resulted in yet another overdose. Imogen, once again, was rushed to Queen Mary's Hospital.

"My father, Christopher Hassall, was an author and a poet," she explained, proudly pointing to shelves of his books.

"He wrote the official biography of Rupert Brooke. Rupert Brooke's bed is my most prized possession—I'd never part with it—no matter how hard up I might be. At the moment, I'm storing it in my spare bedroom—no, I've never tried sleeping on it—I'm reserving that for when I truly need inspiration," she said with a laugh.

"These paintings all around the cottage are by my grandfather—remember 'Skegness Is So Bracing'? I'm having some of them made into mirrors," she said.

"I remember Ivor Novello was a frequent visitor to the house when I was small. My father wrote many of the lyrics for the Novello musicals—remember 'Glamorous Nights' and 'I Left My Heart in an English Garden?'

"It wasn't done in those days to write pop! But he needed the money when my brother Nicholas (also a composer like Imogen's godfather, the late Sir William Walton) and I were small. His real love was poetry—and his really great friend was Sir Edward Marsh, Winston Churchill's private secretary."

The Official Version according to Imogen—nothing but fond memories and family pride. No one disputes that Imogen was very proud of her father's achievements. The rest is, like Imogen, a mass of contradictions.

A touch of sadness crept into the interview when Imogen spoke of a recent bereavement:

Recently, I had the painful experience of losing my 15-year-old doggie friend Ratty. We'd been through so much together—he went with me on tour and slept in my dressing room when I was on stage.

But he was too old and ill to go on any longer. I held him when the vet put him to sleep. It was awful to see him go, but I felt I owed it to him. After all, our pets stay with us when we die, don't they?

The death of Ratso was a grievous blow to Imogen at an especially vulnerable time.

Tentatively, the *Wimbledon News* reporter touched upon the subject of Imogen's stormy love life. Imogen struck a defiant note:

It's true. I've been dated by some of the world's most famous actors. But I'm through being used by men for their ego trips. At the moment I'm living alone—but I'm not lonely. I've got myself together. I'm my own woman nowadays.

The interview was published in the *Wimbledon News* on November 14, 1980. Imogen had two days to live.

Imogen snapped on a beach in Kenya by her friend Suzanna Leigh.

On November 13, Imogen appeared at a local chemist's with a doctor's prescription for 20 Dalmane sleeping pills, 20 Daraprim anti-malarial tablets, 50 Tuinal barbiturate tablets and 25 Valium. The chemist queried the large amounts but was satisfied by Imogen's explanation that she was due to go on holiday.

It was going to be a spectacular holiday — a month-long winter safari in Kenya. Imogen was anticipating it with enormous enthusiasm. She was telling everybody about it, showing off the glossy brochures.

The date of departure was November 16 and Imogen would be traveling with her friend Suzanna Leigh. "Imogen and I were bookends, soul mates."

Suzanna says that she does not recognize the stormy, unbalanced Imogen. They had their little spats, for sure, which they always laughed off afterward, but Imogen never inflicted her demons on her. Suzanna's Imogen did not dwell upon her problems with men and pills. Her friend was "always gregarious, fun." Their shared interests were in simple pleasures, such as plants and gardens at which, Suzanna recalls, Imogen excelled.

But Suzanna did not see Imogen all the time — it was not unusual for a year to go by, she says. And even if her troubles were not a topic of Imogen's conversation, Suzanna was made well aware of what lay beneath the surface.

By chance, Suzanna encountered Imogen at a health farm. Imogen's hands were peculiar, bent back because she had recently attempted to slit her wrists.

Suzanna was appalled. "How could you!"

Perhaps, she suggests, Imogen kept her problems largely to herself because she was wary of the reaction she would get; knowing that Suzanna, being a Catholic, would take a very dim view of the extreme expression of her anxieties, her cries for help.

They went way back, Imogen and Suzanna had wintered together in Africa before, spending days in the bush and on the beach, basking in a simpler and more honest lifestyle. Imogen was hugely popular there, embracing the local community body and soul. She did many good works such as helping to build churches and had a lot of fun judging beauty contests.

Once, Suzanna recalls, in the middle of one such competition, Imo fell into the swimming pool, but carried on regardless, dripping and laughing. "It was a funny, wonderful and truly spiritual time."

This holiday had a particular significance. This was going to be something special.

Suzanna and Imogen were both casualties—the walking wounded of life. This time, once and for all, they were going to get their heads together and sort themselves out!

According to Nick Hirst, by her own standards at least, Imogen had hit rock bottom. But he had the feeling that she was turning things around. "I thought that she had reached a level to re-invent herself with some strength."

He sensed that she had turned a corner, that she was starting to come to terms with herself and was in a position to rebuild her life. Perhaps her collapse and brush with death while on tour had touched upon her vulnerability and given her pause. The grand and dismissive manner that was so often the mask she wore, was, Nick is certain, only a mask. She put it up as a defense, behind which was a very soft, vulnerable, frightened person.

The Imogen that Nick Hirst knew was "the kind of person you could just sit with without talking, a very natural person." Theirs was a comfortable friendship, like brother and sister. They would do routine, ordinary things, such as going shopping in the supermarket for Imogen's groceries, or a quiet lunch in the pub, usually the Crooked Billet or the Hand In Hand. At this time, Nick says, dry white wine was Imo's tipple. She was not drinking spirits, perhaps because of her medication.

Imogen had even taken on a part-time job working in a Putney wine bar. "I bet you never thought you would see Imogen Hassall working behind a bar," she said to Nick. It sounded almost like an apology, as if she was apologizing to herself. "Not to worry," Nick replied. "We've all done it."

There were times, says Nick, in the last few months of her life when Imogen was happy in an uncomplicated way. She was always at her best when she was enjoying the company of friends she trusted.

One of those friends was Gary Hope. During the long interim between the early 1960s and the last 18 months of Imogen's life, she and Gary had hardly seen each other. Gary was married and was raising three children, living in a different world.

But Gary's world fell apart—he was now divorced and another serious relationship had also foundered. "It was a very gray moment in my life. I had my own problems, which were hell, trying to survive, sort my children out, get back on my own feet and so on. It was a very confusing time for me, I was in a very bad state myself."

Imogen and Gary came together again just after Gary's divorce. They saw a great deal of each other—"she was never off the phone to me"—each gave the other a shoulder to cry on, a sympathetic ear. Imogen was captivated by Gary's children. "She absolutely adored them...she worshipped those children."

Gary, often with his children, was a regular at the cottage in Crooked Billet for dinner or Sunday lunch. The children, adults now, remember Imogen fondly and still talk about her.

Imo was always ringing Gary and insisting gaily that he take her up to town. She had a stock phrase delivered in those refined tones for such occasions, "Darling, I'm a rich bitch. I'm going to put on all my furs, because I'm a fucking rich bitch!"

More often than not, Imo would sail into the National Westminster Bank on the King's Road. "Darling, I'll be with you in five minutes!"

Five minutes with Imogen could mean an hour and five minutes. She made many demands on Gary's time and energy, but these were demands that he was happy to meet—"keeping her company for the day, doing this or doing that, going out, that was fun."

He saw the changes. She had become very self-conscious and was always trying too hard to catch the eye. "She had lost her original magnetic appeal."

Gary used to take Imogen to the Chelsea Arts Club. They would talk about Imogen's faltering career. Gary advised her to "stop wagging the tail of the *Sun*, or the *News of the World*, the *Mirror*, what have you. You have qualities as a human being which are much more important than the physical beauty that you feel you have to resort to. If you let that come through, you will be accepted as an actress, you will find that your circle of influential friends will grow and develop and they will look after you and find you the work that you need to do. Don't be afraid of letting that come through."

"Stop all the slit skirts," he told her. "You can't walk about with your tits hanging out and your legs showing."

Imogen listened, but she would also laugh. She would always laugh.

"Her thoughts were all in the wrong place," Gary recalls. "She was having terrible problems with the media. But strip that away, sit with her quietly and talk to her, talk to the real Imo, and you'd see a completely different person."

The real Imogen, says Gary, "was someone that we did love. The higher side, which we all remember and love and talk about, it didn't dominate her life as much as it should have done. She allowed the lower side, which involved the cheap publicity, the cheap thrill, the temporary fix to take over. She was much too flippant in her attitude, she didn't care to concentrate and do the hard work necessary—she took the short cut, the quick cut—ring the press, get a photograph, show a tit, provoke people. The person that those who loved her remember, that had nothing to do with that at all—the real Imo wasn't allowed properly to emerge."

Gary was speaking rationally to an irrational, broken soul. He was asking Imogen to do the impossible.

Imogen's career, as Gary saw it, had come down to doing crap tours for crap money.

She was going to do a tour of Stoppard's *Dirty Linen* and told him boldly that she would refuse unless he was also in it. Gary can recall Imogen tearful and angry when she spoke about being on tour. She said that everyone was always trying to get into bed with her, because they all assumed that she was easy and available.

A male co-star once staged an elaborate campaign to get Imo into his bed. The scenario had him cooking an elaborate dinner for her at his flat. He wrote the script, built the set and rehearsed the actors, roping in reluctant colleagues as fellow dinner guests so it wouldn't look too obvious.

But obvious it was. Imo knew exactly what he was up to. As much as she liked him, and she liked him very much, she simply did not fancy him (the most awful words a man can hear: "I love you as a friend, but...").

Imo duly ate her fabulous dinner, over which her suitor had toiled so arduously. She drank his wine.

The strategic moment arrived, only to have Imo make one of her famous sweeping exits with a single ringing pronouncement, delivered in her grandest, most ladylike tones. "Jamais!"

Backstage, offstage, Imogen was a constant target for the male ego; but even as a teenager she could handle herself. Or so it seemed.

Imogen's fragile self-esteem was dented each and every time she was convinced that a man only wanted her for her body; but she needed the attention and the admiration. She distrusted all but a few rare men, yet she always had to have "input from a male." Perhaps sex was a tranquilizer and was in her opinion all she had to offer—to ensure that she was not left alone for the night.

"What I pitied her the most for," says Nicholas Hassall, "was the destructive attention of the male of the species in hormone over-charged mode."

His sister "took a lot of stick from that kind. To be around when it was happening was to be in on the initial stages of a classical zoo-based anthropological animal cliché. I have always hated the obvious and the blatant way those males attached to her..."

Men, Imogen would complain, only wanted her for one thing, but she was promiscuous. Did something in her seek to drive men to the brink of violence, sometimes beyond; was it an extreme, self-inflicted expression of her self-loathing; or was she finding physical proof of her private, intangible, inexplicable pain?

It is claimed that self-injury and self-mutilation are an expression of an urge to exercise control, at the very least over one's own body, when all else is out of control. No one has suggested that Imogen's bruises were ever self-inflicted, but some recall how she used to show them off. Did her bruises mean that she had won, that she had proved a point? That she was in control?

Imogen and men. A vicious circle that spun her round and round, until she lost her grip and fell off the edge of the world.

In the autumn of 1980, Imogen was resting. To pass the time she found herself a day job.

Walter Randall had first encountered Imogen in the late 1960s, when she strolled into his club on the King's Road in stellar company.

It was a night to remember. A surfeit of alcohol led to words that escalated into fisticuffs—a night encapsulated by the lasting image of a blood-spattered Rolls Royce.

Imogen ended up taking the casualties back to her pad for repairs.

It was in 1980 that Walter and Imogen became reacquainted, when, by chance, a mutual friend, Gary Hope, brought her along for Sunday lunch at Walter's flat in Richmond.

Walter was now the manager of Logan's Wine Bar in Putney. He and Imogen soon became friends. Just how it transpired that he also became her employer he cannot recall. "I don't for one minute think she did it for the money. She did it for something to do, just to see people."

It is traditional for resting actors to find employment in an environment offering ready access to food and alcohol.

"Four quid she used to get"—for working lunchtimes—"she boozed it or ate it."

Imogen was good at her job. She was there mainly for decoration and was immensely popular. People liked her. "She was very good with them and had them in fits of laughter. They just liked her as a person, as a human being. There was no big 'I am, I'm so and so,' no prima donna happenings with her. She was friendly with everyone."

It was not just a job to Imogen, says Walter—"she regarded it as fun, as a social event."

And Imo was making plans. She said that she wanted to stage a Novello production and produce it in tandem with Walter Randall. She had calculated it would cost about £80,000, The owner of Logan's was going to put up half and Imogen said that she would be able to raise the other £40,000.

Crispin Thomas' *Ivor* had opened at the Northcott Theatre in Exeter not long after the start of the *Outside Edge*. *Ivor* featured all the old songs and would have owed the family royalties. So Imogen was going on holiday. She had recently split up with her boyfriend and needed cheering up. So, she was going on a safari for 25 days with her friend Suzanna.

"She said that when she got back," says Walter Randall, "we would sit down and start finding theatres and things like that."

Walter's son Clayton was the DJ in the cellar at Logan's when Imo would come in as a customer. He says that she had other irons in the fire. There would be a part in a play, waiting for her, when she got back from holiday.

The Imogen that Walter Randall saw was cheerful and sociable. But she would also phone him at night when she was feeling down. In the short time that he knew her Imogen took overdoses on at least two occasions.

The police had summoned Gina Batt—still Imogen's friend and also a neighbor to Queen Mary's Hospital where Imogen was recovering from yet another overdose.

The police told Gina that Imogen had been brought to the hospital clad only in a G-string; could she possibly find some clothes for her and bring them? Gina went to the cottage in Crooked Billet. Unable to find any clean laundry she had to wash Imogen's clothes before she took them to the hospital.

Gina was taken aback by the sorry state of the cottage. It was "very dark and dingy and in a mess." This surprised her, because Imogen had always been so house proud. It told Gina just how low Imogen was.

While Imogen rested in her hospital bed it took Gina three days to clean the kitchen. Imogen, obsessed by her weight, lived off a strange menu of diet foods and drinks—strawberry was her favorite flavor. Half-open packets of the stuff were strewn around or congealed in glasses that were stuck to the kitchen counter. There were some white, anonymous pills lying about, but they might have been only aspirin.

According to Gina, Imogen's cries for help were a rehearsed ritual. Gina felt that Imogen had been making these attempts for a very long time, all the way back into her teens.

She would lay out all her props, everything in its proper place—the telephone close at hand; her book containing the circle of names that she would always call on these occasions. Sometimes she would even leave the front door unlocked. Then she would take the pills, pick up the phone immediately and start calling. Someone would always get there on time.

Queen Mary's Hospital, says Gina, knew her well. Once in hospital, Imogen would be impatient and anxious to leave. The remorse would come once she was back home.

Gina took Imogen back to Crooked Billet and stayed with her for four days. While Gina finished cleaning the cottage, Imogen talked. "I didn't mean it, I'm very sorry, I didn't know what else to do. You would have thought that I would have known by now. Once I've taken them I know I shouldn't have done it, but I've done it for most of my life and I don't know how else to do it."

Gina remembers that Imogen made one other single, stark statement—but she never knew what it meant. "I wish it would go away."

Imogen's life amounted to a catalogue of misery. Seeing her mother go into a home had been an ordeal difficult to bear. She was deeply upset when her little dog Ratso, ailing and aged, had to be put to sleep.

And she was back in hospital, according to Suzanna Leigh, having lost another baby. Suzanna says that over the years Imogen had lost some eight babies in all. One was in a taxi on the way to the hospital when the pregnancy was virtually full-term.

This last time the doctor warned Imogen that it was unlikely she would ever be able to have children. She was devastated. Suzanna, inspired by the miracle of Sophia Loren, was planning to take Imogen to a clinic in Switzerland.

Imogen was desperately, incurably lonely. Many of her friends are left with the impression that she was always on the phone to them.

When she was lonely, she would sometimes call her brother.

"She was always thinking about me," says Nicholas Hassall. "The older she got, the more she valued my friendship."

Nicholas is eternally grateful to his sister for respecting his privacy, for being careful to keep him out of the limelight and off the pages of the tabloids. He says that she always trusted him because he did not want anything from her, except her friendship.

But brother and sister were such contrasting people, living very opposite lives. There was little that he could do for her. "We could have been very good friends, but her life was so different—I couldn't stand all that mob she went around with."

In social surroundings Imogen was a commanding figure and Nicholas was naturally withdrawn, self-sufficient, a loner. "When my sister was around, she more or less took over and, frankly, I wanted to keep away. I didn't want to be bossed around by anybody. It's not that she bossed me around, but she more or less took control. She was like that."

Imogen wanted them to be closer but Nicholas says that she could never be close to him. He does not believe that anyone has ever been close to him, except, perhaps, his mother.

And, he says, you could not get close to her.

They saw each other maybe once or twice a year. Many of Imogen's former colleagues are surprised to learn that she had a brother. Most of her friends confirm that they met him—usually just the once—but to them, he was and remains, a shadow.

But she would telephone him when she was lonely and Nicholas did occasionally come to visit and stay in her house. He would spend a day or two with her. They would have a lovely time, he says, laughing and chatting. "Then the climate would change—I'd pack my bags and be off."

Nicholas was not spared the sudden and disturbing mood swings. "One moment you'd get close to her and the next moment she'd be either shouting her head off or telling you to shut up or something."

From age 12 or 13 onward, Nicholas knew better than to stand his ground and fight it out with his sister. Anyway, it was not in his nature.

"I'm not going to have a row with you, Jenny, I'm going to leave."

"Yes, you leave, go on, leave!"

Bags packed, he would be out of the door.

"Ok, Jen, I'm off, bye."

"Yes, I suppose you'd better go, I'm not in a good mood."

"Fair enough, I'll ring you sometime or you'll ring me."

That way, says Nicholas, they stayed friends. "Jenny never so much as once ever spoke unkindly about me. I never heard her once say a single derogatory word about me. I may not have been beyond reproach in her eyes but she never let on once that I could be wrong. Mad, she thought I was, yes! Eccentric even, but she was faithful in her decision about me, that was quite extraordinary, the decision to keep me from her unsavory publicity."

Imogen called him when he was staying at a campsite in Rome, living in an Escort van. She was lonely and down and wanted to come and stay with him.

Nicholas did his best to discourage her—what on earth would she do with herself there? "Jenny, this is not the sort of place for you. I live on a campsite. I'm living in a van. You'd have to stay in a hotel."

"Oh no, I'd live on the campsite!"

"You wouldn't enjoy it, it's not your style." The idea just seemed ridiculous to him—for someone so used to glamorous company and the best of everything to come down and slum it on a campsite. He knew that she would not be happy. Besides, her presence in Rome, he was sure, would soon attract attention. She always drew a crowd.

"It wasn't jealousy on my part. I loved it for her. I just didn't want to be a part of it."

He talked her out of it. "And the next thing I heard, she'd died."

"I'm feeling so lonely," was the last thing she ever said to him.

Jimmy Ellis received a message that Imo was missing her friends from *Outside Edge*. She wanted to see them all together again. "My wife said 'you must go, she sounds really down.' "

There was a grand reunion at Logan's Wine Bar—"we all went and turned it into a party." Imogen was brimming over with her plans to mount a Novello extravaganza. Her enthusiasm was childlike. "Oh, Jimmy, it's wonderful, we'll all go out and do musicals!"

Imogen declared that she was going to cast the entire *Outside Edge* company in her show. Jimmy was the voice of reason. "We'd be disastrous. And don't even think about starring in it. Get yourself well represented. Think of it as independence for yourself. What you'll have will be freedom."

A merry time was had by all. It was good, says Jimmy, to see Imo over her illness and well again. This occurred a few days before her death.

Imogen told the *Wimbledon News* that she loved her new home. Elsewhere, it was reported that she said she hated it and only bought it because Andrew Knox liked it. Contradictions to the last.

Whatever the truth, for the short while that she lived in her new home in Crooked Billet, Imogen was popular with her neighbors. They said she was "a pleasant, seemingly happy person," who was looking forward to going on holiday.

She was the life and soul of a Bonfire Night party, a Village affair. "Everything seemed to be all right that evening," said one of the guests. "She was chatting away to everyone and seemed to be really enjoying herself. It was the first time I had seen her in that mood and it was very good to see."

"She seemed to be happy that evening," said another partygoer. "And I really thought she was at last beginning to integrate herself into the neighborhood."

The wife of the landlord of Crooked Billet's other local, the Hand In Hand, provided a glimpse of the domestic Imogen—the real Imogen. "She used to come and have Sunday lunch with us sometimes. She would take off her shoes and go to sleep after the meal. She was then relaxed and natural—that is how I want to remember her."

But there are also tales of Imogen, drunk and aggressive. She would bring a motley crew home with her to the cottage next door to the pub, anyone who would have a drink with her. And the men now came and went anonymously, literally someone she met in the street, or so it appeared.

Like her houses and her career, Imogen's world was shrinking. But she put on a brave face. "My mates these days are bus drivers and people like that. They're far more reliable than film stars. But I'm very lonely really and very poor."

Nick Hirst was made all too aware of Imogen's loneliness and the contradictions within her. "She needed to have a man like a fish needs water, but she was deeply distrustful of men."

The Crooked Billet: Imogen's last home is just beyond the parked cars, next to the pub.

Sex was not "the primary thing on her mind." Imogen would tell Nick of her great longing for a Mr. Right with one breath; and with the next, would say how she could never trust men.

Obviously, she had been badly wounded by the failure of her two marriages. She saw them very much as her failures and, unprompted, spoke about them at great length and in great detail. Nick defines it as some kind of ongoing self-therapy.

"I need a millionaire to look after me," Imogen would say, but what she really needed, says Nick, was genuine love from someone who loved her for what, not who, she was. Nick suggests that what Imogen needed was one strong, constant man, but all she got was a lot of different men, who only saw a part of her.

Neville Greene was "just a casual acquaintance."

He was in the rag trade and had first come across Imogen during her brief flirtation with the boutique in the Fulham Road. It was about two or three weeks before she died, Neville estimates, that he saw Imogen again on the streets of Putney. He approached her and said hello.

His initiative was rewarded with her telephone number—"you could do that kind of thing in those days."

One evening shortly after, Neville was invited to Imogen's cottage in Crooked Billet. "All I was looking for was sex."

But he found Imogen in a confused state—drugs, he thought at the time, being unaware of the depth of her troubles. "There was no chance in her condition. When she was talking I just listened and made conversation and tried to be light. I could see she was distressed but there was nothing I could do,"

Neville did not take advantage of Imogen's weakness—"because she was a lovely lady."

The last occasion on which Gary Hope saw Imogen was prompted by the accidental death of her cat. The event had distressed and depressed her, so she telephoned to invite him to Crooked Billet.

When Gary arrived, she had other guests, whom he can only remember as a builder and his wife. Imogen was standing out on the village green in front of her home, barring entry to the cottage. "Darling, don't go in there, it's too depressing. We're all going to San Lorenzo's."

Gary protested that he was dressed too casually for dinner in a proper restaurant. "No, darling, I'm a fucking rich bitch. I've booked a table. We're off to San Lorenzo's, so bollocks!"

The foursome duly set off and a very nice time was had by all. They returned to Crooked Billet and at about 10 o'clock the builder and his wife said their goodnights and left the cottage.

Imogen's thoughts now returned to the loss of her pet. Her way of dealing with her bereavement was simple: erase all traces of it. "Darling, you've got a job to do. Get rid of all the cat's food tins and the dishes. I'm going up to bed."

As instructed, Gary removed all the visible evidence that Imogen had ever owned a cat. Promptly, Imogen's voice was heard, coming from the upstairs bedroom. "Could you bring me up a malted milk drink. Don't boil the milk, just hot."

Gary obliged. Climbing the stairs, he entered Imogen's bedroom. There she was on the four poster bed, stark naked.

"Don't go," said Imogen.

Gary just stood there with her malted milk drink in his hand.

"Don't you fancy me?"

"Don't be bloody silly. Of course I fancy you."

"Am I too old for you?"

"You're an absolute idiot. Of course you're not too old for me. I'm still licking my wounds. I'm not in the mood for this right now."

"Well, I want you to fuck me. I want your children. You've got wonderful children."

Gary explained that his children were the product of years of love and hard work and sacrifice, a great deal of conversation and thinking; they did not just spring up overnight. Imogen was not entirely sober and, possibly, had taken some of her pills; but the message sunk in. There were no tantrums.

But she did not want to be left alone:

"Will you at least sleep in that cot?"

Set up in the spare bedroom was Imogen's most prized heirloom, Rupert Brooke's camp bed. By coincidence, Imogen had come to see Gary in a play called *Sweet Wine of Youth*, which was about Brooke and his patron Sir Edward Marsh, Christopher Hassall's friend. Imogen also possessed some of Marsh's silverware, bequeathed by him to Christopher and various other bits and pieces. Gary had portrayed Eddie Marsh in the play. That tenuous connection appeared to mean something to Christopher's daughter.

As a child might, Imogen said: "If you sleep in it I will give it to you."

Gary told her that he would not accept it, nor would he sleep in it. But he set down her milk and said that he would sit with her. "We had this rather long and sweet scene. I sat down on the bed and covered her up and said: 'This is your problem, it's not that I don't want to sleep with you, what man wouldn't; you need more than that from me, you need something else.' "

Gary told Imogen that to climb into bed with her now would be extremely selfish of him. It would be taking advantage of her and violate the trust between them, the mutual need

Imogen with Ratso a few days before her death

that they shared. "I sat with her, we held hands. I talked to her long into the night, until she started to drift off."

When Imogen was asleep, Gary let himself out quietly and went back to his place. It was the last time that he saw Imogen. But he would hear her voice again.

Imogen, meanwhile, was left sleeping, only to wake and be confronted by the daunting prospect of another day. Another day to get through—to occupy herself somehow or call upon someone to keep her occupied till the night came round, the dreaded nights spent all alone that dragged into the early hours when the mercy of sleep might be granted to her.

As her brother observed, "Her life came down to getting through the day."

Imogen's last recorded lover was described by the tabloids as a "burly toolmaker." He said that they had met in the Crooked Billet pub where he and his mates would go on a Saturday night:

"One night Imogen was with some acting friends," he recounted. "And we started chatting."

Imogen had proclaimed that she was no longer interested in becoming involved with showbiz types. She was, she said, looking for an ordinary, reliable man. "I hadn't heard of her before we met. I think she liked that. She used to say she was fed up with all the showbiz hangers-on. She's had enough of being used by famous men who were just on ego trips. After all the glamour, all the jet-setting, she was perfectly happy sitting in her local pub with me. She did go out with famous stars a couple of times in the last few months. But she'd come back and say, 'They're all the same. They don't really care about me.' "

It all began well enough, but her new lover was soon witness to Imogen's alarming mood swings. "We'd go out for a meal and she'd laugh and joke in the restaurant. Then afterwards she'd sink into a depression."

There was also an incident when Imogen found her boyfriend in the Crooked Billet pub chatting to another girl. "Imogen came in and started being abusive. She then threw a drink over the girl."

He obviously began to have his doubts. Perhaps sensing this, Imogen, he said, became ever more demanding. "She was desperately looking for somebody to love her and be a friend. I was happy to be that. But then she wanted more."

Imogen asked him to move into her cottage and live with her. He backed off. "I told her I was happy to be her friend, but not her live-in lover. I was being cruel to be kind."

Gina Batt saw Imogen in the Crooked Billet pub a few days before her death. Imogen spoke about the problems that she was having with her new lover. She accused him of being unreasonable and violent.

When her lover told Imogen that it was all over between them, she took an overdose. Someone came and sorted her out.

On the last Wednesday of her life, Imogen had a guest for dinner.

Sunday she would be off on her safari in Kenya with Suzanna. Imogen wanted to leave the keys to her cottage with young Clayton Randall. He was going to live in and look after the place—a break from sharing a flat with his father and, with Imogen's blessing, have some time and space for himself and his girlfriend.

Clayton always enjoyed Imogen's company. From the very first, she had always made time for him. Whenever she arrived at the wine bar in Putney and he was downstairs spinning the discs, she would make a point of coming down to say hello and sit and talk to him. "I met a lot of people in that profession and she was particularly nice, I thought."

There was never anything sexual between them. "She said she wanted to take me to see her mother because I reminded her of her brother and her mother would have liked me."

And there was no hint of her demons,. "She was very genuine and very nice."

Having been brought up in a show business environment Clayton had seen it all, all the egos and the extremes and outrageousness. The Imogen he knew was exceptional. "She was absolutely lovely. She was actually quite unique in that way, of people in that industry."

That Wednesday night in the cottage at Crooked Billet, Imogen was relaxed and cheerful. She cooked dinner and put on some music. Clayton remembers one track in particular, "Europa," a lush and romantic instrumental by Santana. To this day when he hears it he thinks of her. "She was not depressed that evening at all, in any way, shape or form."

In the course of the evening's conversation Imogen's recent overdose came up. Clayton felt able to raise the subject because Imogen seemed to be on such good form.

There was no mention of boyfriend trouble. Imogen was looking forward to her holiday. And she had a part in a play to come back to. It was definite, Clayton insists, there was work waiting for her on her return.

She had shown him photographs of Andrew Knox, but without any bitterness or pain. "She was absolutely fine."

Clayton wanted to know if Imogen really ever meant to kill herself. "I remember how together she seemed, which is why I was able to ask her about it."

They chatted about suicide in "a matter-of-fact way. She was quite candid, very down to earth."

It was, Clayton recalls, quite a light-hearted conversation. "You don't really intend to do it, do you?" Clayton asked, and, he says, in a very light-hearted way Imogen replied: "No, of course I don't mean to do it."

"One day it'll be too late," Clayton told her. "You'll get it wrong one day, it's a dangerous game to play."

Imogen, says Clayton, "sort of laughed." "Yes, I know," she said. "I know I'm being silly."

Imogen admitted that all she was doing was seeking attention, that someone was always meant to rush round at the last minute and rescue her. "I remember her laughing, like it was a joke."

When their pleasant evening drew to a close, it was arranged for Clayton to come and collect Imogen on the Sunday afternoon to convey her to Suzanna Leigh's.

Imogen's holiday, she said, was going to begin with a flourish. It was all planned. They would drink a champagne toast and then set off for the airport in a Rolls Royce. Imogen was going to do it in style.

The last time he saw Imogen, the toolmaker told the *Wimbledon News*, she found him in the Crooked Billet pub, having a quiet drink with his brother-in-law.

At first, he said, Imogen tried to win him over, but then the shouting began. "Imogen was a really hairy lady—always liable to fly off the handle."

He said that Imogen kicked him and pulled out a clump of his hair. His brother-in-law restrained her, while he made his escape.

Imogen died on November 16, 1980 in the early hours of Sunday morning.

The file on the inquest, preserved at the Coroner's Court in Westminster, is quite slim. The autopsy report notes nothing unusual or suspicious and comes to the straightforward conclusion that "the concentration of barbiturate in the blood was adequate to account for death."

In his statement, Imogen's solicitor said:

> ...She has had problems in the past, in that three to four years ago she received out-patient psychiatric treatment, which ceased a long time ago. She had an ectopic pregnancy. She has taken some overdoses in recent months but I don't think she intended to take her own life. I suspect it did upset her. She had had a previous one.
>
> I spoke to her on the Thursday before she died on the telephone and she was very cheerful and looking forward to her holiday in Mombasa.
>
> Financially she was secure and had no worries in that direction...

Imogen's doctor stated that she had been his patient since October 1979:

> At that time she was very depressed, out of work and taking at least three to five 200 mg. Tuinal a day which had been her habit for many years. She was using them as a tranquilizer.
>
> After much counseling she accepted a job with a Repertory Company and managed an arduous tour of nine months in spite of having a massive hemorrhage in June 1980 from an ectopic pregnancy. She lost the baby.
>
> During this period it was decided that she should be restricted to two capsules of Tuinal a night and she has kept fairly strictly to this regime—to my knowledge. I do not believe that she obtained medication from elsewhere...
>
> I saw her last Thursday, the 13th of November, when she was in extremely high spirits, happy, and looking forward to her holiday in Kenya two days later. She came for a Cholera vaccination.
>
> I gave her enough Tuinal for 25 days, 50 Tuinal...
>
> She had tremors and vomiting if she did not have the Tuinal. She was addicted to the Tuinal.

A supplement to the autopsy report states that the blood barbiturate level was "equivalent to over 15 200 milligram capsules circulating in the blood."

The stark, formal verdict of the Coroner, "Killed herself."

The Coroner observed, "I think this young lady was depressed, but I don't know for certain the reason why."

Why, Imogen? On the very eve of your wonderful holiday?

Nick Hirst was with Imogen on that fateful Saturday. It was a perfectly normal, pleasant afternoon; lunch at the pub, then back to Imogen's cottage.

Imogen was very excited by the prospect of her holiday. She showed Nick all the glossy brochures.

"See you this evening," said Nick as he left. He was going to come back later and help her pack. He left someone who, in his opinion, was on the road to putting her life back together, brick by brick.

He was due to return later that evening at about eight o'clock.

But was it the very last day, the Saturday? Or might it have been the day before—Friday?

After all this time, Neville Greene cannot be positive but he believes that he may have arranged to visit Imogen on what was the last night of her life.

Soup was on the menu—"it was all she could eat." Neville knocked on Imogen's door but got no reply. So he departed, leaving two tins of soup on the doorstep.

Maggie Guess has always believed that on her last night Imogen went back to her home with a couple—drinking companions she met in the Crooked Billet pub.

Apparently there was a row. The girl accused Imogen of flirting with her boyfriend. It flared into a fight.

The wine bar owner received a phone call at the bar later that night. "I've had a terrible time. I've just chucked those people out, will you come over?"

It was Saturday night. The wine bar was packed and there would be a lot of clearing up to do. "Imo, hang on, love, I'll be over when I'm all done..."

There was a lot to do and he lost all track of time.

That version, Maggie recalls, was circulating at the wake held after Imogen's funeral at Logan's Wine Bar. She can recall the wine bar owner mentioning it.

Clayton Randall was working, doing his stint as DJ at the wine bar that night. The bar was always jam-packed and roaring on a Saturday night. It would have been just like Imogen to phone up in the middle of all that and expect to have a chat, but he cannot remember his father ever saying that she had called.

When Clayton and his father returned to their flat there was a strange message on the answer-phone. No voice, just silence. Clayton says that he had been trying repeatedly to call Imogen to confirm the arrangements for Sunday, but the line was permanently engaged.

Nick Hirst, as promised, had returned to Crooked Billet at about eight o'clock in the evening. The last evening of her life, he says, which would have been the Saturday. But might it have been the Friday? Arriving at Imogen's cottage, Nick was about to knock when he heard muffled voices through the front door. This surprised him, because Imogen had not mentioned that she was expecting company. As far as he knew, she would be waiting for him to come and help her pack.

So many years have gone by–all that Nick can recall with certainty is that he heard two strange voices and that they were distinctly male. He could not make out what they were saying; to the best of his recollection the voices were not raised or angry. He detected nothing sinister but felt this was something that he did not want to interrupt.

Shyly, Nick went away. To this day he wishes that he had knocked on Imogen's door.

In the early hours of Sunday morning Imogen called Suzanna Leigh. She sounded unhappy and woozy, but Suzanna just said don't worry, we'll be flying off to the sun in a few hours and everything will be all right.

Suzanna had taken her own sleeping pills and the phone rang for a long time before she answered. Imogen sounded out of it. "Darling, I've thought about it all and I've had enough."

"Oh, my God, don't even think about it!"

"You've got Tim, I've got nobody that matters now the baby's gone."

Suzanna tried to tell her that they could talk about all of this on the plane and on the beach in a few short hours.

"For God's sake don't do anything with those pills!"

Later Suzanna would blame herself for not having taken custody of Imogen's pills—"but taking my life, no matter what the circumstances, would never be an option and I forgot that not everyone thought about suicide like that."

Suzanna was heavily sedated by her own pills and was too far gone to drive over. She approached her lover, beside her in bed, but he had also taken his pills and was unsympathetic. "She's tried it before—maybe this time she'll be successful." In a few short hours they would be winging their way to the sun.

David Wigg was out Saturday night. When he returned Sunday morning there was a message from Imogen. She was crying. "Oh help, help, what am I to do, David, it just isn't worth it, oh help me, help me...!"

"The awful truth," says David, "is you got to the point where you thought, sadly, oh not again. It was so often it happened."

Gary Hope was appearing onstage at the time. After the curtain calls he would unwind in the Chelsea Arts Club before returning home to Richmond Hill.

On this Saturday night there was a message on his answer-phone, "A totally incoherent message."

It was unmistakably Imogen—"but there was nothing to decipher."

She had called so many times before. Gary thought little more of it than that she was obviously "either pissed out of her mind or had taken a lot of her pills."

It was late and he was tired. He decided to call her back tomorrow.

Imogen had no tomorrow. Gary Hope believes that what he heard may have been the very last message that she left. What he heard might have been her dying breath.

Imogen was due to be collected at two o'clock on Sunday, November 16, by Clayton Randall, who had a key so he could look after the cottage in her absence.

Clayton had a mate with him when he arrived at Crooked Billet. He knocked and rang the bell. There was no reply. Clayton noticed that the curtains were still drawn. He tried the key in the front door but found that it was bolted from the inside.

Finding no means of entry at the rear of the cottage, Clayton was able to reach through the cat flap in the front door and undo the bolt. It was a trick that Imogen had shown him. Entering, he called out Imogen's name several times.

Silence. Clayton's friend froze and refused to go any further. The sitting room downstairs was empty. Clayton climbed the stairs to Imogen's bedroom.

He saw her lying on the bed propped against a pillow with her head face down. She was not so much on the bed as in it with blankets drawn across her legs. She looked as if she had simply drifted off to sleep.

When he called out "Imogen" and got no response Clayton tried to lift her arm.

Her arm was stiff and her face had a blueish tint. The bedroom was very hot. His hand had touched a bare arm, but her nakedness hardly registered with him. What really struck him was that the telephone was off the hook and Imogen's hand was resting on the dial.

Clayton had no time to notice anything else. As soon as he realized that Imogen was dead, he ran out to a nearby callbox and summoned the police.

At some point in the day Suzanna Leigh went to Crooked Billet. She says that when she arrived the police were already there.

"She had our tickets in one hand, the telephone hung limply from the other," is how Suzanna remembers it. All she wanted to do was get away from there. She says that a police officer went back inside and retrieved her ticket. "I knew that I had to catch that plane no matter what—one of us had to get this life together...besides, what could I do for her in London other than cry, feel sorry for her and be guilt-ridden...my preoccupation had to be sorting myself out and it was almost as though she was driving me on."

One of the police officers who attended says that there was "nothing untoward, nothing amiss at the scene" which he and his colleagues were presented with when they were called to Crooked Billet.

Unknown to the police at the time there were disturbing allegations made with regard to events that took place during the last few days of Imogen's life—and which remain unsubstantiated and unresolved. Her death, however, is surely just what it appeared to be to the police officers summoned by Clayton Randall.

Two police officers arrived and Clayton took them inside and up the stairs to Imogen's bedroom.

The officers were able to make a detailed appraisal of the scene:

The body was in a double bed, the lower half being covered by two blankets. The body was naked, lying on its left side bent about ninety degrees, the legs were pointing towards the right hand side of the bed. The left arm was underneath her body and head, the right arm was bent so that the hand was resting against her face; there was the main part of a telephone directly underneath the right hand and the face. The hand piece of the telephone was underneath the body and not visible. The head was inclined face down and she had long black hair which had fallen forward over her forehead and covering her right hand.

The blankets were underneath her head and the telephone and underneath the right elbow, across her hips and the small of her back, her right breast was exposed. In front of the body was a copy of the *Daily Express* newspaper dated 15th November 1980, closed and front down. Behind the body was four pillows, between which were two soft toys, that were flattened as though she had been lying on them. To the left of the bed was a side table with a lamp, an empty ashtray and an address book neatly on top of a hard back book. On the right-hand side of the bed was a rocking chair with a cushion on upon which there was a pair of sunglasses, a wet razor and an empty bottle with the lid screwed on labeled Tuinal dated 13/11/80.

On the floor in front of the chair there was a pair of black knee length boots, a black jumpsuit and a red check shirt. At the foot of the bed in the main area of the bedroom was scattered numerous articles of clothing. In front of the window was a chest of drawers upon which there was a television set that was switched off and angled towards the bed, a pile of correspondence including two passports in the name of Hassall one out of date and the other current. At the side of the television there was one box of Daraprim tablets, nearly empty on top of one box of Migraleve (migraine) tablets. On the floor of the first floor landing there was a note written on the rear of a business letter, it was not clearly written, there was also a biro pen.

In the bathroom on the floor there was what appeared to be a running outfit and on the sink there was a tablet bottle with three capsules in it, with no lid on labeled Dalmane and also one tablet bottle with nine tablets in with the lid on labeled Valium SMG and a set of keys.

In the second bedroom, the window was unlocked but retained by the first hole of a retaining arm. There was glass on the floor that had come from a broken picture that was topmost of those stacked against a wall. In the living room on the sofa there was a black handbag containing travelers checks and money on top of which there was a blue shopping bag only containing one red and blue capsule. On the right arm of the sofa there was a red and blue capsule. On the floor by the coffee table there was another red and blue capsule. On the coffee table the ashtray contained numerous cigarette ends and there was a receipt for payment on a holiday to Africa for the 16th November 1980. In the kitchen alongside the sink there was a bottle of tablets labeled Cytacon 50mg with the lid on containing approximately 16 tablets, and also a pot of Golden Health sleeping tablets with the lid on, and quite a few tablets in. In the sink there were glasses and mugs unwashed. The fridge was completely empty, but the freezer had food in. On the work surface there was an empty quarter bottle of Cognac the lid not visible, and also an unwashed plate.

Who knows what hideous mess of confused miseries, anger and self-pity was spinning round and round in Imogen's pill-fogged brain as she sat in bed, telephoning again and again, waiting all alone for someone to come and sort her out.

Imogen's note is scrawled on the back of an undated letter which may have been sent to her while she was convalescing after her collapse during the tour of *Outside Edge* or perhaps another overdose. It confirms that she was up for a part in a forthcoming production of Tom Stoppard's *Dirty Linen*:

> There are 2 good female parts. Maddie is the new secretary who sleeps with anyone and is generally a flighty piece. The other is a Mary White-house type — with a skeleton in the cupboard. Far be it from me to suggest the part Bill may have in mind for you!

Imogen's last words are largely indecipherable, scrawled across the paper in an uncontrolled, desperate and angry hand. The only words that can be made out with any certainty are, "*All you needed to do was talk....*"

And then there is a name, probably that of the toolmaker. The rest is pure guesswork.

> *All you needed to do was talk* (here a name most likely that of her last recorded lover) (and then what may be *AND AS FOR THE REST*, followed by what might be *Including*) (then possibly two more words, indecipherable) (then what might be *you should be*) (then what could be *dead.*)

Few believe that Imogen really intended to kill herself. It was an accident waiting to happen, another cry for help that went over the brink, taken to greater and greater extremes — Imogen, as always, going over the top, going too far, until it all ended in tears.

It appears that she had ritualistically, as she had done so often in the past, set up her props, took the pills and picked up the phone, working her way through her address book.

Only no one responded before the pills took effect. No one came in the nick of time.

Or is the note significant? Does leaving a note mean that this time she intended to die?

Imogen's brother was given the impression that she did mean it.

"I rang up and saidn 'What's happened?'

'She did it this time.'

'What do you mean she did it this time?'

'Well, she left a note saying she was really determined this time.' "

Can those few, scrawled words, written by a hand that was out of control, mean that Imogen was determined to die?

In the inquest papers, Imogen's solicitor is recorded as having made the formal identification of her body. At the time, however, Gina Batt says that the police called her. She says that Imogen's book of phone numbers was open at her page, the Bs. Perhaps Gina's name was first in Imogen's list and that is why the police chose her, just as they had called upon her in the past, when there had been someone to heed Imogen's cry in the nick of time.

Imogen lay on a hospital trolley with a sheet pulled up to her chin. She looked beautiful—although her hair was a mess—"beautiful but empty." Her skin, says Gina, was "like an eggshell."

Did she mean it this time, or was it the inevitable accident; did incident-prone Imo muck it up at last? A friend gave Nicholas Hassall the impression that "she really meant it this time" because she left a note.

But Clayton Randall's dinner conversation with Imogen on the previous Wednesday convinced him that she had no real intention of taking her own life. He believes the note was there for the sake of appearances. "If somebody rushes round to rescue you, it looks better if you've gone through the whole charade."

The door was bolted, which did surprise him. Odd to leave the door so securely barred if you're expecting rescuers. Perhaps she just forgot. She was hardly rational. Gina Batt said that Imogen sometimes left the door unlocked.

And Clayton found her in the bed. She was not on the bed as though she had laid down to die. She was under the blankets and had her hand on the telephone; she was still trying to call someone when she lapsed into her final sleep.

It just happened to be the wrong night. On a Saturday night everyone would be out treading the boards if they were lucky enough to be in work or partying. If they came home at all it would be very late and they would be very tired. And Imo had called like this so many times before. They would ring her back tomorrow.

Who was she trying to call?

It will never be known just how far she got in her address book.

In Imogen's left hand was found a business card with a home telephone number scribbled on the back. It belonged to Neville Greene.

Her agent, David Daly, told the newspapers that she sometimes called her solicitor or her accountant.

She spoke to Suzanna Leigh on Sunday—woozy in the early hours. Gary Hope and Walter Randall found strange messages on their answering machines.

Imogen made the front pages on Monday, November 17. When Nick Hirst saw it, he was shocked, but there was also an inevitability about it.

On that Monday night Nick drove through the fog to the Crooked Billet pub, trying to resolve the mystery of the two muffled male voices that he had heard through Imogen's front door.

He questioned all the regulars and others as to whether they had seen Imogen leave the pub with anyone, but came away without an answer.

The burly toolmaker told the reporters that he was convinced that Imogen had been trying to call him. "I now just wish she had been able to get through that last time. I cried all day when I found out what happened...Now I wish I'd done as she wanted. I'd have done anything if I'd known she was going to take it so badly."

Gina Batt recalls bumping into him not long after Imogen's death. "I didn't do anything to her," was the first thing he said.

Clayton Randall was surprised by the sudden emergence of the toolmaker as a self-proclaimed leading player in the drama of Imogen's final days. "A boyfriend came forward. I don't even remember the guy. If she had this boyfriend, she never brought him down to the wine bar."

But Clayton notes that she did tend "to lead separate lives." It was not unusual for Imogen's various friends to be unaware of each other's existence.

One overpowering unanswered question remained—the puzzle of the extraordinary timing of Imogen's final cry for help, the very eve of her much anticipated holiday.

Imogen was found dead on the Sunday afternoon. She was still alive it appeared in the early hours of Sunday morning, still trying desperately to find someone to come to her rescue.

On Saturday morning Suzanna Leigh received a frantic phone call. "Something terrible's happened, you've got to come over!"She found Imogen in what she describes as a severely distressed mental and physical state. She said Imogen had been beaten, her face was battered; her hair had been torn out by the roots and her scalp was still bleeding.

As Suzanna did what she could to comfort her distraught friend and bathe her wounds, a story emerged. "I was raped."

Imogen told Suzanna that on Friday night she heard the front doorbell ring and peering through the spyhole she saw a man that she knew well.

Imogen opened the door only to have a second man burst in upon her. This second man, although obviously a companion of the first, was a complete stranger to Imogen; and his brutal assault began without any preliminaries.

The man that Imogen knew simply stood by and let it happen. Suzanna says that Imogen must have resisted fiercely, judging by the injuries to her face and body.

Imogen did not want to go to the police. When pressed by Suzanna, she refused to name the first man. "I've got to cope with who it was...I can't get my own head around it...I'll tell you when we're sitting in the sun...I'll tell you on a beach with a tequila sunrise in my hand..."

According to the inquest papers, Imogen phoned her doctor later that Saturday to ask his advice about bruises to her face and scalp; sustained in a "brawl at her home." That was all she told him.

The tabloids were well represented at the inquest. One reporter recorded the doctor's description of Imogen's injuries as bruises to her "head and ear"—"she was feeling sore and concerned with the physical aspect of her bruises," implying that the doctor's impression was that Imogen's main concern was with the cosmetic effects of her injuries.

The autopsy was carried out on November 17, the Monday following the alleged Friday attack. The report noted only "recent bruising to both temples"; there is no mention of any other sign of injury—there is no mention of any evidence of sexual assault. "At that time," testified Imogen's doctor, "she was only concerned with the physical injuries and did not appear to be unduly depressed."

Clayton Randall recalls that the police questioned him for the rest of the day—"I can never remember having any arguments with Imogen and we were always the best of friends," he said in his statement.

The police attempted to locate the toolmaker, but came up with nothing after numerous inquiries. This was noted with no suggestion that any further action be taken.

There is a scribbled note appended to the handwritten witness statement of a police Sergeant at Wimbledon police station. That short statement pertains to the failure to establish the "witness," the toolmaker's exact address (there is no witness statement from the toolmaker among the inquest documents). The Sergeant's note appears to read:

> I do not know where she was (the next word could be either driving or drinking). I have made substantial inquiries. Nobody saw her—Nothing of a sinister nature.

"I was raped" is what Suzanna says Imogen told her.

Imogen's brother offers a more complex hypothesis:

> Such behavior must have been initially precipitated by Jenny's extraordinary insensitivity, callousness, to *some* of her paramours. In other words she *must* have led them on. She was not naïve, and she may have even

wanted subconsciously to set up a situation where violence ensued. She must have had a masochistic streak in her. I know she felt *deeply* inadequate...these violent confrontations must have exacerbated her unstable mental state which led her to taking her own life...the incident must have left her feeling so degraded that she soon became overwhelmed by the knowledge that she must have brought it on herself by her own eccentric behavior. She was more than humiliated. She was overwhelmed briefly by the knowledge that this particularly shameful character deficiency had brought her yet again to a humiliating incident all because of the less savory part of her nature.

Did Imogen tell the undistorted, unembroidered truth? Or is her account some kind of embellishment—Imogen's re-interpretation—of what she described to her doctor simply as a brawl?

"A brawl at her home," the doctor typed in a letter to the Coroner. But he, or someone, has added in pen, "I believe it was the Crooked Billet"—the Crooked Billet. A newspaper account of the doctor's evidence at the inquest hearing gives it as "a pub fight." Is that, in fact, where the brawl took place, in the Crooked Billet pub and is that all it was?

"Actress Imogen Hassall died only hours after a blazing row with a boyfriend in her next door pub," reported the *Wimbledon News*. That was how the toolmaker told it, his story of the night Imogen confronted him in the Crooked Billet and how he had to be rescued by his brother-in-law.

There was no doubt in anyone's mind that Imogen's death was straightforward, a cry for help that went wrong, the inevitable accident waiting to happen. All the physical evidence pointed to her lapsing into her final sleep while still trying to phone anyone and everyone that she could think of.

But, for all that she was wont to embellish a tale and whatever the underlying psychological complexities may be, it would seem that something brutal happened on the Friday night, be it a brawl or a rape or even both.

It may explain the two anonymous male voices that Nick Hirst heard, muffled by Imogen's front door. Can he be certain, after all this time, that it was the very last night of Imogen's life, the Saturday, or might it in fact have been Friday, the night on which Imogen alleged that she had been raped, the night of the brawl?

Of course, those voices may have been completely innocent.

All alone in the early hours of Sunday morning, sleepless and lonely, did the trauma—and self-loathing—of whatever happened on that Friday night come crashing down on her? And so, on the very eve of the wonderful holiday that she had been looking forward to so much, she felt desperate enough to take her pills, pick up the phone and cry out to the world: "Come and sort me out!"

Imogen's funeral was on an appropriately bleak November day. She would have been pleased by the turn-out:

> More than 50 mourners attended the funeral service of actress Imogen Hassall who died of a large overdose of drugs. Show business personalities joined friends and relations at a simple service at the chapel in Gap Road Cemetery, Wimbledon...which included the 23rd psalm and a reading from St. John's Gospel.
>
> The coffin was then carried by four pallbearers to a grave at the far end of the cemetery.

Friends still remember that long, sad procession under a cold gray sky.

Clive Graham sums up the mood as one of "genuine grief and loss."

"I've never known so many people to be quite so thoroughly depressed," says Jimmy Ellis. "Showbiz funerals often have a buoyancy about them, but we were all so heavily bad, so desperately depressed."

Andrew Knox was there supporting Eve Hassall. No one can remember seeing Nicholas, but he was also at the graveside, although he did not stay long afterward.

Geoffrey Davies says that Andrew Knox was "beside himself with grief."

According to John Kane, Andrew "felt immense guilt over Imogen's death—the failure of the marriage and Imogen's suicide really damaged him enormously. He saw himself as a white knight and he was devastated."

A message on one of the wreaths read: "Our grateful thanks for all you did for the spastic people—from all at the Spastics Society."

In his capacity as Vice-President of the Stars Organization for Spastics, David Jacobs said, "Imogen was a super girl and a real stalwart of the spastics. She was always one of the first to help. She will be greatly missed."

Imogen, consumed by her midnight miseries, was convinced of her utter loneliness. She was laid to rest surrounded by friends.

Gina Batt told the *Wimbledon News*:

> She was a very lovely lady who got very lonely. The fact that so many people were here for the funeral meant that she had more friends than perhaps she realized.

"She felt she had no real friends," the toolmaker had once said. "But in reality everybody loved her because although she was famous, she was still so friendly and ordinary."

The trade papers noted her passing. *Screen International* was considerate:

> Imogen Hassall, who will sadly be better remembered as the perennial starlet rather than the busy actress, has died of a drug overdose, aged 38.
>
> Daughter of the late lyricist Christopher Hassall, she worked in films, TV and stage from 1964 and was married twice—to director Kenneth Ives and actor Andrew Knox.
>
> Her films included *The Long Duel*, *When Dinosaurs Ruled The Earth* and *Carry On Loving*. In the last, she played cleverly against type, a dowdy miss who eventually flowers, and proved categorically she could act.

The Stage, however, was less charitable:

> Imogen Hassall was found dead at her home in Wimbledon on November 16. She was 38. The daughter of author Christopher Hassall, she was better known for attending premieres than for her abilities as an actress, though she appeared in a number of films and plays, the most recent being *Outside Edge* in which she toured earlier this year.
>
> She was twice married, first to Kenneth Ives, the television and theatre director, and secondly to actor Andrew Knox, from whom she separated 18 months ago.

Tuesday's Child

Imogen died as she had lived, in a flood of tabloid headlines. Most simply churned out the familiar tales of her stormy love life and her other misfortunes—the source of so much easy copy in times past. But there were other, more sympathetic voices:

> Actress Imogen Hassall always knew that despite the glitter of her public life she never really won the prizes.
>
> But her personal grief was greater than that—behind the image of a fun-loving glamorous girl she was really a lonely woman longing for a baby to love.
>
> When the publicity her life-style created died away she found herself alone with her personal tragedy about which only a few close friends would listen.

> There will be people who will say that my friend Imogen's life ran out when the show-biz money stopped coming in.
>
> They couldn't be more wrong...
>
> It wasn't wealth that Imogen needed—she needed to be taken seriously as an actress by the film industry. And she never really got that reaction.
>
> For somebody depicted as a confident sex-starlet she was a very vulnerable person.
>
> I remember a call from her maid when Imogen took an overdose from which she recovered in St. Stephen's Hospital.
>
> Maybe, if she thought she would lose admiration when life took its toll of her beauty, she didn't want to recover.
>
> If so, her friends, including people like those of the Spastics charities she worked for, would have dearly loved to tell her she was mistaken.

> This is to Imogen, with love, affection and much, much sadness. The open season for jokes about 'The Countess of Cleavage' will probably start now that Imogen Hassall has taken her life.
>
> She may have appeared a wacky, starstruck flopperoo, but I knew her as a nice lass who suffered too many heartbreaks, too many miscarriages.
>
> A lass who suffered from having a high intelligence, a superb body, a pixie's face, but just not enough real talent to keep her from the pill bottle and disaster.
>
> I hope that those who felt pain at Lady Barnet's death can bring themselves to feel the same pain for poor little beat-up, battered Im, as I knew her.
>
> The occasional letter will not drop on my desk any longer. They will not tell me about wanting to go and buy every book in Foyle's but wondering whether people would recognize her. As if she didn't really want them to.
>
> I'll miss Im, I'll always wonder whether I did as much as I could to help her. I'll always wonder whether we all did as much as we could to help her...

Many of Imogen's friends echo those sentiments and some still blame themselves.

Nick Hirst wishes that he had knocked when he heard those mysterious voices.

Gary Hope wishes that he had not gone to bed thinking I'll ring her back tomorrow.

Suzanna Leigh blames herself for telling Imo don't worry, tomorrow we'll be flying off to the sun, everything will be all right. If only she had thought to take Imogen's pills away with her when she rushed round to Crooked Billet on Saturday morning.

But how can you help someone who cannot help herself? And if not then, it would have happened another day. There was an inevitability about it.

In her correspondence Joan Hassall wrote, "I sometimes think sadly that Imogen's beauty and charm raised expectations which she had not the qualities to realize...her life had got into a sad muddle. It was such a waste of beauty and charm. It was not a total shock as she had tried three or four times before, but it had always seemed more like a cry for attention and to be fussed over...I am sorry for Eve..."

BARBARA:... Remember Imogen?

KENNETH: Now whatever happened to her?

BARBARA: She killed herself. She was 37.

KENNETH: Well I suppose that explains it.

BARBARA: Why do so many people live unhappy lives?

KENNETH: We don't like ourselves. We grieve for the person we dreamed
of being but never grew into.

Enter the cemetery by the main gate in Gap Road, Wimbledon. Then walk straight ahead, as far as you can go, all the way across to the gates at the back at the far end.

Facing those gates, turn left down the narrow path that runs parallel to the back railings. A few graves along from the gate on the right hand side of the path is grave KA 1454. That is Imogen. She lies beneath a simple white marble slab now dark and discolored:

IN
LOVING MEMORY
OF
IMOGEN HASSALL

BORN 25th AUGUST 1942
DIED NOVEMBER 16th 1980

The local Council trims the grass although nettles are always sprouting. Someone had been leaving flowers for her regularly, anonymously, perhaps a standing arrangement. The flowers appear to have stopped in late 2000, so perhaps the arrangement was for 20 years from Imogen's death.

Her grave is overlooked by the rear balconies of a row of drab, three-story Council flats. Their narrow gardens with washing on the line, run down to the iron railings of the cemetery, a few feet from the grave. One can usually hear raised voices, radios and dogs barking as life goes on in the background. The grave is partly screened by trees, especially when the leaves are out in summer and the aura around it is peaceful.

Trains can be heard in the distance as they pass through Wimbledon Station on their way to and from London; the world on the move, while for Imogen time is standing still.

Imogen's neighbors remember the crowd at her funeral; it was a big event. An old man, one of the gravediggers now retired, recalls being told to make this one special. He says that Imogen lies in the best soil in the cemetery.

In the Summer, children play in the gardens and their broken toys sometimes find their way over the railings and onto the grass beside Imogen's grave. She would be happy and sad to hear children playing close by.

Otherwise she has the occasional visitor and a spectacular variety of bird life; patrolling cats and dogs; spiders, grasshoppers and snails. And the eternal wind in the treetops and passing clouds high above, forever.

She can sleep now. No more pain.

No more laughter and excitement.

Nicholas Hassall is left to muse upon what might have been, "I miss the sister that she would have been for me. The friend that she could have become to her beatnik brother."

He says that the most enduring tribute to his sister are the loving memories of her friends. "Her friends saw the caring, gentle person."

She compensated for the turmoil and disappointments of her private life by giving her affection to her friends and the people she worked with. "She got on extremely well with people—if anything, she loved them in a sense...she was good at bringing out the best and the affection...she was good with everybody."

Imogen, says Nicholas, took after her father in that respect. Both of them kept their friends and their friends adored them. "That was a good quality, a wonderful quality she had."

She loved her friends and would do anything for them. They saw the storms, but remember her laughter, her kindness and generosity. "She loved her friends and they loved her...with all the psychological problems she had, she could still maintain those friends—that was something in her life."

Her friends still miss her.

"...the lights change. A tune begins: 'For All We Know.' Out of the shadows comes Sid. He sits at the table and deals the cards. Imogen appears and joins him. They smile, happy to be in each other's company. They pick up their hands. Sid stakes his watch. Imogen smiles, takes off her top and puts it on the table. The lights fade.

FILM CREDITS

1965—*The Early Bird*—a Norman Wisdom comedy about a milkman. Imogen comes and goes in the blink of an eye, as Miss Cartwright, "Sir Roger's secretary."

1967—*The Long Duel*—somewhere on the North West Frontier… Imogen is "Tara," the wife of a Dacoit tribal chieftain—Yul Brynner—at war with British imperialism, personified by Harry Andrews and Trevor Howard. Heavily pregnant, Tara flees into the hills with her lord and master, only to die offscreen in childbirth, twenty minutes into the film.

1969—*When Dinosaurs Ruled The Earth*—a Hammer film – the epic tale of tribal tensions in a fanciful, very unscientific Stone Age, following the perilous adventures of an escaped, beautiful blonde sacrificial victim, Victoria Vetri, pursued by the chief of the Meat Eaters, Patrick Allen. Clad in a Stone Age bikini, Imogen plays Ayak, one of the Fish Eaters; a Jurassic good girl who goes bad when she is replaced in her handsome boyfriend's affections by the new and exciting blonde.

Mumsy, Nanny, Sonny and Girly—a thriller, in which Michael Bryant is terrorised for the apparent murder of his girlfriend—Imogen in flashback.

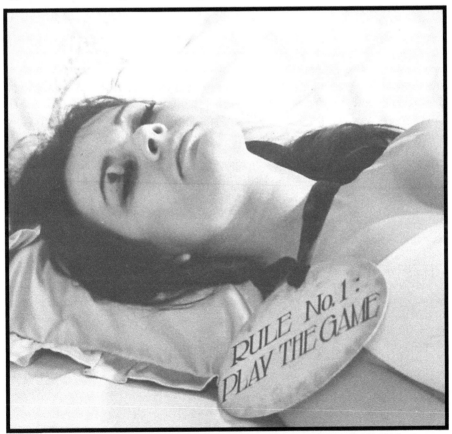

Imogen comes to a sticky end in *Mumsy, Nanny, Sonny and Girly*.

1970—*Carry On Loving*—marks an attempt to depart from the historical romps and return to the old-fashioned seaside postcard antics and real-world settings—this time a dating agency—of the earlier films in the series. Imogen plays Jenny Grubb, a shy wallflower who is transformed into a gorgeous glamour girl.

Reviews: "…Imogen Hassall proves that she has comic talent as well as other more noticeable attributes…"

"…she played cleverly against type, a dowdy miss who eventually flowers, and proved categorically she could act…"

Incense for the Damned—a veritable cult classic, based on the novel *Doctors Wear Scarlet* by Simon Raven. The plot concerns a strange vacation to Greece, by a young and handsome (but impotent) Oxford don, played by Patrick Mower. When he fails to return to the dreaming spires, his friends and fiancée follow his tracks, only to learn that he has fallen under the spell of the mysterious and beautiful Chriseis (Imogen). Imogen's Chriseis is the daughter of darkness, a vampire—but is her lust for blood real, or a perversion that provides the only means by which the young academic can achieve sexual gratification?

The Virgin and the Gypsy—a tale of forbidden love, by D.H. Lawrence. Imogen plays a gypsy girl, sullen and smoldering, whose man forsakes her for an English rose.

Tomorrow—alien abduction and a pop band, directed by Don Kirshner and starring Olivia Newton-John.

El Condor— a Western, shot in Spain, starring Lee Van Cleef and Jim Brown as two amiable rogues, out to steal a fortune in gold from a local warlord. Imogen is Dolores, a humble village girl, selected to entertain one of the warlord's officers. Her performance earned her a special mention in the film review column of *Mayfair* magazine:

"An unexpected bonus for western enthusiasts in *El Condor*, now on general release, was Imogen Hassall's revealing nude scene."

1971—*Take A Girl Like You*—written by Kingsley Amis and directed by Jonathan Miller, the story of a North Country lass (Hayley Mills) struggling against all the odds to preserve her virginity.

1974—*White Cargo*—a low-budget spy spoof, starring David Jason, a saucy, seaside postcard comedy, about a Walter Mitty character, prone to 007 fantasies, who foils a gang of white slavers, operating out of a Soho strip club. Imogen plays Stella, an undercover policewoman disguised as one of the strippers.

1979—*Licence To Love And Kill*—a B-movie secret agent caper, starring Gareth Hunt of *The New Avengers* fame.

TELEVISION CREDITS

1963—episode of series *Moonstrike*—"A Sunday Morning"—based upon the true-life exploits of the Special Operations Executive, during World War II, aiding the Resistance, in Occupied France. Imogen appeared as a French girl.

Episode of crime series *Scales of Justice*—"Position of Trust."

1964—episode of series *The Saint*—"Sophia"—Imogen was cast in the title role, as a Greek innkeeper's daughter, embroiled in archaeological skulduggery.

Episode of series *The Sentimental Agent*—"Not Quite Covered"—Imogen turns up as a Middle Eastern beauty, mixed up in an insurance racket.

1965—episode of series *No Hiding Place*—"The Reunion"—the archives list Imogen merely as an un-named cast member.

Imogen with Patrick Macnee on the set of *The Avengers*

1966—edition of *Theatre 625*—a dramatisation by the BBC of Evelyn Waugh's "Sword of Honour."

1967—episode of series *The Saint*—"Flight Plan"—Imogen is Nadya, a Middle Eastern bad girl, involved in the theft of a top secret military aircraft.

Episode of series *The Avengers*—"Escape In Time"—Imogen goes from Arabia to India, as Anjali, a bad girl once again, a cog in an evil organisation that helps smuggle wanted criminals to safety.

1968—episode of series *The Champions*—"Reply Box 666"—Imogen comes and goes even before the opening credits, as an anonymous temptress of uncertain but definitely exotic stock.

1969—episode of series *The Saint*—"The People Importers"—Imogen is Malia Gupta, an Indian girl, a thoroughly modern girl, a Chelsea Girl, a model, assisting the Saint in his crusade against crime.

1970—pilot episode of series *The Persuaders*—"Overture"—Imogen plays a French girl this time, making her entrance in yet another skimpy bikini, the romantic interest for Tony Curtis and Roger Moore.

1971—episode of series *On The House*—"The Secret Life of Reggie Cattermole."

Documentary—*Celluloid Love–The Hassall Family*—in which Imogen is body-painted by Peter Blake, the man who designed the cover for "Sgt. Pepper."

1972—Spoof on advertising—*Images*—featuring a comedy sketch that Imogen wrote herself.

Episode of series *Jason King*—"Stones of Venice."

THEATRE CREDITS

1962—Royal Shakespeare Company—*Curtmantle*—by Christopher Fry—the reign of Henry II, about the man, and "...the interplay of different laws: civil, canon, moral, aesthetic, and the laws of God."

Troilus and Cressida—Shakespeare—a tale of doomed love during The Trojan Wars.

The Devils—by John Whiting—Based on *The Devils of Loudon* by Aldous Huxley—possession, nuns and priests and persecution.

June 1963—New Theatre—*Strike Me Lucky*—by Jon Cleary, author of the best-seller *The Sundowners*—the disruptive effects, the stirrings of passion and greed, that the discovery of gold has upon the inhabitants of a sleepy New South Wales township. Imogen was cast as Teresa Da Vinci.

August 1963—New Arts Theatre—*The Afternoon Men*—a dramatisation of the Novel by Anthony Powell, up-dated from the 1920s to the 1960s. Imogen played a very English Harriet.

1964—Duchess Theatre—*The Reluctant Peer*—by William Douglas Home—about a peer who renounces his title in order to become Prime Minister, much to the consternation of his family. Imogen appeared as Rosalind, the reluctant peer's daughter, who has a communist boyfriend.

Review: "...and there must be a welcome for Imogen Hassall..."

August 1965—Yvonne Arnaud Theatre—*Milestones*—by Arnold Bennett and Edward Knoblock—an upper crust family saga set entirely in a drawing room in Kensington Gore, between 1860 and 1912. Imogen was The Honourable Muriel Pym.

November 1965—Yvonne Arnaud Theatre—*The Vortex*—by Noel Coward—Imogen was Bunty Mainwaring.

Review: "...Imogen Hassall was fascinatingly hard and brittle as the bright young thing engaged to Florence's son..."

1968—Wyndham's Theatre—*The Italian Girl*—a dramatisation of a novel by Iris Murdoch. A complex, sometimes bizarre, and often comic family drama. Imogen played Elsa Levkin, who belonged "to the race who are hunted all over the world and must either hide themselves or die."

Review: "...quite haunting..."

Sept-Nov 1971—Duke of York's Theatre (and on tour)—*The Jockey Club Stakes*—a comedy by William Douglas Home; devious doings in the horse racing world. Imogen was cast as Lady Ursula Itchin, the spoiled, headstrong daughter of the Chief Steward, the Marquis of Candover.

Reviews: "That well-known lady, Imogen Hassall, has a surprisingly small part for her billing. Perhaps it's the fact that the character, Lady Ursula Itchin, is supposed to be a silly nonentity, and Miss Hassall's impression on the play is disappointing."

"Lady Ursula was delightfully played by Imogen Hassall."

August 1972—Marlowe Theatre, Canterbury–*The Little Hut*—a lightweight piece popular in the 1950s.

Reviews: "Miss Hassall and her fellow artists...worked like demons to tighten and trim the production into a well-timed and homogeneous whole."

"Miss Hassall displayed more than the obvious sultry beauty as she played her lovers off against each other."

June-July 1973—on tour—*Barefoot In The Park*—by Neil Simon.

Reviews: "Sadly, Neil Simon's 'Barefoot In The Park'...was billed as though it was Imogen Hassall's 'one-woman' show, as though Miss Hassall was the leading light and everything else was to move in her glow like so many moths. Miss Hassall was bright in a bouncy sort of way, but was hardly what one had anticipated...the leading light was not going to dazzle anyone, at least not in this context."

"Imogen Hassall seems determined to play capering Carrie at the fastest possible tempo..."

"Imogen Hassall gives a very decorative performance."

Oct-Nov 1973—on tour—*The Mating Game*—A lavish London apartment with only one bed in it. Draycott Harris, a smooth, suave bachelor who is a TV star and his brother, loveable, cuddly James. Then add two delectable girls, Honey Tooks and Julia Carrington. The referee is Mrs. Finney, a dragon of a charlady. Then sit back and enjoy the fun. Imogen was Julia Carrington, the short-sighted and censorious secretary.

1974—Christmas "Panto"—*Puss In Boots*.

Sept-Nov 1975—on tour—*A Bit Between The Teeth*—a Brian Rix farce.

Reviews: "...not only voluptuous but clever with it..."

"...great skill..."

"...Imogen Hassall, exposed in one sense but hidden in another (behind doors, curtains, and under an eiderdown) timed all her antics to a nicety..."

"...Imogen Hassall does not have much of a part—although she does have a lot of everything else, all of which is made to waggle..."

December 1975—Christmas "Panto" again—*Babes in the Wood.*

June-July 1976—on tour—*Killer*—the sinister plot concerned a successful public relations man, who has clawed his way to the top, only for a stranger to emerge from his murky past and destroy him. Imogen had the role of the PR man's glamorous and efficient secretary, with whom he might, or might not, be having an affair.

Reviews: "…happily, Imogen Hassall brought elegant beauty to the unrewarding part of the secretary…"

"…Imogen Hassall prowls elegantly…"

September 1978—on tour—*Say Who You Are*—a comedy by Keith Waterhouse and Willis Hall, an expose of feminine stratagem, presenting the modern image of the single girl on the sexual merry-go-round, sowing the seeds of marital discord. Imogen took the role of the bachelor girl, Valerie, who is forlornly in love, but not for keeps.

Feb-Aug 1980—on tour—*Outside Edge*—Richard Harris's comedy about a cricket club. Imogen played Ginnie, who spends much of her time, bikini-clad, reclining on a sun-lounger in her garden, reading magazines.

Reviews: "Raven-haired beauty Imogen Hassall is certainly bowling the fellows over in her latest role. For the sultry actress has the men in a spin when she appears in a skimpy bikini during Richard Harris's hilarious new play…"

"…both decorative and delightfully dismissive, using an elegant figure and throaty voice to delineate Ginnie, 'the scourge of Sainsbury's.'"

"…one other of the cast of nine deserves special mention: Imogen Hassall, as the poisonously jealous, neurotic wife of Bob…spitting venom from her sun lounger…"

Acknowledgments

Nicholas Hassall—This book owes an incalculable debt to Nick Hassall. His unique insight shone a light on his family and illuminated the darkest recesses of his sister's damaged psyche. There could have been no book without his cooperation.

Chapter 1

"All around…of the Atlantic"—This synopsis of the year 1942 is derived from the part-work history of World War Two: *Images of War, The Real Story of World War II*, Marshall Cavendish Ltd, 1988.

Hassall, Novello and Marsh—Accounts of Christopher Hassall's professional and emotional relationship with Ivor Novello and Edward Marsh are derived in part from two books: *Ivor: The Story of An Achievement*, W. MacQueen Pope, W.H. Allen, 1951, Hutchinson and Co (Publishers) Ltd, 1954; and *Ambrosia and Small Beer*, Christopher Hassall, Longmans, 1964 .

John Hassall—Although my account of Imogen's grandfather is drawn from the recollections of the family and friends of the family, there is an excellent and lavishly illustrated book: *The John Hassall Lifestyle*, David Cuppelditch, Dickle Press, 1979.

"Soliloquy To Imogen"—*Penthesperon*, Christopher Hassall, William Heinemann Ltd, 1938

John Counsell and Eve Lynett—*Counsell's Opinion*, John Counsell, Barrie and Rockliff, 1963

Britvic—Information kindly provided by Britvic Soft Drinks Ltd.

Elmhurst Ballet School—*At Your Service, Elmhurst Ballet School 1923-1998*, Jennifer Rice, 1998. Many thanks are also due to Patricia Eccles, Old Elms Association.

Chapter 2

Royal Ballet School—The description of auditions for and the regime at the School is taken from *Life At The Royal Ballet School*, Camilla Jessel, Methuen, 1979.

Rapier Players—The potted history of the Rapier Players is but a tiny fragment of the immense help given to me by a remarkable theatre archivist, John Foster. The constant flow of information that John was able to provide: credits, cast lists, theatre programs, etc., laid the foundations for all of my research. It all began with him. John is always happy to help and may be contacted at 15 Pine Street, Langley Park, Durham DH7 9SL, UK.

Chapter 3

Hassall correspondence—Christopher Hassall's papers, an enormous collection, are now held by the Keeper of Manuscripts, Cambridge University Library, West Road, Cambridge CB3 9DR, UK. I also owe a great debt of gratitude to Christopher Hassall's former secretary, Gillian Patterson, to the friends of Joan Hassall named in the text, and to Imogen's cousin Mark Hassall for his interest, enthusiasm and encouragement. Thanks are due also to Brian North Lee. Brian's concern for the reputation of all concerned, and especially Joan and Christopher, was a welcome reminder to me to try and be fair and balanced.

Royal Shakespeare Company—The account of Peter Hall at the RSC is taken from Simon Trussler, *The Cambridge Illustrated History of British Theatre*, Cambridge University Press, 1994.
"Tonford Manor…of land"—*Kent Messenger*, October 1963

It meant that sex…sex was fun for women. Bliss!"—*Yesterday's Britain*, Reader's Digest Association, 1998

"a double image…could not take it"—*News of the World*, July 18, 1971

Chapter 4

Christopher Hassall's "credits"—*Who Was Who*, volume VI 1961-1970, Adam & Charles Black, 1972

Christopher Hassall and William Walton—The sources for my account of this are four books: *William Walton, His Life And Music*, Neil Tierney, Robert Hale; *The Music of William Walton*, Frank Howes, Oxford University Press, 1974; *William Walton, Behind The Façade*, Susana Walton, Oxford University Press, 1988; *Portrait Of Walton*, Michael Kennedy, Oxford University Press, 1989.

"I had to tell my father...in the film world"—*News of the World*, July 25, 1971

Chapter 5
"The slinky...Douglas-Home"—unidentified article in the *Daily Mirror*, c.1963

Cleo, Camping, Emmanuelle and Dick—When I heard that Imogen was going to be in a play at the National I contacted the author, Terry Johnson. We exchanged scripts and it is from the then current draft of the play that these extracts are taken. The script is now published by Methuen Publishing Ltd.

"I fall in love...years and years"—Robert Ottaway, *Daily Sketch*, July 30, 1969

"The sun was shining...their profession"—*Chelsea Bird*, Virginia Ironside, Secker & Warburg, 1964

"Although I was...sense of humour"—*News of the World*, July 18, 1971

"Monte Carlo 1966...swimming pool"—*Daily Mirror*, April 25, 1966

"I went to several orgies...in those circumstances"— *News of the World*, July 18, 1971

Chapter 6
"She has the chameleon character...on talent"—Robert Ottaway, *Daily Sketch*, July 30, 1969

When Dinosaurs Ruled the Earth—For an excellent and very informative account of the making of this film, from which is taken the quote by Jim Danforth: see "When Dinosaurs Ruled The Earth" by Mark A. Miller, in *Guilty Pleasures of the Horror Film*, edited by Gary J. Svehla and Susan Svehla, Midnight Marquee Press, 1996. Thanks are due to Mark for his enthusiasm, encouragement and assistance.

"People say bosoms are out...in the matter"—Alix Palmer, *The Sun*, February 2, 1970

"With a family like that...share of struggling"—Alix Palmer, *The Sun*, February 2, 1970

"I moved in with an old brass bed...on silly things"—Alix Palmer, *The Sun*, February 2, 1970

"...as soon as you get through the door...owns it herself"—Ray Connolly, *Evening Standard*, June 15, 1970

"Since it was the middle of the afternoon...its greatest effect"—Ray Connolly, *Evening Standard*, June 15, 1970

"I remember having wanted...more often than not"—*News of the World*, July 25, 1971

"I had a competition... at ballet school"—Ray Connolly, *Evening Standard*, June 15, 1970

"Imogen has courted her publicity...professional deserts"—Robert Ottaway, *Daily Sketch*, September 22, 1970
"The big hallo at first nights...her real talent"—Robert Ottaway, *Daily Sketch*, September 22, 1970
"She wants now, she says...would they?"—Ray Connolly, *Evening Standard*, June 15, 1970

"Well, its been a helluva week...You're welcome"—Donald Zec, *Daily Mirror*, July 15, 1970

Nobody recalls...ballet and repertory"—Donald Zec, *Daily Mirror*, July 15, 1970
"Certainly she is the most sought-after female...never be the same"—Donald Zec, *Daily Mirror*, July 15, 1970

"Today the 'clothes-peg'…be herself"—Robert Ottaway, *Daily Sketch*, September 22, 1970

"Its easy to scoff…permanently on the map"—Robert Ottaway, *Daily Sketch*, September 22, 1970

Chapter 7

"Men these days…of doing it"—*News of the World*, July 18, 1971

"There was a time…had a ball"—*Radio Times*, November 11, 1971

"A lithe, tanned girl…I have what it takes"—*Scottish Daily Record*, September 21, 1971

"That well-known lady…is disappointing" Newcastle, *The Journal*, 1971

"Mum's The Word For Miss Sexpot…give birth to a child"—*Daily Mirror*, January 16, 1971

"Four babies…the flavour was honey"—*Daily Mirror*, January 16, 1971

"You know, he won't marry me…a home and a family"—*Daily Mirror*, January 16, 1971

Loss of baby—My thoughts on the death of a child are hardly my own. I am not qualified. They come from a book treatment by a friend of mine who endured that terrible loss—and from: "Birth Day Sadness", Kathleen Jones, *Community Outlook*, April 1989; "When A Baby Dies," Gill Mallinson, *Nursing Times*, March 1, Vol. 85, No. 9, 1989.

"the first man with whom I fell in love…Mrs Hassall"—*News of the World*, July 18, 1971

"My father and I…breaking up a marriage"—*News of the World*, July 25, 1971

"It was lovely at the fair…I can speak from experience"—*News of the World*, July 18, 1971

Chapter 8

"Having lunch with Imogen Hassall…if you let them"—Chris Kenworthy, *The Sun*, August 3, 1972

"Imogen, who appears…dancing on the tables"—Chris Kenworthy, *The Sun*, August 3, 1972

"Actress Imogen Hassall arrived by bicycle… no laughing matter"—*The Sun*, June 24, 1975

"He was a very sweet, charming man… enjoyed their breakfast that morning"—from an unidentified newspaper interview

A Ticket To The Carnival—Barrie Stacey, 1987

"Sadly…hardly what one had anticipated"—*The Whitehaven News*, 5 July 1973

"All those enticing poses…to some extent forgotten"– *The Whitehaven News*, 5 July, 1973

"She told me… a bit of ballet as well"—*The Whitehaven News*, January 2, 1975

"Imogen Hassall—the girl dubbed the Countess of Cleavage…I can't see how things can get worse"—Stuart White, *News of the World*, June 29, 1975
"I thought I was forgotten…Some people don't understand that"—source unknown, September 18, 1975

"I still love him…it doesn't seem likely"—source unknown, September 18, 1975

"Still, with so much to look forward to…worst time of my life"—source unknown, September 18, 1975

"Actress Imogen Hassall today pleaded…go to a doctor"—Bradford, *Telegraph and Argus*, October 21, 1975

"Actress Imogen Hassell is in…waking up in hospital"—Ian Waterman, *News of the World*, July 20, 1975

"In fact, when we originally met I should be so lucky"—Michael Cable, *News of the World*, May 6, 1979

It's bull that we had a poor sex life…we just couldn't live together"—Polly Hepburn, *News of the World*, May 6, 1979

Chapter 9

"Just recently…I'm my own woman nowadays"—George Mink, *Wimbledon News*, November 14, 1980

Suzanna Leigh—Much of what Suzanna has to say was taken from the draft manuscript of her very entertaining autobiography *Paradise, Suzanna Style*, Pen Press Publishing, 2000, which Suzanna was kind enough to let me delve into.

"She used to come…how I want to remember her"—*Wimbledon News*, November 21, 1980

"My mates…and very poor"—*Daily Telegraph*, November 17, 1980

"I hadn't heard of her…being cruel to be kind"—Greg Miskiw, *Sunday Mirror*, November 23, 1980

Inquest docs—I was granted access to these papers by way of a letter of introduction from Nicholas Hassall. My thanks go also to the Coroner, Dr. Paul Knapman and his staff.

"I now just wish…take it so badly"—John Clare, *News Of The World*, November 23, 1980

"More than 50 mourners…far end of the cemetery"—*Wimbledon News*, November 28, 1980

Imogen Hassall, who will sadly…she could act"—*Screen International*, November 22, 1980

"Imogen Hassall was found dead…18 months ago"—*The Stage*, November 27, 1980

"Actress Imogen Hassall always knew…only a few close friends would listen"—John Jones, *Daily Express*, November 17, 1980

"There will be people…she was mistaken"—David Wigg, *Daily Express*, November 17, 1980

"This is to Imogen…as much as we could to help her"—Peter Thomas, *Daily Express*, November 21, 1980

Postscript: Imogen now has her own website, which can be found at: http://ukstarlets.users.btopenworld.com/
Well worth a visit.

Photograph Acknowledgments

Cover: Imogen on a beach in the Bahamas in July 1969 (picture taken by Larry Ellis)

Frontispiece: A haunting portrait (provided by John Stoneman)

Such a force of life (provided by Mark A. Miller)

Introduction
Just being herself: on location for *Incense for the Damned* (provided by Paul Sproxton)

Imogen was always ready with a pose (picture taken by Larry Ellis).

Chapter 1
A young Christopher Hassall painted by his sister Joan (1930/31) (National Portrait Gallery).

Eve Lynett as a rising young actress in *Children in Uniform* (1932) (original theatre program, provided by John Foster)

The poet by Joan Hassall from the title page of *Penthesperon* (provided by Brian North Lee)

Imogen as a happy baby (provided by Nicholas Hassall)

Imogen with a favorite toy dog—as an adult she would have many beloved real dogs (provided by Nicholas Hassall).

Imogen with her big brother Nicholas (provided by Nicholas Hassall)

Little Imogen strikes a serious pose for the camera (provided by Nicholas Hassall).

Imogen with classmates in the dance studio at Elmhurst (provided by Jennifer Rice and Elmhurst Ballet School).

Students in leotards and their colored sashes drill on the tennis court (provided by Jennifer Rice and Elmhurst Ballet School).

Jenny and fellow classmates pose in their Victorian costumes complete with parasols (provided by Jennifer Rice and Elmhurst Ballet School).

Dress rehearsal on the tennis court (provided by Jennifer Rice and Elmhurst Ballet School)

Life Story by Imogen Hassall, age 12 (provided by Jackie Ingham)

Little Imogen would become a Daddy's girl (provided by Nicholas Hassall)

Chapter 2
Sweet 16—Scarlett O'Hassall and the Rapier Players in *The Amazing Adventures of Miss Brown* (provided by Jennifer Lessimore)

...*Miss Brown* was set in a select academy for young ladies and chronicled the hero's endeavors to gain access to his beloved by disguising himself as Miss Brown (provided by Jennifer Lessimore).

Chapter 3
Imogen's long-suffering Aunt Joan, whose patience was severely tested by her niece (provided by Brian North Lee).

Imogen, front and center, strums her lute in the Royal Shakespeare Company's *Curtmantle* (1962) by Christopher Fry (Zoe Dominic).

Imogen as a possessed nun in *The Devils* (Shakespeare Centre Library, Stratford-upon-Avon)

In *Troilus and Cressida* Imogen was a mere observer as a handmaiden of Helen of Troy (Shakespeare Centre Library, Stratford-upon-Avon)

Chapter 4

Christopher Hassall on his way to La Scala, Milan, seen off by his wife Eve and daughter Imogen (original clipping, Evening Standard).

A portrait of the young actress with the world at her feet (Theatre Museum, Covent Garden; V & A Picture Library)

Chapter 5

Imogen in distinguished company: with Sybil Thorndike in *The Reluctant Peer* (anonymous clipping found in the Theatre Museum, Covent Garden)

Imogen's appearance with Charles Gray in *The Moon and Sixpence* for BBC TV is not included in her list of credits (picture taken by Larry Ellis).

The Avengers "Escape in Time" featured Diana Rigg as Mrs. Emma Peel and Imogen as Anjali (BFI Stills Dept).

Patrick Macnee as John Steed with Imogen in *The Avengers* "Escape in Time" (BFI Stills Dept)

Charlotte Rampling, Imogen and Virginia North promoting *The Long Duel* (BFI Stills Dept),

Swinging London comes to Monte Carlo (Syndication International).

Chapter 6

Tara (Imogen) flees into the hills with Sultan (Yul Brynner) in *The Long Duel* (BFI Stills Dept).

Imogen's finest hour: *The Italian Girl* (anonymous clipping found in the Theatre Museum, Covent Garden)

The Italian Girl: tragedy befell Imogen in art as well as in life (Illustrated London News Picture Library).

Low on the billing but prominent in the advertising (anonymous clipping found in the Theatre Museum, Covent Garden)

Sexy cave girls from When Dinosaurs Ruled the Earth: Imogen, Victoria Vetri and Magda Konopka (provided by Mark A. Miller)

Hammer's primarily male audience liked nothing better than a prehistoric cat fight in this publicity shot for *When Dinosaurs Ruled the Earth* (provided by Mark A. Miller).

A stunning studio portrait of a very glamorous cave girl (BFI Stills Dept)

John Stoneman still treasures this autographed photo (provided by John Stoneman).

Imogen puts the bite on Patrick Mower in *Incense for the Damned* (provided by Midnight Marquee Press).

Imogen turns on her sunny side for an interview with Paul Sproxton (provided by Paul Sproxton).

Imogen plays a sullen and smoldering Gypsy girl in *The Virgin and the Gypsy* (BFI Stills Dept).

Imogen as homely Jenny Grubb with Terry Scott in *Carry On Loving* (BFI Stills Dept)
Carry On Loving: the Grubb clan interviews Jenny's prospective suitor (picture taken by Larry Ellis).

Imogen informs Terry Scott that those falsies do not belong to her (*Carry On Loving*) (BFI Stills Dept.).

Imogen pauses to pose on the Pinewood lot during the filming of *Carry On Loving* (picture taken by Larry Ellis).

Imogen told Jim Danforth on the set of *When Dinosaurs Ruled the Earth* she didn't know if her breasts were a "blessing or a curse" (provided by Mark A. Miller).

Imogen's main attractions opened the doors at premieres, galas and first nights (provided by Donald Coe).

Imogen with Linda Hayden, Richard Harris, Lulu, Maurice Gibb and Honor Blackman leaving Heathrow for the Limerick Film Festival in Ireland ("PA" Photos).

Imogen and Ingrid Pitt (*Today's Cinema*, November 10, 1970, provided by Donald Coe)

Man lands on the Moon while the Sun shines on Imogen Hassall (picture taken by Larry Ellis).

Producers dismissed Imogen as a clothespeg for see-throughs (BFI Stills Dept.).

Imogen in the gardens of Pinewood Studios (picture taken by Larry Ellis)

Imogen and Ratso (Atlantic Syndication Partners)

Imogen with Roger Moore in *The Saint* (BFI Stills Dept.)

The pin-up (provided by Mark A. Miller)

Chapter 7

An unlikely couple: Imogen cuddles up to Wilfrid Hyde White (Syndication International).

Imogen and Kenneth Ives pose on their wedding day (News International Syndication).

Imogen looks positively doting in this still from *The Virgin and the Gypsy* (BFI Stills Dept)

Imogen's listing in the 1972 British Film and Television Year Book (provided by Walter Randall)

Alan and Imogen out on the town (provided by Alan Whitehead).

Imogen with Ratso and friends at Alan's pool (provided by Alan Whitehead)

Imogen in sunnier and happier times (provided by Alan Whitehead)

Chapter 8

Imogen meets Archbishop Makarios, President of the Republic of Cyprus (BFI Stills Dept.)

Imogen and the bicycle (News International Syndication)

Thirty-something and still a pin-up (*The Guardian*)

A flyer for *The Mating Game* (from the original, provided by John Foster)

Imogen portrays a policewoman in the spy spoof *White Cargo* (1974) (picture taken by Larry Ellis.)
Imogen tops the bill—on tour in panto (from a clipping in *The Whitehaven News*, December 26, 1974).

Imogen and the cast of *Puss in Boots* (provided by Caroline Lange)

Imogen was offered a tour with Brian Rix in *A Bit Between the Teeth* (*The Journal*, Newcastle)

A poster for *Killer* (from the original, provided by John Foster)

Andrew (top left) and Imogen: mixing work with pleasure (from the original flyer, provided by John Foster).

Imogen struts her stuff but hardly in the manner of a serious actress (provided by Mark A. Miller).

Imogen and Andrew's marriage was made in tabloid heaven (News International Syndication).

Chapter 9

Outside Edge: Amanda in the white hat, Maggie in fur, Jimmy seated second from left with Norman on his left, Imogen is back row left (provided by Maggie Guess)

Imogen's autograph in a stage door keeper's guestbook (provided by Tony Burns)

Happy New Year—Imogen is ready to party (provided by Suzanna Leigh).

Imogen snapped on a beach in Kenya by her friend Suzanna Leigh (provided by Suzanna Leigh)

The Crooked Billet: Imogen's last home is just beyond the parked cars, next to the pub (postcard published by J. Arthur Dixon Ltd: C.R.H. Photographic Ltd.).

Imogen with Ratso a few days before her death (from an original clipping, *Wimbledon News*)

A break in the filming of *Incense for the Damned* (provided by Paul Sproxton)

Imogen in her prime (picture taken by Larry Ellis)

As Ayak in *When Dinosaurs Ruled the Earth* (Kobal Collection)

The way her friends like to remember her (provided by Alan Whitehead)

Film Credits

Imogen comes to a sticky end in *Mumsy, Nanny, Sonny and Girly* (Kobal Collection).

Television Credits

Imogen with Patrick Macnee on the set of *The Avengers* (BFI Stills Dept.)

If you enjoyed this book,
please call or e-mail for a free catalog.

Midnight Marquee Press, inc.
9721 Britinay Lane
Baltimore, MD 21234
410-665-1198
MMarquee@aol.com
www.midmar.com

Lightning Source UK Ltd.
Milton Keynes UK
UKHW021826210321
380738UK00007B/747

9 781887 664479